Additional praise for *Rebels and Runaways*

"*Rebels and Runaways: Slave Resistance in Nineteenth-Century Florida* is a marvelous history of the complex ways enslaved blacks resisted slavery and how their determined efforts impacted the larger American experience. Rivers is to be commended for telling the complicated and compelling story of the fight enslaved blacks faced against terrorism over their bodies, minds, and souls in America."

—Martin Luther King III, President and Chief Executive Officer, The King Center, Atlanta, Georgia

"In this masterful undertaking, Larry E. Rivers fulfills a promise to illuminate the humanity of enslaved Floridians and argues convincingly that the Second Seminole War was 'a Negro, not an Indian War.' *Rebels and Runaways* makes it impossible for scholars to ignore the level of discontent among slaves in Florida."

—Wilma King, Arvarh E. Strickland Distinguished Professor of History, University of Missouri, Columbia

"*Rebels and Runaways* is the most important study of African American slave rebellions since the publication of Herbert Aptheker's *Negro Slave Revolts*. Larry E. Rivers does for the history of slave resistance in the United States what C. L. R. James's *Black Jacobins* did for the Haitian Revolution. Rivers faithfully portrays the aspirations of enslaved Africans in Florida with sensitivity, and he opens a new chapter on the history of slave revolution and race war in the Americas. This book will have a profound impact on the field for generations to come."

—Paul Ortiz, associate professor of history, University of Florida

"*Rebels and Runaways* is groundbreaking because, unlike other similar studies to date, it analytically addresses the Atlantic worldview held by some rebels and runaways and their impact on the multi-level patterns of slave resistance that developed over time in Florida. It focuses also on what these various levels of slave resistance meant to the overall expansion and development of the country as a whole. This is a solid and engaging study."

—Freddie L. Parker, professor and chair of history, North Carolina Central University

I0893570

Rebels and Runaways

THE NEW BLACK STUDIES SERIES

Edited by Darlene Clark Hine
and Dwight A. McBride

A list of books in the series appears at the end of this book.

Rebels and Runaways

Slave Resistance in Nineteenth-Century Florida

LARRY EUGENE RIVERS

University of Illinois Press

URBANA, CHICAGO, AND SPRINGFIELD

© 2012 by the Board of Trustees
of the University of Illinois
All rights reserved
Manufactured in the United States of America

♾ This book is printed on acid-free paper.

Library of Congress Cataloging-in-Publication Data
Rivers, Larry E., 1950–
Rebels and runaways: slave resistance in nineteenth-century Florida /
Larry Eugene Rivers.
pages cm. — (New Black Studies Series)
Includes bibliographical references and index.
ISBN 978-0-252-03691-0 (cloth: alk. paper)
1. Slave insurrections—Florida—History—19th century.
2. Fugitive slaves—Florida—History—19th century.
3. Slaves—Florida—Social conditions—19th century.
4. Slaves—Florida—History—19th century.
5. Florida—History—1821–1865.
I. Title.
E445.F6R57 2012
306.3'620975909034—dc23 2011051423

For

Betty Jean, Larry Omar, and Linje Eugene

I am bound for Canaan land,
To that happy golden strand.
There I shall receive a blessing
For the work I've done below.

There I'll meet my loved ones gone on,
To receive their just reward;
What a meeting that will be
On that bright celestial shore.

—From "Canaan," a gospel song

Contents

Florida: A Runaway Haven
(We are headed to Florida)
TEN DOLLARS REWARD

Ranaway from Abbeville District, S.C. on the 9th June, a white girl and a young negro man. The girl is called MARY CONN, is about 18 years of age, low built, round faced, her face is very full of pimples, and has a strong course voice. The boy is about 25 years of age, called Stephen . . . near 6 feet high, a likely fellow, a thin visage, pretty black complected, and a large mouth . . . and shows the white of his eyes very much. . . . It is supposed they design going to Florida. . . . The above reward will be given for lodging the negro in any jail. . . . (Signed) JAMES CONN, JOSEPH CONN. Abbeville, S.C.

Milledgeville Georgia Journal,
June 26, 1821

Rebels and Runaways

Introduction

No close examination of American slavery can better expose the institution's cruel realities than a careful look at the many and varied ways in which its victims resisted their bondage and oppression. This argument, of course, is not a new one. Over a decade past, John Hope Franklin and Loren Schweninger's seminal work *Runaway Slaves: Rebels on the Plantation* took on the subject in a comprehensive manner by focusing directly on slave flight and rebellion throughout the South during the period 1790 to 1860. Their study showed, as the authors remarked, "how a significant number of slaves challenged the system and how the great majority of them struggled to attain their freedom even if they failed." Franklin and Schweninger drew attention, as well, to "how slave owners marshaled considerable effort to prevent the practice of running away, meted out punishments to slaves who disregarded the rules, and established laws and patrols to control the movement of slaves." They added of their research: "It exposed the violence and cruelty that were inherent in the slave system. It illustrates, perhaps better than any other approach, how enslaved blacks resisted with various forms of violence and how slave owners responded, at times brutally, to demonstrate their authority over their human chattel."[1]

Given the extended time frame they considered and a focus that covered most states in the South, Franklin and Schweninger admirably captured the overall essence of regional slave resistance and of the experiences of bondpeople as they resisted. As would be true of any large study of the kind, however, their need for generalization due to constraints of time, resources, and space limited Franklin and Schweninger's ability to reveal in great depth the multilayered and richly textured experiences of bondservants who resisted, rebelled, or ran away from their owners in each state of the South. The loss of such rich experience unfortunately can prove highly detrimental to achieving understanding and helpful insight.

Now that over a decade has passed since the release of *Runaway Slaves*, the time has arrived for another look at the subject, one that not only tests the conclusions offered by its distinguished authors but also affords the kind of in-depth look that a more general survey cannot hope to offer. A state study would fill the bill, and, to this author's mind, Florida provides an excellent laboratory. Its experience may not be typical of the South as a whole, but this very fact may be telling on the more general experience. As a locale not often considered in studies of American slavery, its story comes as a fresh one. In some respects, it may even come as a startling eye-opener.

Accordingly, this study aims to examine slave resistance in Florida while incorporating perspectives that reach beyond its borders to embrace a regional and even larger context. In doing so, it builds upon the foundation laid by Franklin and Schweninger and also upon the works of scholars such as Jane Landers, Michael Gomez, John Blassingame, Lawrence Levine, Margaret Washington Creel, Walter Johnson, Sterling Stuckey, Freddie Parker, and Gwendolyn Hall. Taken together, these historians of slavery, among other things, offered highly useful tools for conceptualizing and analyzing the slave's experience in the Old South and beyond. These authors noted, for example, that a supportive African, Caribbean, and African American culture helped slaves to maintain a sense of agency and humanity. They noted also that the political organization and collective actions of bondservants as they addressed the hegemony of masters and owners remained rooted firmly within the slave community.

The time frame utilized for this look at slave resistance in Florida, it should be pointed out from the start, is considerably shorter than the 1790 to 1860 period adopted by Franklin and Schweninger. For one thing, Florida historiography already benefits from Jane Landers's excellent *Black Society in Spanish Florida*. This award-winning volume brilliantly analyzes the lives of Africans, persons of African descent, and enslaved blacks in Spanish Florida up to 1821. Landers's work covers many aspects of the African and African American experience under Spanish rule, especially the complex and international world that linked the Caribbean and Africa—and Indians, blacks, and Europeans and their governments and leaderships—to North America. Landers drew also upon African, European, and indigenous models to re-create the black Spanish experience in the "circum-Atlantic periphery of Florida." Some blacks, she emphasized helpfully, were at home on international waters and used the port of St. Augustine and other outlets to connect blacks in Florida to other ports on both sides of the Atlantic as well as to the Caribbean.[2]

As Landers further detailed, some blacks developed maroon societies, not to mention stable communities. In the latter case, Fort Mose, founded in 1738, probably stood out as the first "southern" free black community. It lay a mere two miles north of St. Augustine, Florida's gateway to the Atlantic. Black communities such as Fort Mose helped their inhabitants to establish cultural ties to other Africans, Spanish, Native Americans, and Anglo Americans. The interactions among these groups certainly played complex and varied roles that would contribute to setting the stage for the evolution of slavery in Florida following its cession to the United States in 1821.[3]

Other Florida scholars, too, have joined Landers in setting firm foundations for this study. Their work is noted more closely in the chapters that follow, and all deserve recognition for their contributions. I would underscore here, though, the fact that Kathleen Deagan, Daniel L. Schafer, and Canter Brown Jr. have added significantly to scholars' understanding of the interactions between blacks, whites, and Indians in Florida, particularly in northeast Florida and the peninsula. In a general sense, they have explored the power and culture of these groups from the Spanish period to and through the Civil War. Their studies did not purport to focus specifically on slave resistance or on how it changed over time between 1821 and 1865; yet, each of these scholars has provided factual detail, revelations, and insights that have proved invaluable to me.

Mention of the Civil War compels me to add that the time frame of this study, which begins three decades after that adopted by Franklin and Schweninger, extends five years longer than theirs so as to encompass Civil War resistance. As will be explored in depth, violent resistance to slavery in the form of slave rebellion and even open warfare marked Florida's experience and profoundly affected the nature of Florida development, politics, and race relations. Seen within that context, the Civil War years provided a further laboratory for testing. The results, again, may prove surprising to many readers.

The issue of perspective, as well as that of time frame, commanded my early attention. As I had done with my earlier book *Slavery in Florida: Territorial Days to Emancipation*, I committed from the beginning to allow the voice of the slave as an active participant to be heard insofar as I was able to do so. On the one hand, I can applaud countless works on slavery for the lasting contributions that they have made and yet, on the other hand, I can rue the fact that, to greater and lesser degrees, they have bled the humanity from their subject. Let us with every step taken remember that our subjects were human beings filled with all the talents, intelligence, and shortcomings of other human beings. They did not exist simply as statistics, and I do not believe their story should be told as if that were all that their lives and experiences constituted.[4]

A few comments on overarching context may help to set the stage for what follows. Slavery had defined colonial Florida during the Spanish and British periods that extended from 1565 to 1821, and the "peculiar institution" continued to dominate during the territorial and statehood periods that followed. This proved true in terms of cultural, social, political, ideological, and economic systems. Importantly, the legal structure in Florida quickly evolved after 1821 from a somewhat more fluid set of racial codes in place at the end of the second Spanish period to a far more stringent system of laws reflective of other Deep South states. Boasting a frontier society for much of the territorial and early statehood periods, Florida nonetheless presented complex day-to-day realities that defied simple description as to either time or place. Within that reality, law often ceded authority to local custom and practice with results that stood in direct contrast to what lawmakers and their planter backers had intended.

Enslaved persons in Florida meanwhile comprehended in important ways the world they and the slaveholders had made and continued to make. Sometimes they interacted with whites and Indians on a daily basis. They also traveled or else heard word of others' travels. Thus, they often managed to know something about the trials and tribulations of their enslaved brothers and sisters in other parts of the South, in the Caribbean, and even in Central and South America. Since Florida and Floridians profoundly affected the lives of whites, enslaved blacks, and Indians all along the Atlantic coastline during the time frame under study, what happened in Florida very well could have influenced attitudes and behavior in the Lowcountry of South Carolina or even in the Bahamas, as well as in other parts of the Atlantic world.

Given the relative complexities of their experiences as suggested by such broad knowledge, it should come as no surprise that slave resistance in Florida came in diverse and sometimes apparently contradictory forms. This work, as a result, attempts to share the slaves' stories as daily dissidents, runaways, violent rebels, saboteurs, and revolutionaries. It aims in doing so to identify forces that shaped the slave's world and made resistance or revolution more possible at certain times and in certain places. The stories, when taken as a whole, should be appreciated as nothing less than remarkable. At least, I consider them so.

The proximity of enslaved Floridians to race war, slave revolution, and societal violence should be emphasized from the outset as major factors in development of resistance patterns. From Spanish days, Florida's geographical proximity to the Atlantic and the Caribbean made it ripe for resistance and revolution. The French sugar island of Saint Domingue lay not far distant across the waters, and by the late 1790s veteran Haitian revolutionaries had resettled in La Florida with responsibilities for the colony's defense, facts that set in place patterns of militancy coupled with military competence. Florida also stood out as a haven that attracted runaways from up and down the Atlantic coast and other parts of the developing cotton, tobacco, and rice kingdoms. With immense reaches that remained poorly policed and sparsely populated well into the nineteenth century—historian James M. Denham in fact has referred to Florida before the Civil War as a "Rogue's Paradise"—maroon communities existed, sometimes thrived, and always offered hope. They meanwhile served occasionally as headquarters for organizing rebellion.[5]

And, make no mistake about it, race war—sometimes combined with slave rebellion—afflicted Florida time and again. Scholars in denominating major slave insurrections generally refer to those associated with Gabriel (Virginia, 1800), Denmark Vesey (Telemaque) (South Carolina, 1822), and Nat Turner (Virginia, 1831) and to the Louisiana revolt of 1811. None of these, however, came close to comparing in size, intensity, or duration with Florida's Second Seminole War of 1835–42, what I call the Black/Indian Rebellion. Despite its traditional name, this upheaval involved maroon insurrection and slave revolution. Army general Thomas Jesup simply stated the facts when he insisted, "This, you may be assured, is a Negro, not an Indian war." No other resistance movement experienced in the United States that was led by blacks and supported by self-determined black runaways endured as long as did this war. The revolution did not last several months but for years. In the process, it rocked the very foundations of Florida's slave society and, with it, the nation.[6]

Whether resistance involved revolution or other actions, questions of culture, the role of the politics of collective action (the importance of which Walter Johnson has noted), and the impact that political movements carried deserve to be explored. As will be seen, acculturation played significantly in the actions of slaves through the antebellum era. The agency gained thereby permitted bondservants—largely American-born English speakers who had assimilated in good part into Anglo-American society—a basis for asserting themselves and otherwise making their views known to those who saw themselves as the masters. When combined with Florida's Atlantic world locale and traditions of militancy, the brew for resistance and rebellion simmered and eventually boiled over. The results were evident through the Civil War.[7]

This study additionally aims to pay due attention to process, development, and change over time. Florida—or, at least, significant portions of it—passed through two basic stages of evolution during the territorial and early statehood periods, including as a frontier region and as a plantation region dominated by slaveholders. Yet, these changes did not occur at the same time or to the same degree in West, East, Central, and South Florida as they did in the principal plantation region of Middle Florida (the panhandle area centered on Tallahassee). The frontier era, for example, lasted longer in Central and South

Florida, areas that lagged behind in development until nearly the twentieth century. It was there where maroon communities thrived and where access to the Atlantic world came with relative ease. There, too, resistance pulsed and rebellion was born.

Hosts of other factors influenced slave resistance. Where enslaved people lived made a difference but so, too, did their status, gender, work routines, and work experiences. As to geography, the enslaved typically worked differently in West and East Florida compared to bondservants who labored in Middle Florida. In the former locales, the task system could be seen in use at every hand, while in the latter, the gang system predominated. It was in Middle Florida, though, that most slaves lived and where, by the Civil War era, 80 percent of Florida's commodity exports were produced.

Organizationally, the examination of slave resistance that follows covers its subject thematically and, within themes, chronologically. Three parts, inclusive of eleven chapters, consider nonviolent and day-to-day resistance, running away, and violent resistance. I have attempted to impose a logical progression within these categories, although the reader should keep in mind that the highly complex nature and diversity of Florida's experience tends to interfere with and often confound logic and easy progression. In such cases, reader patience and persistence will be most appreciated and, I hope, rewarded. An afterword briefly presents my thoughts in summation.

I noted earlier my personal and professional commitment to underscoring the humanity of enslaved persons as opposed to approaching the subject of slave resistance purely as a cliometric exercise. This is not to say that I do not have respect for statistical analysis or believe that statistical analysis should play no part in a study such as this one. Having now pursued an understanding of Florida slavery for well over three decades, I have accumulated a mass of documentation from which I felt a limited number of statistical comparisons could be drawn with a measure of helpful validity. This research base consists of oral testimonies, former slave narratives, newspaper advertisements for runaways, census returns, ledgers, wills, court records, and similar documents. The text points out where statistical measures are taken from this database. The documentation is maintained in my personal collections located in Fort Valley, Georgia, and Tallahassee, Florida. Significant portions of it also have been placed on deposit at the Southeastern Regional Black Archives Research Center and Museum, Florida A&M University, Tallahassee.

Through the full extent of my career as a historian, I have benefited from the generous contributions and support of others. My ability to undertake a study such as this one has depended absolutely on those contributions and that support; this study profited from their sharp critiques and helpful suggestions. They come from all walks of life, political persuasions, and economic backgrounds. Naturally, many are scholars of solid reputation. Florida for many years was understudied, even as it grew into the fourth largest state in the nation. Fortunately, that condition no longer prevails. Thanks to individuals such as Canter Brown Jr., Jane Landers, Daniel Schafer, Kathleen Deagan, James M. Denham, and Edward Baptist, we know much more about blacks, whites, and Indians—and their interrelationships—as well as about the influence of international events on the peninsula from the Spanish eras to the antebellum period. The groundbreaking studies derived from the work of these scholars, along with those of other respected colleagues, clearly have influenced my own.

Let me acknowledge that I owe an especially deep debt of gratitude to my colleague and friend Canter Brown Jr. Truly a scholar of Florida's nineteenth-century experience, his generosity has produced insights of significance into the history of the South and of antebellum Florida in particular, while his skills as a researcher and editor have proven invaluable. Through a collaboration that now has lasted twenty years, he always has desired to be of assistance and never has let me down. Canter's wife, Barbara Gray Brown, also has been very encouraging and supportive of my research and writing endeavors over the years. For this, I cannot thank them enough.

I offer thanks to my former professor Donnie D. Bellamy, retired Regents professor of history at Fort Valley State University (FVSU), for his encouragement over the years and for introducing me at a 1970 seminar to fellow FVSU alumnus John W. Blassingame. John, in turn, inspired me to major in history at FVSU. For that, I am eternally grateful. I thank as well my two major advisors—David Killingray and Peter D. Fraser—at Goldsmiths, University of London. Their guidance lies securely within this book's heart.

Many others deserve recognition as well. I thank the three additional examiners who reviewed this material, Vivien Miller, Melvyn B. Stokes, and Richard Halpern. Each shared insights and suggestions that improved the study. Several anonymous readers for the University of Illinois Press similarly critiqued several drafts of the manuscript. I benefited tremendously from their suggestions to apply new approaches to the study of slave resistance, ones that I am convinced made this a better book.

The following individuals, over three decades, offered their support and truly merit my thanks: Darlene Clark Hine, Patricia Griffin, Lewis Baldwin, Dennis Dickerson, Julius Scipio, Lisa Scipio, Min Tau Chow, Shelisha Williams, Nancy Hewitt, William W. Rogers, Maxine Jones, Wilma King, Bob Hall, Aubrey M. Perry Sr., Charles U. Smith, Frances J. Stafford, James M. Denham, David Jackson Jr., Roland M. Smith, Michael Gomez, Orville Vernon Burton, David J. Coles, Jerome Clayton, Beth Boyett, Jody Norman, Mary Ann Cleveland,

Cynthia C. Wise, Dorothy Williams, Randi Bailey, Joe Knetsch, Peter A. Krafft, Nathan Woolsey, Elizabeth Alexander, Bruce Chappel, Freddie L. Parker, Mark I. Greenberg, Susan Parker, Magen Wilson, Taryn Rodriquez-Boette, Charles A. Tingley, Fay Farmer, Bonney A. McClellan, George Chapel, Charles Carroll Fishburne Jr., Miles Womack, William G. Dayton, Rosemonde Russell Lowe, Therese Lewis, James James, Sonya Pridgen, Lambide Moore, Niera Marshall, Anthony Dixon, Tom Muir, and Lyle Britt. My appreciation goes out additionally to Julie Bush, who meticulously copyedited this manuscript, and to Yvonne Oliver and Anna Holloway for their assistance in reading proofs.

I owe great thanks to Joan Catapano, Daniel Nasset, Larin McLaughlin, Vijay Shah, Kelly Gray, Jennifer Clark, Joseph Peeples, and other members of the University of Illinois Press. Their patience, assistance, and urgings over the past eight years, as my stints as dean of a college of arts and sciences and as university president provided enormous distractions, proved key elements in my ability simply to get this done for publication.

My rock in a weary land has been my family. I can never repay them for their generosity and overall support. My parents, Felix and Lavonia Rivers, have gone on to glory; I wish they could have lived to read some of what I have tried to write about the human experience in America. My seven siblings offered moral support over the years; for that, I want to thank Raymond Sr., Allen Sr., Felix III, Donald, Phyllis, Harriet, and Trisha. I thank my mother-in-law, Annie M. Hubbard of Dry Branch, Georgia; my sisters-in-law, Willie Mae, Delores, Bernice, Regina, Nell, Cynthia, and Cathy; and my brothers-in-law, Charles, Robert, Roy, Thomas Jefferson, and Charlie.

To our young men who now are out of the house at last—Larry Omar, a college professor, and Linje Eugene, an attorney—thanks, guys, for your love, support, and understanding. And finally, I can never say thank you enough to my bride, Betty Jean Hubbard, whom I met as an FVSU student in 1969, for her guidance, unconditional support, and patience over these many years. This book is dedicated to them for making my life meaningful, worthwhile, and fulfilling.

Responsibility for interpretation of events and errors of fact is mine alone.

PART ONE

Resistance by Wiles

1. Day-to-Day Resistance

I rather be beat to death than worked to death.
—Octavia Stephens to Winston Stephens, March 2, 1862

The majority of Florida's enslaved blacks of the nineteenth century lived and worked in "slave labor camps," as Peter Wood articulated the situation; most did so as nonviolent dissenters, even though many men, women, and even children physically resisted slavery and its cruelties. This resistance occurred despite the fact that bondservants understood the dire, self-destructive, and even deadly consequences of outright rebellion or retaliation. As early as 1828—only seven years after the United States had assumed control over the former Spanish colony—this reality had hardened into law. That year, Florida's criminal code was amended to create latitude for the exercise of cruelty by slave owners through the stipulation that "Slaves, Free Negroes, and Mulattoes" could suffer whippings and even death depending upon the severity of the infraction committed. Historian James M. Denham correctly noted that "with some minor revisions, the code remained in force throughout the entire antebellum period, and all blacks—bond or free—were subject to its proscriptions."[1]

In the circumstances, the enslaved usually and creatively opted to utilize a wide variety of options when it came to forms of dissent. Most commonly, their actions understandably were based on a conservative approach. That typical nonviolent approach being the case, it should be emphasized that numerous individuals refused to hide behind deferential facades when addressing their discontentment or dissatisfaction with their lot; they simply spoke their minds. Others stole food, hogs, cattle, sheep, poultry, money, liquor, cotton, indigo, corn, and just about anything else they could get their hands on. Added to those ranks were slaves who revealed their irritation with what they had to wear by making or acquiring additional clothing. Others simply worked slowly or carelessly. Some bondservants quietly resisted by learning to read and write. They might also have destroyed wagons, carriages, or equipment or mistreated livestock. Most at some time feigned illness for brief reprieves from work routines. Bondpeople, as Kenneth M. Stampp aptly noted, became a daily "troublesome property" for their owners.[2] This clearly was the case in Florida.

Appropriately, then, this chapter explores the various forms of conservative resistance used by slaves in Florida and often elsewhere within the slave empire of the United States. William Dusinberre called these types of actions or inactions nonviolent "dissidence." Indeed, bondservants actively, though discreetly, resisted their owners on a day-to-day basis. In doing so, many slaves believed that they could either get away with their recalcitrance or use it to negotiate concessions from their masters. Since enslaved blacks knew that violent attack could mean immediate death, they naturally and intelligently sought other means of expressing their discontent concerning plantation or farm regimens. Sometimes they made life uncomfortable for their masters, and sometimes, in the process, they made life uncomfortable for themselves.[3]

Scholars of the subject have reviewed newspaper accounts, plantation journals, diaries, ledgers, letters, and personal notes of slaveholders to determine what whites thought of the reasons for the rebellious nature of their bondservants. As Gerald W. Mullin, John W. Blassingame, Merton Dillon, Douglas R. Egerton, and others have suggested, however, another way to understand the objectives of individuals who resisted bondage would be to focus on the slaves themselves. For studying nineteenth-century slave resistance, slave narratives and testimonies—as well as the writings of bondservants—can be useful in understanding how enslaved blacks reacted to their bondage. Failure to appreciate what such sources have to offer can easily lure the historian to misleading insights and misdirected conclusions.[4]

With an important exception that will be considered in due course—that of the Second Seminole War (or the Florida Black/Indian Rebellion) era of 1835–42—few of Florida's slave owners overtly expressed concern about possible massive violent uprising by their bondservants. Yet, they sought and enacted various laws suggesting otherwise. By virtually copying the laws of the older slave states, Florida's slave owners presumably sought to shore up their control over their property. Day-to-day reality popped such bubbles of optimism. Many slaveholders knew that placing laws on the books to control the bondservant was one thing, while enforcing those laws in a consistent manner over a sustained period of time clearly represented a distinctly separate matter. The laws framed to control slaves, as it turned out, did not apply neatly to managing the realities of life on farms and plantations.[5]

Daily Existence

Although masters appreciated that the enslaved could commit sudden and sometimes unprovoked acts of violence toward members of the slaveholding class, the bigger problem they recognized involved the day-to-day dissidence of "their people." Indeed, this dissident army, as John Hope Franklin and Loren Schweninger fittingly called them, left an indelible impression on the minds of many Florida masters. An apostate host, it consisted of slaves who had become acculturated or assimilated into Florida's slave society. Which is to say, the dissident army included nearly all of Florida's slaves.[6]

And the numbers of Florida's rebels and runaways grew with an ever-increasing slave population. A few statistics can help to make the point. Although less populous than most of its southern counterparts, Florida grew steadily after 1821. Its numbers of persons held in bondage, meanwhile, expanded at a much faster rate than in most other southern slave states from 1830 to 1860 (the exception was Arkansas). Census takers reported the facts: Florida's enslaved population increased by an astonishing 298.2 percent between 1830 and the Civil War's beginning, from 15,501 persons to 61,745.

As tables 1 and 2 illustrate, Florida counties increased from sixteen in 1830 to thirty-seven in 1860, all holding enslaved workers. In 1830, the population of

Table 1. Florida Population by County, Number of Enslaved Blacks, and Their Percentage in Each County in 1830

County	Total population	No. of enslaved blacks	Percent of population
Alachua	2,204	597	27.0
Duval	1,970	1,018	51.6
Escambia	2,518	885	35.1
Gadsden	4,895	2,501	51.0
Hamilton	543	61	11.2
Jackson	3,907	1,854	47.4
Jefferson	3,312	1,610	48.6
Leon	6,404	3,152	49.2
Madison	525	263	50.0
Monroe	517	66	12.7
Mosquito	733	657	89.6
Nassau	1,511	793	52.4
Santa Rosa	868	349	40.2
St. John's	2,538	1,030	40.5
Walton	1,207	280	23.1
Washington	978	385	39.3

Source: United States Census Office, Population of Each State and Territory (by counties) in the Aggregate and as Whites, Free Colored, Slave, Chinese, and Indian, at All Censuses, 1790 to 1870 (Washington, D.C: Government Printing Office, 1872), 18–19.

Table 2. Florida Population by County, Number of Enslaved Blacks, and Their Percentage in Each County in 1860

County	Total population	No. of enslaved blacks	Percent of population
Alachua	8,232	4,457	54.1
Brevard	246	21	8.5
Calhoun	1,446	524	36.2
Clay	1,914	519	27.1
Columbia	4,646	2,063	44.4
Dade	83	2	2.4
Duval	5,074	1,987	39.1
Escambia	5,768	1,961	33.9
Franklin	1,904	520	27.3
Gadsden	9,396	5,409	57.5
Hamilton	4,154	1,397	33.6
Hernando	1,200	200	16.6
Hillsborough	2,981	564	18.9
Holmes	1,386	112	8.0
Jackson	10,209	4,903	48.0
Jefferson	9,876	6,374	64.5
LaFayette	2,068	577	27.9
Leon	12,343	9,089	73.6
Levy	1,781	450	25.2
Liberty	1,457	521	35.7
Madison	7,779	4,249	54.6
Manatee	854	253	29.6
Marion	8,609	5,314	61.7
Monroe	2,913	451	15.4
Nassau	3,644	1,612	44.2
New River	3,820	744	19.4
Orange	987	163	16.5
Putnam	2,712	1,047	38.6
Santa Rosa	5,480	1,371	25.0
St. John's	3,038	1,003	33.0
Sumter	1,549	549	35.4
Suwannee	2,303	835	36.2
Taylor	1,384	125	9.0
Volusia	1,158	297	25.6
Wakulla	2,839	1,167	41.1
Walton	3,037	441	14.5
Washington	2,154	474	22.0

Source: United States Census Office, Population of Each State and Territory (by counties) in the Aggregate and as Whites, Free Colored, Slave, Chinese, and Indian, at All Censuses, 1790 to 1870 (Washington, D.C: Government Printing Office, 1872), 18–19.

bondservants in ten counties (or 62 percent) ran 40 percent or higher. Thirty years later, with twenty-one more counties, still only ten (27 percent) claimed enslaved populations of at least 40 percent. Here the state's slave belt centered.

It bears mention that, by 1830, over 98 percent of Florida slaves had been acculturated into Anglo-American society, at least in terms of being American-born and adopting, if only partially, the Christian religion of their masters. As will be seen later, the Middle Florida region, stretching through the panhandle from Jackson County on the west to the Suwannee River on the east, consisted of six counties where over half of all enslaved blacks lived and worked by 1860. There, they engaged in Protestant worship, typically as Methodists, Baptists, Presbyterians, or Congregationalists. In West Florida—principally the Pensacola vicinity and adjacent areas—and East Florida, including the northeast and the peninsula, centuries of Spanish influence persisted in various degrees in various places. So, at locales such as Pensacola, St. Augustine, and other locations, worship might include Roman Catholicism. Baptist and Methodist itinerant preachers began to appear in East and West Florida only in the 1820s and 1830s after Spain's cession of the colony to the United States in 1821. The few slaveholders and bondpeople who lived in the central and southern regions of the peninsula may have identified with any of the aforementioned religions, or they may not have claimed Christian religious faith at all.[7]

In addition to influences surrounding acculturation, attitudes and actions of individual masters also must be considered in any discussion of how blacks reacted to their enslavement. A master, for example, could opt—and many did—for a paternalistic approach based upon persuasion, incentives, or a simple give-and-take. But, because of the refusal of some bondservants to be driven beyond a certain point in their work routines, the master's persuasive manner might well not alter work performances.

The experience of a woman named Holly helps to make the point. According to her sister Margrett Nickerson, Holly refused to be pushed at any rate of speed other than the one she established for herself. Nickerson recalled, "Holly didn't stand back on non' uv em, when dey'd get behin' her, she git behin' dem; she wuz dat stubbo'n and when dey would beat her she wouldn't holler and jest take it and go on [at her own pace]." Margrett meanwhile also resisted working other than at her own pace. She remembered that, when she had to "tote tater vines on my haid," overseer Joe Sanders would hurry her and other slaves, "beatin' us with strops and sticks." She told of an incident when the overseer beat her and another slave for working slowly, leaving Margrett crippled. Her injuries proved permanent, even though her father "would try to fix me up cose I had to go back to work nex' day." She added, "I never walked straight from [that] day to now."[8]

Sometimes, tenacious behavior by the enslaved, while raising the ire of slaveholders, surprisingly sparked little or no further response. Emmaline's example illustrates the point. She, like many other enslaved blacks, was a commodity supplied by the international slave trade, or "Black Mother." But, the migration of bondpeople not only encompassed travel from various parts of Africa to North America. The journey for many, much like that of Emmaline, began or continued with bondservants and their families being uprooted from the Upper South (Delaware, Maryland, Virginia, and the Carolinas) to the Lower South for the purpose of making owners wealthy. In Emmaline's case, as a Maryland-born bondservant, she had been uprooted and forced to migrate to the fertile, but also violent, Florida frontier. The dynamic of relocation that touched Emmaline, as several students of the subject have noted, emerged during the Great Migration of the 1820s and 1830s, one of the largest, if not the largest, forced removal of enslaved blacks in US history. On a personal level, Emmaline's experience united her with several thousand black migrants compelled to accompany planter families from Upper South states to Florida.[9]

In Emmaline's case, the family that mandated her move was that of prominent Maryland planter and politician William Wirt, who relocated her and twenty other slaves to the new town of Tallahassee in 1828. If her journey reflected that of other captive laborers who traveled with their planter owners from the Upper South to Florida, the trek would have unfolded as arduous at best. This was seen in the case of northern Virginia's Thomas Brown, who, with his family and 140 slaves, also came to Leon County. In 1827, Brown reflected on this particular trip by observing that white men rode on horses and the white women rode in wagons. Most adult bondservants and children walked the two-month journey on foot at fifteen to twenty miles per day. Once the caravan stopped for the evening, the bondpeople had to cook and provide musical entertainment for the whites. They passed the night in "'open tents [on] one long strip of cloth,' while whites slept in tents with walls and doors." Thus, having likely walked the two- or three-month trip from Maryland to Tallahassee, Emmaline and her fellow Wirt slaves surely were exhausted. Nonetheless, Laura Wirt Randall, whose husband, Thomas, had charge of her father William's plantation, voiced complaints shortly after their arrival that Emmaline was working too slowly.[10]

That proved only the beginning of Emmaline's Florida experience with dissidence. On another occasion, Randall noted that Emmaline did not want to wash clothes. "She is very slow and loitering," the owner insisted. Another day, Laura complained that Emmaline had taken a whole day scouring one side of the porch. After seven months, Emmaline had not changed her behavior to Randall's liking. In frustration, Laura told her father that the bondservant had become too "impudent and unmanageable." Emmaline could have been protesting her uprooting and separation from family and friends in Maryland, but, the reason notwithstanding, she successfully resisted owner demands. Not insignificantly, as an acculturated house servant with religious underpinnings, Emmaline, along with other uprooted Maryland slaves, did work feverishly to build a small church of their own within three months of their arrival.[11]

The slaveholder, of course, might choose to be an absentee owner, in which case overseers typically undertook to regulate bondservant life and duties. Some of these individuals tried to pattern their behavior after the paternalistic gestures of the employer, as was the case with Judge Roberson. He sought to use kindness instead of more direct persuasive actions. The enslaved, unfortunately for Roberson and his employer George Noble Jones, perceived their supervisor to be weak and took advantage of him. Jones's bondservants on his several Middle Florida plantations clearly understood that their master lived primarily on his larger Savannah estate and came to look after his interests in Middle Florida only periodically. With the knowledge, they played games of deception with the overseers. Some even would pretend to be at the worksite when actually sleeping in their cabins.

D. N. Moxley, overseer on another Jones plantation, recognized what was happening under Roberson's watch and came to look upon his peer as an inept manager. He related his opinion to fellow overseer John Evans, who in turn wrote the owner. "Mr. Moxley sees that he had to flog one of the Judge hands out of the Quarters for sleeping all morning until an hour or two after sun before he left for the mill," the letter read. "Ansler is the boy's name. Mr. Moxley ses that the Judge has not bin on the canal in nearly two weeks where the hands are at work. If this be the case they aint hurting themselves at work very much." The bondservants had come to expect a certain management style from Roberson, since he oftentimes did not spot-check their work, and they acted in their own interest accordingly. Notably, although Roberson allowed the bondpeople much more latitude than did either Moxley or Evans, Jones declined to replace him.[12]

Bondservants would have known that their behavior of laboring at a slow pace could be self-destructive—after all, they faced potential flogging for poor work performance; still, they oftentimes did not modify that behavior until concessions were made. Take the case of Die, for instance. The bondwoman was another of George Noble Jones's slaves who had been whipped by the overseer for working slowly and for otherwise not performing her duties. Yet, she had persisted in her refusal. Frustrated with her actions, the overseer sent the recalcitrant woman to another Jones plantation, where the attitudes of the bondservant slowly began to change. As a result, Die's new overseer then asked that she be left under his supervision, since she had no problems working for him. He went on to observe, "I have not had a cause to strike her a lick." Sometimes being disagreeable earned the enslaved a measure of satisfaction, even if for a short period of time.[13]

The numbers again can offer a bit of insight. Out of over 1,403 pertinent references from Florida probate records, slaveholders' journals, diaries, ledgers, and letters from 1821 to 1865, a total of 267 bondservants were cited at least one time as being lazy or as performing work routines poorly. Focusing specifically on gender, men made up 48 percent; women, 52 percent. Most of the references came from the 1850s. In fact, prices of staple crops began slowly to increase during that decade, after a scandal known as the Union Bank debacle had undermined a Florida banking scene already shaken by the Panic of 1837. Rising prices and improving conditions likely caused authority figures to push bondservants to produce more. D. N. Moxley in 1854 noted to Jones: "I regret to Say to you that I never have had as hard work to git cotton picked and that don in good order befor. it seames that those peaple [slaves] was determe to not pick cotton." Since there would be little in the way of recompense for what amounted to a lifetime of hard free labor, Florida bondpeople, like those on Jones's El Destino plantation, felt little incentive to work at any other than the slowest pace they could manage.[14]

Actually, there was more to it than that, at least from the bondservants' perspective. While the golden decade of the 1850s spurred enslavers to maximize productivity on farms and plantations, slaves perceived something else. They viewed masters as increasingly harsh and unwilling to recognize the reality of a give-and-take dynamic to the relationship. Faced with the dilemma, they continued to perform "lazily" or "poorly," if not more so.[15]

Petty Theft

The pace of work represented only the first step in the slave's nonviolent resistance. Pilferage was a second one, especially in Middle Florida. Many bondpeople in fact found it necessary to steal to supplement their diet. In most cases cited from the late 1820s to the early 1840s, slaves stole from the plantations and farms where they lived. Much like the experience in the rest of the South, slaves did not regard raiding the pens and barns of their masters as theft. They simply were taking what they had helped to produce. Instead, enslaved blacks saw stealing as taking from other bondservants. But the focus of their stealing tended to change by the mid-1840s. They had acquired enough confidence and knowledge of the region's geography by then to pilfer from other plantations and farms. Some slaves took it as a game to see if they were smart enough not to get caught. Others supplemented their material conditions by selling contraband property in the black market.[16]

Dick was one individual who thought of it as a game when he stole from his owner, although he later entertained second thoughts about his unsavory conduct. Like other slaves with a sweet tooth, his list of desirable acquisitions included various fruits. Dick particularly gained notoriety when it came to watermelons. He eventually quit his larcenous ways only after a dog grabbed him by the "seat of his pants." Meanwhile, John Gamble, a Middle Florida slaveholder, experienced problems with George stealing peaches. And over in East Florida's Duval County, cooperative slaves staged nighttime raids on W. B. Fickling's estate. The estate administrator spent countless hours in ultimately frustrated attempts to curtail the theft of oranges, grapefruits, watermelons, and other fruits. With the owner deceased and the administrator too busy to watch carefully over the estate, enslaved persons perceived a great opportunity to steal for consumption or trade in the black market.[17]

The change over time in patterns of theft and pilferage was not so subtle or insignificant as might be imagined, especially in Middle Florida. From the mid-1840s to the 1860s, as slaves became more assimilated and more familiar with their environment, increasing numbers confidently left their home venues to try their skills elsewhere. From extant evidence, slaves ventured forth to steal something twice as often from the mid-1840s to the 1860s than had been the case from the late 1820s to the early 1840s. For example, during the late 1850s, William E. Kilcrease's Gadsden County estate administrator knew he had his hands full with the 144 slaves on the plantation, a responsibility that encompassed their rebellious actions off the place as well as on. In his case, the character and behavior of the slaves under his charge came to the county judge's attention. Several times the executor reluctantly paid out funds for restitution when slaves refused to accept the limits of their residential plantation when it came to liberating pigs and other desirable commodities. On a single occasion, the administrator paid W. M. B. Jones as much as twenty dollars for hogs stolen by the estate's charges.[18]

As the Kilcrease bondservants' behavior evidenced, pigs stood out as a commodity of choice to steal. Pig theft particularly caused dilemmas for some overseers who were unable to curtail the practice and also unprepared to admit the same to their employers. A. R. McCall preferred not to consider at all that slaves were stealing hogs; instead, he merely acknowledged that the hogs had neither improved nor increased under his management. Henry Wirt confronted the same situation when the disappearance of hogs on his parents' plantation proved chronic. "The negroes have been behaving so badly about the hogs," he complained to his mother. "Mr. Anderson [the overseer] will know [what to do] without any suggestion how to punish them for their rascality." But, Anderson appeared to have little luck in stopping the pilfering of pigs. In another instance, Amon DeLaughter enjoyed little more success than his fellow managers when he caught and whipped "Birl and Isaac" for stealing a hog.[19]

Chickens stood second to pigs on the list of choice foods to steal. Louis Goldsborough was only one of many overseers who dealt with epidemics of chicken stealing. "Our chickens were frequently stolen at the old cabin," he expressed on a typical occasion. The overseer/manager sought to rectify the problem by directing carpenter William to build a sturdier structure, one that Goldsborough could admire for its potential to stop thievery. "This shall now, I hope [allow us to] have plenty of fresh eggs and young chickens to boot," he remarked gleefully. Goldsborough's optimism found itself quickly dashed, though, for bondservants shortly after helped themselves to the chickens and eggs from the "new cabin."[20]

During the early 1850s, overseer Amon DeLaughter, like Goldsborough, faced rampant theft, whether from the enslaved on the plantation or from the surrounding community. He regretted the fact that chickens were stolen with impunity. Understanding the games bondpeople played, he sometimes caught the rogues, but most of the time he did not. For several years, his journals indicated the thefts but no punishments. Slaves were winning this power struggle, at least until one slave was caught. In 1854, the overseer delighted in finally nabbing Jack for the infraction. The malefactor thereafter suffered a whipping at the overseer's hand. Two weeks later, the frustrated overseer recorded that the "stealing of chickens" had started again.[21]

Pigs and chickens were not the only foods stolen by the enslaved. Crops such as potatoes, collard greens, and squash—for that matter, everything edible—disappeared at one time or another from plantations and farms. Daniel and Scot stole potatoes from owner Nancy DeLaughter, earning a whipping when identified. Henry W. Todd, the executor of a Gadsden County estate, could not stop residents or nonresidents from stealing. Much like the Kilcrease slaves, these pilferers not only took hogs from the home place and from neighbors in the area but also nabbed collard greens, squash, tomatoes, corn, and other vegetables with seeming impunity.[22]

Sometimes, even the most assimilated bondservants surprised their owners by stealing. Quite a few bondservants acted differently, indeed, when out of view of their owners, and it was evident that a part of a slave's personality, as was true for Randall Jr., simply could involve duplicity. The young man had been born on Edward Bradford's Leon County plantation. His father served as coachman, and both parents were house servants. As was true earlier with Virginia and Maryland traditions, where children often followed in learning the skills and duties of their parents, the younger Randall was being trained to take his father's place.

In a sense, that's where Randall's problem started. In the slave community hierarchy, he and his parents were looked upon as privileged bondservants. One privilege permitted, and often required, movement, and in his subsequent travels with his father, Randall Jr. learned about the outside world. When eventually tasked by the owner to take goods to Tallahassee, Randall Jr. devised a plan to steal bacon from the plantation smokehouse and barter it for whiskey when he and his companion Molly got to the capital city. The master discovered the plot. As Bradford's daughter recalled, these bondservants suffered consequential punishments. Randall Jr. nonetheless had moved toward adoption of the dual personality resorted to by so many of his fellow bondmen and bondwomen. He presented one face to the owner while taking advantage of what the owner provided to him, in his case helpful knowledge of the world outside plantation bounds, to more easily pilfer while participating in the larger economy. Randall Jr. and others easily could present one person at one time and another at a different time.[23]

To summarize, Florida slaves who stole exercised this nonthreatening form of resistance throughout the territorial and antebellum periods. Stealing symbolized defiance of the master's authority. The majority stayed on their own plantations and farms when stealing, but this dynamic began to change over time, at least in certain areas, as others began to venture away from their domiciles more frequently during the mid-1840s to the 1860s. From the 1,403 sources mentioned previously, bondservants who stole food or other materials at least once appeared 351 times during the period 1821 to 1861. Authority figures noted that those who pilfered were male 97 percent of the time. The incidence of theft increased by a ratio of two to one from the mid-1840s to the 1860s. With women working as cooks, seamstresses, and housekeepers in close proximity to valuable movable property, we can only speculate that slaveholders often turned a blind eye when things went missing from the house or simply did not record losses in journals, log books, or diaries. "As the persons in charge of food preparation for both whites and their own families," Jacqueline Jones notes, "women at times clandestinely fed runaways in an effort to keep them out of harm's way." In many ways, bondwomen truly controlled the kitchens of antebellum Florida.[24]

Pride in Work as Well as in Pilferage

The point that enslaved women controlled the kitchens of Middle Florida permits a greater one to be made. Whatever level of dissidence otherwise may have prevailed, privileged slaves as a rule took pride in their work. Many of these cherished positions—cooks, house servants, wagoners, carpenters, bricklayers, and seamstresses, just to name a few—required special skills and often years of experience. These bondservants, whether pilferers or not, generally were more concerned about the quality of their bondage than their liberty. When owners sought to take these cherished positions from those who held them and move the dispossessed to some type of field work, those affected often expressed their frustrations in a manner that prompted descriptions of them as surly. Enslaved blacks hoped, in this case, to use nonthreatening resistance to get their former positions restored. Charles, a man owned by Ellen Wirt McCormick, took pleasure in his position as a house servant. For a while, he had been hired out to work in Tallahassee in the same capacity. When the bondservant got wind that his master planned to sell him as a field hand, he took action to squelch her plans. At the first opportunity and with no facade of deference, he sharply told his prospective buyer that he had "never been in the field and done any hard work." Upset by this episode, the owner recorded, "Of course, Mr. Crong declin[ed] closing the deal."[25]

As with Charles, Henry Minor had his quality of life challenged when the owner confronted him with field work. A newcomer to Wirtland plantation, the bondservant had been accustomed to laboring as a hireling in Tallahassee. In town, he did not have to concern himself with such lowly efforts as planting, plowing, hoeing, and picking cotton. Plus, he was away from the owner's watchful eye. Now, the bondservant expressed through his inactions that he did not care for planting, picking cotton, or harvesting crops as a field hand. When the overseer instructed him to plant trees, he grew petulant and made it clear that he would rather be sold. Irritated by the attitude, Mrs. Wirt attempted to assert hegemony over the laborer's life by insisting, "He is not his own master, to come and go as he pleases to the arrogance of his owner." Nonetheless, Henry continued to make his concerns about work preferences known. He, unlike many other bondpersons, paid little deference to the all-powerful white authority figure, offering insults about wanting to be sold rather than do the assigned work. In violent frontier Middle Florida, Henry needed to exercise caution about what might have been perceived as insults, for they could lead to punishment and even death. He acted nonetheless.[26]

Catherine Randall faced a similar challenge with her bondservant Eliza as did Ellen Wirt McCormick with Lucy. Eliza proved disagreeable after being asked to work in the field. Yet, when Catherine conveyed to her husband Eliza's sentiments, Catherine suggested that the bondservant did not mind continuing to cook, even though she balked at doing anything else. Catherine specifically quoted Eliza as saying she believed her task was to cook, "and [she had] a notion that nothing else [is] to be expected of her." Illustrative of the fact that such battles persisted between owners and digruntled and not-so-subtle bondservants over work assignments, Ellen Wirt McCormick observed of her slave, "Lucy is unfit for field" work but "make[s] no objection to cooking for them." As often was the case with other slaveholders, the McCormicks needed Lucy to help in the fields and said as much to her. "So, as soon as she [Lucy] is well [she must comply]," they recorded. On the other hand, no evidence comes to hand that suggests Lucy actually returned to the field.[27]

Care should be taken to understand that Eliza and Lucy may have been ill-prepared for their new work routine upon arrival on the Middle Florida cotton frontier. Although not set immediately in Florida, the experience of Lydia, who was forcibly removed from her Maryland home to a large cotton plantation in South Carolina, echoes tellingly. Charles Ball, born in 1780 on a Maryland plantation, ended up on the same plantation and later told Lydia's story in his own autobiography. Ball recorded that blacks in the slave community considered Lydia "a great beauty among people of color." She had been trained from childhood to be a house servant for her white female master until being sold to Wade Hampton I. As was the case for many planters on the expanding Florida frontier, South Carolinian Hampton needed field workers and not house servants to turn cotton into cash. Lydia's beauty, light-skinned complexion, and history as a waiting maid, however, did not keep Hampton's overseer from abusing her. Ill-prepared to work in the fields, Lydia lamented, "I have several times been whipped unmercifully because I was not strong enough to do as much work with the hoe, as the other women, who . . . have been accustomed from their infancy to work in the field." Ball claimed that Lydia soon died from "hardships and suffering" at the hands of an "inhuman" overseer. Lucy's and Eliza's lives may not have ended as tragically as did Lydia's; but, given that they had been raised as house servants in Maryland as well, they may have had similar experiences to Lydia's. Of the two Middle Florida bondservants, Lucy, at least, may have prevailed by successfully avoiding arduous field work.[28]

Reflecting the layers of complications that underlay the tapestry of bondage, assimilated bondservants who were skilled or semiskilled—and who took pride in their work—more often challenged the slaveholder over the conditions of their enslavement than did slaves with lesser skills. This was true in Georgia, Alabama, and the Carolinas, as well as in Florida. Sometimes, for example, the bondservant's desire to be as far away from the master and his family could trump the conditions of servitude. As historian Jacqueline Jones has observed, "Interviews with former slaves suggest that the advantages of domestic service over field work for women have been exaggerated in accounts written by whites."[29]

Claude A. Wilson illuminated this case with a reminiscence. "[My] mother was very rebellious toward her [house] duties," he recalled, "and constantly harassed the 'Missus' about letting her work in the fields with her husband." Wilson's mother probably did not want to remain under the constant eye of the mistress, nor did she want to be on call at all times or to face the potential of sexual exploitation by whites in such a close environment. As Jones noted, "For any one or all of these reasons, black women might prefer field work to housework. . . . The master's house offered no shelter from the most brutal manifestations of slavery." In a test of wills, the house servant continued to be very testy with the master about her domestic duties. The Columbia County owner eventually allowed Wilson's mother to labor alongside her husband.[30]

In an effort to instill the qualities that masters believed were most desirable in acculturated bondservants, domestic work assignments almost always kept the enslaved worker under constant surveillance of slave owners. Some bondpeople worked but forthrightly criticized their domestic work routines in hopes of being dismissed from such chores by their masters. At Wirtland, the owner disapproved on one occasion of the way a house servant was carrying out her work assignment. He noted that she had become unmanageable and started working to her own "liking." William Wirt's troubles did not stop with this particular house servant, for ultimately he had to eject another woman from the kitchen who believed that she, too, had been overworked. This and similar evidence suggests that nineteenth-century Florida women did not clamor for domestic work, as perhaps was the case for eighteenth-century bondservants.[31]

2. Stepping Up the Degrees of Resistance

I am doeing all I noe to make the slaves work.
—John Evans to George Noble Jones, September 2, 1852

The practice of dissidence by enslaved Floridians involved degrees of intensity, as would be expected. Escalation could occur in a variety of ways and manifest itself very privately or quite publicly. Sometimes the results evidenced themselves immediately; other times discovery or recognition might not occur for a while. The actions could be of the simplest nature or reflect considerable intelligence and creativity. Complications, as always, abounded.

When bondpeople perceived that owners and overseers had overstepped their bounds with regard to the slave community, for instance, some protested by temporarily not working. An instance arose on one of George Noble Jones's plantations when an overseer, the sawmill manager, courted the favor of one particular female slave. Eugene D. Genovese, addressing such situations, claimed that white men directed their attention toward "single girls by using a combination of flattery, bribes and the ever-present threat of force." Indeed, George Noble Jones's overseer Jonathan Roberson used flattery and bribes. He thought that he easily could place one foot in the world of the enslaved and keep the other in the world controlled by powerful whites. He was wrong, and the effort did not sit well with the plantation's male bondservants. Given that male slaves outnumbered the females of marriageable age, these men viewed Roberson as an unwanted and unfair competitor. And, beyond the question of indignities of sexual exploitation, these men wanted the overseer to stay out of the business and private affairs of the slave community. They sent him a clear message of their disapproval by their inaction: they simply refused to work for him. This situation appears not to have changed over time. Over the three-year period of Roberson's employment as overseer, according to surviving documentation, bondpeople on that particular plantation seemingly worked when they wanted to.[1]

A similar situation occurred at another plantation owned by Jones when slave complaints and grouchy ways reverberated in the wake of overseer actions. John Evans should have surmised that he was not making his management of the men any easier when he, like Roberson, interfered in the internal affairs of the slave community by fathering at least two children, a boy named Robert and a girl, Mary. Their mother was Mariah, an unmarried slave. Much like the situation at Jones's El Destino plantation, where the incident involving Jonathan Roberson occurred, men of courting and marriageable age at Evans's Chemonie plantation outnumbered eligible females. This may not have been the only reason why males became antagonistic toward Evans, but it could account for some of the plantation's troubles. No wonder that Evans often complained to the owner that he was behind in his work. "I am doeing all I noe to make the slaves work," he exclaimed.[2]

Such token acts against servitude and interference in the affairs of the slave community repeatedly challenged the authority of whites during Florida's antebellum period. Given the callous manner in which slaveholders could sell, split, and abuse slave families, as well as mortgage them for cash, it is not surprising that slaves fought authority figures the best way they could as they endeavored to reconfigure and protect their lives and families in an unstable and threatening environment.[3]

Admittedly, much of what is known about the enslaved in nineteenth-century Florida comes from sources that focus purely on the large slaveholding Middle Florida region of the panhandle, for these planters wrote more about their perceptions than did other slaveholders in the territory and state. But, glimpses of the daily struggles between master and the enslaved in East and West Florida can be gleaned as well by focusing on plantations large and small.

In Putnam County, for instance, Winston Stephens owned about eight individuals. Not unlike many of his peers, he believed himself to be a caring and amiable master. In a pattern often repeated, Stephens's slaves perceived the matter quite differently. As a result, their owner's amiable nature did not keep his subjects from griping about their work routines. Burrel, born in Florida and quite articulate, had risen to become the trusted driver of the bondservants on his master's farm. When he concluded that the bondpeople were being pushed too hard, however, he made his complaints known to the owner's wife, Octavia. He chose to avoid subtle talk; rather, he spoke openly and directly about the amount of work the bondservants were being ordered to perform.[4]

Similarly, after the passing of her husband, Frances Blitch of Marion County found herself in charge of farm management. This proved no easy task. She especially experienced frustration with her slave Horace. The forty-year-old refused to work as he once had when her husband supervised the farm, leaving the impression that he would take to the woods should Frances attempt to compel him. She concluded that the bondservant had become "profitless troublesome and expensive to said Estate" for he had a "habit of absconding."[5]

Hiring Out

From 1821 to 1850, Florida bondservants generally looked favorably on the thought of being hired out. This situation began to change, though, with the coming of the mid- to late 1850s and the Civil War. In the latter era particularly, with southern men leaving for the war, fewer and fewer remained behind to see to the necessary work. Hired bondservants accordingly were expected to labor harder and longer during this period. Many responded by fighting the conditions of their employment. This, in turn, produced threats from masters, masters' spouses, and masters' agents that the bondpeople would be hired out if they continued to challenge authority.

The Stephens family provides such an example. With her husband away fighting for the Confederacy, Octavia Stephens, still in her early twenties and not long a newlywed, managed the farm alone, doing all that she could to keep the slaves under her strict control. As was the case for Frances Blitch and countless other white women of the South, Octavia found herself buffeted by the challenge. Left alone with slaves, especially male bondservants, she encountered enormous difficulties in managing them. Writing from the army on one occasion, Winston Stephens complimented his wife for speaking "so short" to driver Burrel. Clearly, though, that approach failed to accomplish the desired goal, for in December 1861, the husband wrote again instructing his wife to inform Burrel and the others, by way of a threat, that he would "hire the whole of them out" if they continued their cantankerous ways. Apparently, Burrel, through his actions, manifested a belief that, in the absence of Octavia Stephens's husband, he then was the man of the white and black families on the farm.[6]

Over time, the Stephens farm bondpeople continued to challenge Octavia's authority, and owner Winston eventually made good on his threat to hire some of them out in the vicinity. This naturally did not sit well with the hirelings, and they expressed their discontent about the quality of their work assignments and their overall treatment. After being whipped several times for not working to the satisfaction of their new employer, the Stephens's bondservants reported their "mistreatment" to the owner on their weekend visits to the farm. Octavia listened to the allegations, but she still sent them back to complete their lease agreements with their temporary master.[7]

There even were examples of owners who chafed so strongly at an individual's behavior that they simply refused to hire out such a bondservant. Instead, owners sold recalcitrant slaves to others who intended to hire them out. An instance of such an arrangement arose in Alachua County as early as 1840. Corinna Aldrich reported the incident to her brother, the artist Mannevillette Brown. "Aunt Hall has returned to Jacksonville," she wrote. "I believe she has gone to Charleston to buy a nigger. . . . She had a man—he did not suit her, and I bought him, and have hired him out at $125 per month. He will keep me in pin money." Aldrich concluded, "He is an old Jackass—Edward & Charles offered to hire him for her, but no, she would sell him."[8]

Feigned Illness and Women

As enslaved persons in nineteenth-century Florida were becoming more assimilated, they persisted, as has been seen, in devising schemes and coordinating efforts to make the conditions of their enslavement more endurable. As a part of this process, the feigning of illnesses marked the entire era, and the practice does not appear to have changed substantively over time. In fact, feigned illness ranked near the top in the enslaved person's arsenal of token resistance to bondage, representing, as it did, a step-up in intensity of resistance to work-pace demands. As historian James Oakes noted, thwarting this nonviolent form of resistance already had plagued slaveholders throughout the eighteenth century. James Carter, a member of one of Georgia's wealthiest and earliest planter families, helps to underscore Oakes's argument. Carter experienced so much trouble managing his bondservants that he was advised "to sell about half of his Negroes, those that are unfaithful, [and] those women that pretend to be always sick."[9]

Yet Carter, along with nineteenth-century slaveholders throughout the South, had to be careful in determining whether their bondservants were faking or truly were ill. On the one hand, slaveholders knew that, by forcing sick laborers back to work, they could damage their investment permanently or even destroy it. They understood as well that all women experienced certain "female problems" that sometimes required time off from their regular work assignments. On the other hand, owners and drivers could not consistently concede the upper hand to these bondservants in the slave community. In this matter, slaveholders particularly walked a tight rope.[10]

Gender played a part in this dynamic form of resistance. As Deborah Gray White has noted, "The most common form of female-defense was feigning illness." Accordingly, female slaves professed illness more often than males. This fact did not change from the eighteenth to the nineteenth century, at least in

Florida. Throughout the territorial and statehood periods, bondwomen proved more effective than males at using illnesses to get sporadic days off from their burdensome work routines and more persistent in doing so.[11]

Some slave women, in fact, enjoyed a great deal of success in getting more than just a few days off from field work. Take the case of Hannah. For her and many females, giving birth—together with related complications—provided relatively easy opportunities or pretexts for work stoppages or slowdowns. A slave of William D. Moseley, Hannah remained sick for fifty-two days prior to the birth of her mulatto son. But, unlike many slaveholders in Middle Florida who instructed their overseers or bondwomen to administer medicine or home remedies to the medically needy bondservants, Moseley called upon a medical doctor to attend to Hannah and her infant. Two weeks later, the owner described the bondwoman as "still very sick" from childbirth, and the records he kept do not indicate when she returned to work. A larger question of course can be asked: who fathered Hannah's mulatto child, owned by Moseley? According to former slave Harriet Jacobs, "Southern women often marry a man knowing that he is the father of many little slaves." Charlotte Martin, a former bondservant born and raised on a Florida plantation, echoed Jacobs's sentiments when she said, "Sometimes the master himself had sexual relations with his female slaves." Sexual slavery, or, as Brenda E. Stevenson aptly noted, "concubinage," became an unfortunate form of forced labor and a way of life for many enslaved females. Indeed, in Florida slave society, most members of white society generally knew those men who took enslaved women and young girls as concubines and fathered mulatto children with them but only whispered their names in private company.[12]

Much like Hannah, Nelly, one of the Wirtland slaves, also took privileges as a new mother to prolong her stay away from the fields. "Nelly has never been in the field since the birth of her child," Ellen McCormick informed her mother, "having been a good deal invalid ever since, suffering with pains and a constant visitation of month[ly] sickness until last month when she misset." McCormick added, "So soon as she is dismissed from the hospital and doing [better], she will go into the field again." In the meantime, Nelly worked in the house doing a "little sewing." But Ellen wanted Nelly to return to the fields as soon as possible. "I shall not keep her from the field when she can otherwise [be out there]," she insisted. Seemingly, Nelly did not return to the field during a convalescence period of about three months—a period considerably longer than most slave women enjoyed. As long as they did not overdo using illness as an excuse, many bondwomen could take a few days off without suffering adverse consequences. Nelly, though, managed to negotiate more time off than the average slave could expect on the large plantations in Middle Florida.[13]

The process of determining whether enslaved blacks actually were sick bedeviled owners and overseers through the antebellum period. It was true that the incidences of illness in Florida women increased substantially from the 1820s to the 1840s. In one incidence occurring during the early 1840s, ships from the Caribbean brought yellow fever to Middle Florida. Black and white inhabitants were stricken with the deadly plague, and fatalities ran high. Given that Florida mimicked other tropical environments by hosting diseases such as yellow fever and malaria—carried to human victims quite efficiently by mosquitoes and other insects—it became increasingly more difficult for owners to make timely determinations of slave health.

So, masters had to play detective in evaluating the true health conditions of their bondservants. One case involved Sally, a slave belonging to Thomas Randall. In 1828, the slaveholder was compelled to spend valuable time looking carefully at her claim, eventually concluding that Sally "is not much sick and supposes her privileged [by not having to work]." Twenty-eight years after Randall's experience with Sally's attempt to deceive him about the state of her health, men such as overseer A. R. McCall continued to face the reality that bondservants were using various bogus illnesses as a reason for avoiding work. Ellen was one of them. McCall acknowledged as much in 1856 when he proclaimed that Ellen had not really been sick but was only trying to "deceive" him to keep from doing any work.[14]

Over time, Florida bondservants—whether from necessity or not—seemingly became better and more convincing actors and actresses in their efforts to resist their enslavement. Given that both master and bondservant wore masks of deception, blacks sometimes played the helpless obedient slave while whites played the good and caring master. One particular slave sought to manipulate the paternalistic facade of her master to her advantage. This otherwise quiet and obedient bondservant convinced her Leon County master and overseer that she could handle only "light" chores around the house since she could not walk or work without the assistance of crutches. Wanting to appear caring in front of the rest of the slave community, the master allowed the slave a schedule that involved only such "light" duties.

Wearing her mask of deception, the bondservant managed to manipulate the master and overseer, who did not know her nearly as well as they had believed. Indeed, some bondpeople did not need to be within the master's view in order to evidence a highly refined and deceptive side of their character and personality. Such was the case with this particular woman. According to the memory of her fellow slave Uncle Demps, the woman put on such an act that, in today's vernacular, she might have won an Academy Award. As it turned out, the master and the overseer after seven years learned of her great talent as an actress. At the Civil War's end, this allegedly calm and sedate women, now free, threw down her crutches and walked briskly out of her former owner's house, never to be seen again. Persons such as she, as they engaged in their day-to-day resistance, perceived how to squeeze out small liberties that allowed them to exhibit some degree of self-determination in a system designed to rob them of body, soul, and mind.[15]

The Rest of the Feigned Illness Story

Although women more commonly feigned illness, men managed their share of such deception too. Much like their female counterparts, men also wore a mask of deception, claiming to be sick in order to secure a day or more off from work. By way of illustration, Washington held the record for sick days on Charles Bannerman's plantation. In a three-month period, the owner recorded that the bondservant lay out sick for forty-five days. Possibly Washington did experience various illnesses in disease-ridden Middle Florida, but available evidence suggests that a desire to avoid required work routines played a major role in the way he presented his case.[16]

Louis Goldsborough, a son-in-law and overseer on William Wirt's large Jefferson County plantation, witnessed the same dynamics at play during the 1830s. "The Negroes are all well," he observed at one point, "saving a couple of them who complained yesterday of pains and colds." The overseer often would allow these "sick" slaves a few days off to recuperate. It seems that Wirt's brother-in-law John Gamble also saw his share of "sickness" among slaves for years after Goldsborough's report as male bondservants continued to claim illnesses in order to get periodic relief from their various work routines. The planter recorded, for example, 119 days lost in 1835, 80 of them to various illnesses among his bondservants.[17]

From the 1830s to well into the 1850s, certain trends manifested themselves with respect to illnesses of male and female slaves. Particularly, bondpeople on nineteenth-century farms or plantations routinely took "time off" during the height of the planting or harvesting season, much as did other slaves on plantations and farms through the South during this general period. Based upon newspaper advertisements and other documentary accounts, table 3 illustrates that more runaways departed farms and plantations during the height of the harvesting or cotton-picking season, from September to December, than at other times. Writing about enslaved blacks on George Noble Jones's El Destino and Chemonie plantations in Middle Florida, Kathryn T. Abbey noted that "slaves frequently ran way, usually because they were being hard pressed during the harvest time." The next largest group left during the months of April to

Table 3. Florida Runaway Seasonal Trends

	1821–40 percentage of enslaved blacks	1841–60 percentage of enslaved blacks
January–March	15	16
April–June	26	27
July–August	24	25
September–December	35	32

Sources: Florida and Georgia extant newspapers, 1821–60, as well as other documentary accounts.

June, or what may be generally referred to as the clearing and planting season. With the exception of the first quarter of each year, slaves could be expected to abscond at just about any time of the year.

Admittedly, much sickness could have arisen from the strain of work or the season. Still, during the cotton-picking season in September 1839, Ellen Wirt Voss complained that "almost every man, woman, and child with two exceptions have been sick." Her brother Henry Wirt echoed her words by observing that their mother's bondservants constantly reported sick during the planting season. "I think Charlotte [a bondservant] told me their was more sickness during the months of May, June, and July among the negroes that she had ever known," Henry recalled on one occasion, likely with a sense of befuddlement as to what it all meant.[18]

Using available Florida probate records, diaries, journals, notes, and letters, an idea can be gained of the frequency with which authority figures recorded illnesses and accidents that kept slave workers from laboring, at least in Middle Florida, from 1821 to 1865. In these sources, 356 slaves were listed as being ill at least one or more times. With the exception of special notations concerning women with "female problems," most entries merely named the slave and described him or her as "ill" or "sick today." When compared to males, females reported illnesses 73 percent of the time from 1821 to 1865. Men could have been sick just as much as women, but it is clear that slaveholders took particular care to note when their female bondservants were alleged to be in poor health. Of the women noted as being ill, 72 percent were between the ages of thirteen and thirty-seven. Since these generally represented the reproductive years of women, masters may have been more interested in keeping consistent health records of female bondservants. The females, after all were primarily responsible for perpetuating the "peculiar institution" by their reproduction of slave offspring.

Paternalism and Dissidence

In creating their own world, bondmen and bondwomen fashioned the slave community as the viable core of their universe. Its protections surrounded men and women who lived each day of their lives subject to the ever-present threat of physical abuse, sexual exploitation, sale, and forcible removal and separation from family members. Much as was the case with thousands of other bondservants uprooted from family members in moves from the Upper to the Lower South, arrivals in Florida were compelled to reconfigure the slave family in the new land. As they created their own new world and community, they secured the slave family at its center.[19]

Although they generally did not recognize the slave family in a legal sense, the larger number of slaveholders at least apprehended its importance to individuals and the overall slave community. Middle Florida slave trader and planter Achille Murat understood the importance of role-playing within the context of family. In fact, the slaveholder considered himself, like many other slave owners in the region, to be a "father rather than . . . a master" to bondpeople. As patriarchs of the white and black extended family, most—or at least many—at various times tried to exhibit a paternalistic nature in dealing with their bondservants. They knew that by compromising and offering incentives to their enslaved workers, they stood a better chance of bringing peace to their farms and plantations. With any luck, it could make them very successful and wealthy to boot.[20]

Men such as William Wirt and his son-in-law Thomas Randall hesitated little in considering themselves paternalistic slaveholders. Sharing a plantation with Wirt, Randall believed he could keep the bondpeople in the slave community "happy and contented" by offering to bring a slave from Maryland to be united with her husband on the owner's Florida plantation. As a part of the larger forced removal of bondservants from the Upper South to the Lower South, in 1828 Randall and the Wirt family had brought a group of men, women, and children with them from Maryland to Leon County. In the process, bondpeople who came with the Wirts and Randall or otherwise were settled in Middle Florida were torn from homes, families, and other relationships in Maryland, Virginia, and the Carolinas during the 1820s and 1830s. It was an experience hard for any survivor to forget, and, while Randall may have felt that a single gesture could overcome the legacy that had been created, he and others like him time and again grappled with the frustrations that persisted.[21]

The facts in Randall's case were these. David, who had been purchased from Nicholas Thomas in Maryland by Randall's father-in-law, Wirt, had an abroad marriage (these were marriages bondservants unwillingly left behind in their forced removal from the Upper South). After being away from his wife and children, the bondservant demonstrated his masculinity by standing up and asking Randall in no uncertain terms to sell him if his children and wife were not purchased. The newly arrived overseer, wanting to show his paternalistic side in the process of keeping harmony in the slave quarters, knew that a man like David "would infect the whole body of the black community with his despondence" if conditions did not change. Randall subsequently purchased David's wife and younger children, and they joined him on the Wirtland plantation. "I regret I was not at home to witness the reunion of David and his wife," Randall ultimately informed Wirt. "They are very happy."[22]

But were men like Randall, Wirt, or even Murat paternalists in the truest sense of the word? And was David really happy and forgiving? Forceful removal of human beings from their homes and from older family members such as mothers and fathers, together with the painful ordeal of relocation to Florida, called into question whether any genuine paternalistic sensibilities were at play with Wirt, Randall, or their peers. How could an owner or manager purport to treat his or her "people" with kindness and concern and at the same time pull asunder their families and kinfolk? Randall's actions admittedly were unusual in this case, for most slaveholders who settled in the region from 1821 to 1840 sought to get rich quick and demonstrated nowhere near such regard for the slave family or community. It unfortunately became more common for slaveholders to tear slave families apart in the search for cheap land and those ever-desired quick profits.

Perhaps no one knew about the importance of paternalism more than Zephaniah Kingsley, an experienced slave trader and owner, who lived in East Florida under Spanish rule. Unlike the majority of Middle Florida farmers and planters, Kingsley had been an Atlantic world traveler, having obtained slaves in Gambia, Saint Domingue, and Cuba, as well as in other parts of the Caribbean. And from his experience, Kingsley learned a valuable lesson: he came to understand that enslaved blacks in that region worked better and more efficiently under the task system than they did under the gang system.[23]

Subsequent experiences reinforced for Kingsley the insight he had gained. He grew more convinced that his enslaved laborers were less ill-tempered when given the opportunity to work under the task system. The work routine permitted his bondservants to complete their assignments by two or three o'clock each day, allowing them time for personal matters and concerns. Kingsley believed that this approach helped to minimize day-to-day dissidence on his East Florida estate and, by extension, would achieve the same results elsewhere. The use of the task system came into widespread practice in East and West Florida where small and medium-sized plantations existed, whereas the gang system reigned supreme in the Middle Florida plantation belt.[24]

On the plantations and farms of nineteenth-century Florida, enslaved people, like their counterparts throughout the South, rarely rose up in rebellion against their masters. In their daily dissidence, slaves, as Gerald W. Mullin noted for eighteenth-century slaves in Virginia, more commonly used inward or non-threatening forms of rebellion that did not undermine Florida's slave society in any profound manner. As seen in this chapter, these could involve work stoppages and feigned illnesses, among other things. Yet, enslaved Florida blacks often did not bite their tongues when expressing thoughts about their work routines. These tactics could have proven self-destructive and even fatal in a violent Florida frontier area, but slaves still used these token forms of rebellion to wrest concessions from their masters as they strove to create, preserve, and protect family and community.[25]

PART TWO

Running Away

3. Away without Leave

Such gallow-birds as flock here every winter . . .
—*Apalachicola Commercial Advertiser,* March 11, 1844

A drama played out at St. Augustine in 1830 that was to see itself repeated countless times during Florida's pre-emancipation era, a circumstance that spoke volumes about slave humanity and the courage to resist. The story commenced when Mary A. Sanchez purchased a man named George from the estate of the "late Col. Weeks" of the Ancient City. Then, shortly after George arrived at his new home, he ran away. As sometimes happened, the new owner never recaptured her fugitive. His reasons for departure are not known with certainty. As discussed in this chapter, though, George's thinking may be surmised in a manner that permits insight on a broader basis into the courageous attempt of a single bondman to discard his chains.[1]

The causes of flight were many. In Mary Sanchez's case, the slaveholder faced what many owners experienced when enslaved blacks feared the transition from one owner to another: they simply ran off. The event easily could have occurred for a host of reasons. Individuals and groups time and again seized opportunities to abscond from the farms and plantations of Florida due to, for example, a change in venue, a breakdown in plantation management, the death or replacement of owners, or alterations in the master's household finances that might portend a modification in their status. Others disappeared because of abusive treatment by authority figures. Some could not stand the pain of separation from spouses and absconded in an attempt to reunite with family members.

The very nature of Florida's development over time caused bondpeople within and outside its boundaries to view the peninsula as a runaway haven. Not surprisingly, then, nineteenth-century bondpeople escaped from farms and plantations—and enslaved persons from other jurisdictions absconded to the peninsula as well. Many whites understood this fact and reflected on what they perceived as the high incidence of truancy in Florida. A St. Augustine journalist expressed in 1824 what many others knew to be common and had feared for years: many newcomers refused to settle in the territory "because they are liable to the loss of their negroes by elopement."[2] The intra- and interstate flight of bondservants would continue to mark nineteenth-century Florida until freedom came for all, and, as had been the case in 1824, the territory and state's image as a haven for runaways remained a constant source of concern to whites.

As early as 1828, slaveholders, many of whom ranked influentially in territorial political and legislative circles, foresaw a serious problem with laborers departing their domiciles. During that year, the legislative council prohibited slaves from "lurking" around places where they had no permission to visit. The law declared that "many times slaves run away, and hide, and [are] in swamps, woods, and other obscure places killing hogs and committing other injuries to the inhabitants." A newspaperman expanded upon the point in 1834: "There are few things which have been subjects of greater complaint for the last two or three years than runaway negroes." The journalist went on to portray the problem's depth. Fugitives, he insisted, "are permitted to go at large, and plunder the public."[3]

Lurking

As apparently was true with Mary Sanchez's George, Florida bondservants often "took off" as an expression of their disapproval at being sold to a new owner. Sanchez sent out notices that all would be forgiven if George voluntarily returned to her. But the slave owner, like so many other masters, deceived herself into believing that bondservants such as George wanted to remain slaves. Meanwhile, no one apparently asked George or other bondservants their thoughts about being stolen, sold, and enslaved.[4]

Many owners, though, seemed more concerned about their slaves "lurking" than they did about escapees completely separating from slavery by running off. Middle Florida bondpeople—and most of Florida's enslaved population lived in that region of the panhandle centered on Tallahassee—as a general rule saw little of the outside world beyond their masters' gateposts. So, while the region's slaveholders compelled enactment of tough laws to curtail any "outside" movements of their bondpeople, they aimed special attention at addressing the more localized version of flight.[5]

As would be the case with other stringent measures designed to regulate slave life and behavior, however, the "lurking" statute proved mostly unenforceable.

At times—or, at least it so appears from surviving accounts—lurking became commonplace. Available evidence suggests many of the reasons. From 1821 to 1850, when bondservants were "lurking," they primarily were visiting family and friends and generally not, as many whites believed, stealing from other plantations and farms. This pattern did change somewhat by the 1850s, as discussed in chapter 1. The surviving documentation also suggests something that slaveholders did not want to admit: their own workers often were the culprits who engaged in the pilfering that was blamed on lurkers.[6]

For males, more times than not, lurking involved a desire "to be with their wives or companions." Tom did not appreciate the forced separation from his wife after being purchased by Sarah Knighton of Jefferson County. He disappeared from the plantation shortly after arriving at his new home. Knighton believed that Tom could be found "lurking around the plantation of Asa May and estate of Richard Cole, as he has a wife at the latter place." In the same way, Nelson, described by his owner as "a very black boy, 22, high forehead," was "probably lurking around Tallahassee to be with his wife."[7]

Similarly, bondwomen also lurked around plantations and farms to be with their husbands. Sophia, a woman in her early twenties who was described by her owner as "thick set, not very black," departed her home plantation, according to the master, "to be in the neighborhood of Strawberry Mills [where her husband lived]." I. R. Harris, the executor of Daniel McLaughlin's Gadsden County estate, noted that Hattie was lurking around nearby Leon County to be with her husband. Obviously, women desired to reunite with their loved ones just as much as men did.[8]

Regardless of gender, some fugitives suspected of "lurking around" or "lying out" did so with the support of friends or to be among friends. As Eugene Genovese has noted, "While in slavery, blacks protected each other much more readily than they undermined or betrayed each other." This seems to have been the case with sixteen-year-old Elias, who departed his Jefferson County home. The young man found support among his friends while "lurking alternately between his neighborhood and that of Samuel Parkhill's in Leon County." As had been true with Elias, Charlotte found support among fellow bondservants and was traced to a certain slave community not far from where she lived. She obviously had protection there since she reportedly would frequent "certain Negro Quarters" and managed to do so usually without being detected by her master or the slave patrols.[9]

In the 1,403 plantation records, journals, letters, and 711 Florida and other newspaper advertisements that served as a research foundation for this study, the word "lurking" or "prowling" appeared 228 times from 1821 to 1860. Some 12 slaves lurked and prowled more than once. Of 216 slaves who were recorded as lurking or prowling at least one or more times, 86 citations were noted from 1821 to 1840, with men making up 82 percent and women 18 percent. This changed somewhat from 1841 to 1860, with these same sources citing 130 slaves lurking. Men made up 79 percent and women 21 percent. The incidence level of slaves lurking or prowling around from 1841 to 1860 increased by 50 percent when compared to the period from 1821 to 1840. From the survey, family, friends, and the overall slave community offered individuals cause to "lurk or prowl around" other neighborhoods. Nonetheless, the majority who "lurked around" ultimately returned to their domiciles.

While some persons lurked to be with loved ones and friends, other disgruntled absconders took off because they were upset with work routines. Most returned to their homes with the intention of bargaining with overseers and owners over their assignments. While the statistics are not conclusive, overseers appeared to encounter more problems of this nature than did owners. In order to understand why this might be so, a closer look at overseers appears in order. According to William Kauffman Scarborough, overseers, generally speaking, could be broken down into three classes. They were "the sons of planters, a floating population of amateur overseers, and the general body of professional managers."[10]

Amon DeLaughter fell into Scarborough's first group, the young sons of planters. In Amon's case, however, he managed the family plantation not for his father but for his mother. In fact, mother Nancy DeLaughter of Madison County represented a bit of an anomaly. She numbered as one of the mere 5 percent of females who qualified as planters, with twenty or more enslaved workers in Middle Florida, during much of the territorial and antebellum periods. Much as Charles Wilhelm Bulow had done several decades before in uprooting his "nearly 200" bondpeople from South Carolina to the peninsula, DeLaughter in January 1851 took her twenty enslaved workers with her from South Carolina's Edgefield District to her lands in Madison County, Florida. Shortly after their arrival, Amon took on responsibilities as overseer. Scarborough praised men like Amon DeLaughter, for he was a son of a planter. He noted that the "general reputation of this group was superior" to that of the other two groups. However, because he found himself taking constant recourse to corporal punishment, young Amon thought of himself as a complete failure as an overseer. As he noted in his journal, "I am now 20 years of age & my time has been but ill spent." In fact, after about three years of overseeing for his mother, he begged her to relieve him from such arduous duties.[11]

The specific incident that gave rise to Amon's resignation decision leaps from the pages of his journal. In early 1851, he faced a runaway problem with several individuals who maintained an "impudence" toward work. After he whipped several bondservants for poor performance, these slaves took off. Like many enslaved blacks in Middle Florida, they voluntarily returned a few days later. To demonstrate his hegemony over the twenty-two bondservants under his supervision—and, inadvertently, his lack of managerial skills—he made examples out of them by applying the whip to these disgruntled absconders in a severe, not to say brutal, manner. The bondservants under his control thereafter continued nonetheless to exhibit, in his eyes, so much rebelliousness that he hoped he could be trained for another profession for which he was more suited. At age twenty-three, Amon noted, "I have quit attending mothers business and I hope she may do better." As it turned out, his mother would hear none of it. In the next day's journal entry, he wrote, "I resume mothers business again." By 1860, Amon was still serving as overseer of his mother's plantation but appeared to be less than enthusiastic about his duties, saying, "I am now 26 years old & have done very little for the world at large."[12]

The fact that slaves often absconded when flogged for poor performance could be seen in examples ranging through the territorial and antebellum periods. Some three years after DeLaughter's experience, for instance, four women ran off after being whipped by the overseer for picking disappointingly small amounts of cotton on another Middle Florida plantation. Knowing that lawyer W. G. M. Davis would listen to them, they ran off to nearby Tallahassee to tell him of their plight. After Davis examined their bodies, he reported to townspeople that D. N. Moxley, the overseer, had badly whipped the women. John Evans, the overseer on another of the owner's plantations, informed the owner that he had examined their backs himself and "did not see anything that was cruel about them." Like some slaves who ran off to get relief from hard work routines, the four women soon returned and resumed picking cotton.[13]

Permanent Flight

Unlike the four Middle Florida women who temporarily resisted their treatment at the hands of authority figures by going to the town to get some relief, other determined fugitives evidenced greater decisiveness and commitment to flight, for they had no intention of returning to their domiciles to resume old work routines. Many of them roamed far and wide in their quest for freedom. Acculturation, literacy, skills, and confidence levels all factored in the tenacity of some of these runaways as they strove to secure freedom outside of the plantations, farms, industries, or urban areas where they once had lived and worked. As previously noted, for centuries the very nature of Florida's development had prompted fugitives within and outside its boundaries to view the peninsula as a "runaway haven."[14]

Achille Murat, a man associated with Napoleonic aristocracy, faced a similar situation to that of Mary Sanchez when his newly acquired slave Chester arrived at Lipona plantation. As one of Jefferson County's largest slaveholders, Murat, too, learned the reality of this state of affairs firsthand as he began a search for Chester only "two months" after his arrival in 1830 from North Carolina. Chester's plan of escape must have been a good one since Murat does not appear ever to have recorded the recapture of this bondservant. Much as with George and Chester, Mary, a bondwoman on another Middle Florida plantation, absconded after only a month of working on her third master's estate. As her experience suggests, disgruntled runaways continued to plague Murat over time. In 1845 he lost John, for example, to elopement. A year later, Tim got as far as Thomasville, Georgia, before his recapture.[15]

John Gamble—another wealthy white man, one who forcibly had uprooted his bondservants from Richmond, Virginia, to Leon County during the late 1820s—similarly experienced problems shortly after arriving in what was to become the Sunshine State. Significantly, surviving evidence suggests that Gamble endured serious runaway problems throughout the 1830s because his bondservants simply did not like their new home. These uprooted bondservants had been compelled to leave family and loved ones behind. The situation involving Gamble and runaways had not changed for the owner by the 1840s. For example, when slaves purchased by him from one particular planter disappeared in 1842, his overseer found most of the fugitives at a familiar plantation among family and friends. They had settled in at the new location with no intentions of returning to the Gamble plantation, at least not until forced to do so. Ultimately, they were returned to their new owner, took their punishment, and went back to work. Still, punishment did not deter some, for they continued to run away to be with family and friends.[16]

Enslaved workers who experienced ownership by multiple masters appear to have run away with greater frequency than those who had only one master. Based upon public and private sources concerning Florida runaways from 1821 to 1860, 279 listed two or more previous owners. A total of 134 had one previous owner from 1821 to 1840, with women making up 53 percent and men 47 percent. From 1841 to 1860, 145 slaves—51 percent women, 49 percent men—were listed as having two or more owners. It would appear from the data that men and women averaged about the same number of owners during much of the period under study. Meanwhile, 61 percent of the 279 slaves listed as having one or more previous owners were between the ages of fourteen and forty-five.

As has been reported for Virginia, North Carolina, and South Carolina, a bondperson might well have experienced three previous owners before being placed on the auction block for the fourth time. This nearly was the case with Lawrence, who fled Tallahassee before he could be bargained away yet again. For his part, Oral disappeared from Pensacola prior to his third change of ownership, this time to Tallahassee's mayor B. C. Willis. As was true with Oral, Matthew absconded from Henry Bird's Tallahassee estate before being sold on a third occasion. Other examples abound. After acquiring Dennis on consignment, the Tallahassee slave-trading firm of Hughes and Patterson lost the bondservant to flight. Fearing that he would go on the auction block for the second time in Middle Florida, Will departed Apalachicola several days after his owner's death.[17]

As in eighteenth-century Virginia, some persons ran away when new overseers took over the management of farms or plantations or else might opt to depart to demonstrate their disenchantment with new rules and directives. As historian Philip D. Morgan noted, workers resisted when a new overseer took over management of the Virginia Richneck Quarter as early as 1737. Levels of resistance to new overseers seemed only to increase over time in Florida.[18]

Some individuals persisted in resisting changes in their work routines brought on by a new overseer. Mariah's case illustrates this fact. The Florida bondwoman did not like the management style of new overseer A. R. McCall in 1840. Under former overseer John Evans, she likely had enjoyed special privileges around the place, since Evans had fathered at least two children by her. When McCall took over, things changed for Mariah, and she grumbled about it. After telling her child Mary not to obey the directives of the new overseer, Mariah openly defied him as well. As a result, the new overseer flogged Mary and started to do the same to Mariah, who fled the place. Mariah ultimately appeared back on the plantation to face her punishment. McCall made his point, but Mariah had made hers as well. The overseer of William Harris's plantation in Leon County experienced a similar problem, with one big exception. Within one month of the new overseer's arrival, bondservant Jack had absconded, never to be seen again.[19]

Former bondpeople maintained memories of fellow slaves who fled plantations and farms because of abusive treatment from both overseers and drivers and related the tales to interviewers well into the twentieth century. According to Shack Thomas, one "hard" overseer "used to 'buck and gag' us." This meant a form of corporal punishment that constrained a slave painfully. The practice led some to run away. Upon their capture, they were "gagged and tied in a squatting position and left in the sun for hours." Some runaways, Thomas claimed, were "suspended by their thumbs for varying periods." Douglass Parish claimed to remember overseers on other plantations who beat slaves to death. The former bondservant could have been speaking about such occurrences on the plantation where he lived and worked but chose not to further discuss the incidents with the interviewer. He noted instead that the master would simply show a "black whip which *was usually sufficient*" in making them stand in fear. Louis Napoleon gave the impression that his former master did not allow the driver to whip his charges for fear they might run away. But when slaves did abscond, the master flogged them himself.[20]

Others were inclined to run away when personnel in the "big house" changed. According to historian Jacqueline Jones, some planters' wives took their frustrations out on bondservants, as in the case of Mary Minus Biddle. The one-time bondservant recalled that her master's first wife "was a very kind woman." Upon her demise, the owner relocated from Escambia to Columbia County, where he remarried. At that point, the slaves grew apprehensive and uneasy about the new wife, who, according to Biddle, was a veritable terror. "She was always ready and anxious to whip a slave for the least misdemeanor," she recalled. Fearing that Mary and others might run away because of this abuse, the master "told Mary and her mother that before he would take the chance of them running away on account of her [his wife's] meanness he would leave her." The master obviously did not leave his wife soon enough, since Mary ran away to avoid a flogging. Finally, some relief did come from the mistress's abusive ways. This did not occur because the master divorced his wife; rather, it happened because her angry son-in-law fatally shot her.[21]

Assignment to relatives of owners or to the administrators of owners' estates provoked some persons to disappear. When William Norwood took over the operations of brother Jonathan Thomas's Gadsden County plantation, ten of thirty-two slaves ran away. No available record reports their capture. Sam fled the premises of the late Robert Sturges when a new overseer took charge. Thomas Munroe, executor of John W. Malone's estate, faced runaway problems shortly after taking control of Malone's Gadsden County plantation. Within one month, five of twenty slaves had disappeared from the property.[22]

Other types of slaves fled also. Owners used to hiring out bondpeople knew that the highly skilled and assimilated ones enjoyed wide mobility as well as status. With such confidence in themselves, these enslaved blacks usually moved outside of the plantation or farm unafraid. John D. Parish yearned, for example, for the capture of Sam Jones, his highly skilled carpenter. Having acquired a knowledge of the geography of Middle Florida as a hireling and able to converse with whites, the bondservant avoided the catchers with relative ease thanks to the fact that he had a "pass to hire his own time." There is no indication that the artisan was captured or otherwise returned to the plantation.[23]

When working conditions were not to the liking of hirelings, many successfully absconded. John, a hired-out slave of James Gadsden, disapproved of the poor working conditions at his new employer's establishment, so he took off in protest. What started out as a trickle in the 1830s with this type of departure became a flood by the 1850s as slaves increasingly ran away from the arduous and dangerous work required of them by various rail systems and construction outfits then operating in Florida. Another John and a man named Albert were hired out for such labor around 1840. Shortly after, they escaped to remain at large for over two years. In a similar situation, large Leon County planter Benjamin Chaires advertised his hireling as missing from the "St. Joseph Rail-road." The fact was that, by the 1840s and 1850s, slaves who had been uprooted from their Upper South homes during the 1820s and 1830s had become more familiar with the geography of Florida. In the process, they had grown more confident in absconding.[24]

Some Florida owners permitted slave traders, as their agents, to hire out their property, a fact that created another dynamic in the runaway equation. Some of these firms and individuals cared little about the treatment of the slaves or the working conditions under which they would have to labor. Charles DuPont of Gadsden County possessed many slaves. Some he hired out himself, while others were given to trading companies to lease out to whites. Only one of DuPont's many slaves by the 1840s was classified as native-born African. Named Aleck, he had the scars of his country on his face. The bondservant must have been quite acculturated because he could speak some English, and he had had at least two previous owners. The sources remain silent, however, on his skill level or occupation. In any event, Aleck's master planned to hand him over to the trading firm of R. J. Hackley of Tallahassee to be leased. Hackley, in turn, hired out the bondservant to John R. Lloyd. Ill-disposed toward his new employer, old Aleck had been assimilated enough into society to have the confidence to flee three months later. Not knowing the working conditions and possible treatment they would receive, several slaves simply disappeared from the Tallahassee slave-trading firm of Hughes and Patterson before they could be hired out.[25]

The problem with leased laborers who were runaways grew so severe over time that local governments called for attempts at resolution. For instance, Middle Florida's Gadsden County saw citizens determined to control slave movement by curtailing the idea of bondpeople hiring themselves out. The county's grand jury declared, "The permission by some owners of slaves in the county to hire themselves out [is against the law]." Their neighbors to the south in the port cities of St. Joseph and Apalachicola voiced similar complaints. The *Apalachicola Commercial Advertiser* declared it "an evil not to be borne . . . such gallow-birds as flock here every winter from abroad to be hired out." As the item suggested, bondservants from around the state seemed to be drawn to these particular ports. The writer of the newspaper had it right, for many bondservants by the 1840s knew the geographical landscape in and around these port towns. Many loved to live and work around seaports where they could meet people, hire their own time out, catch up on news and gossip, and see themselves as a part of a larger Atlantic world community—even if those were not the words they would have chosen to express their desires.[26]

Runaways' knowledge of Florida's geopolitical landscape was something that masters typically underestimated. For hundreds of years, hired-out maritime workers had traveled to ports of the panhandle and peninsula and along the Atlantic coastline, trading their skills for remuneration. This practice did not significantly change during the territorial and statehood periods. Instead, it expanded. Maritime slaves who could read and write also usually could access newspapers and information, thus gaining entry to windows on the outside world.[27]

Attitudes about Freedom

As difficult as it may be for modern readers to believe, large numbers of East Florida slaveholders thought that semiskilled or skilled enslaved mariners were comfortable with their enslavement, since their conditions had been ameliorated with the type of work they performed. Not so. The ever-present desire for total freedom pulsed in the minds of many, if not most, bondservants. Enslaved persons, especially those in the maritime industry in East Florida, would seize any opportunity to remove the shackles of slavery completely by absconding.[28]

In assessing the question, the point should be noted that slaves' worldviews in West and East Florida were more diverse than those of their Middle Florida counterparts. Many in the East and West lived in coastal areas along the Gulf of Mexico and, as mentioned, understood something about the world outside the plantation, farm, or small industry. Some probably had met slaves imported illegally from the Caribbean—Cuba in this instance—into the various port towns in their regions, as the *Pensacola Gazette* had described in 1837. So, with their skill and literacy levels and knowledge of peoples from other Atlantic world outposts, it became increasingly more difficult to know if some of these assimilated yet freewheeling bondservants were runaways or not.[29]

Florida blends land and water to people. Situated to the south of Georgia, with Alabama, Mississippi, Louisiana, and the Gulf of Mexico to the west and north and the Caribbean to the southeast, Florida became a conduit for connecting people to the Atlantic world. With relaxed enforcement of laws, numbers of bondservants moved about during Florida's Spanish eras with relative freedom for over two hundred years. However, the moderately free mobility of bondservants changed somewhat when the United States took control of La Florida in 1821. Regardless of treatment or freedom of movement, the desire for complete liberty remained for many bondservants.[30]

Individuals time and again felt so desperate to secure freedom that they even took canoes, small boats, or rafts to aid in their escape. For years, many of these individuals had worked in the maritime industry as pilots, boatmen, shipwrights, coopers, or longshoremen. They knew about the various waterways leading to the Atlantic Ocean and the Caribbean. As Jane Landers found, many of these blacks were at ease traveling the international waters of the Atlantic. Middle Florida fugitives Dick, his wife, Margaret, and their five-year-old son were unsuccessful in navigating the waters of the St. Marks River in their attempt to get to the Gulf of Mexico and the Atlantic Ocean. Sadly, they were "picked up at sea in a canoe a few miles from St. Marks." Some obviously sought to get to the Caribbean, probably the Bahamas, by way of Key West. This likely was the case of three fugitives who arrived from places unknown at Key West in "a small boat."[31]

Bondservants in Florida continued to perceive the Atlantic as a means of travel that ultimately would bring them freedom. Many sought to stow away on ships and other vessels in their quest for liberty, and southern states sought to enact laws to halt such activities. In 1822, South Carolina became the first state to pass what was known as the "Negro seamen acts." The measure, according to Philip M. Hamer, required that "free Negro employees on any vessel which might come into a South Carolina port be imprisoned until the vessel should be ready to depart." White South Carolinians hoped the law would forestall black mariners from assisting runaways by hiding them on seafaring vessels. Some ten years later, in 1832, Florida followed suit by enacting a similar law. This act permitted black seamen to be jailed until their ship or vessel departed port towns. Another Florida law simply restricted free blacks from coming into the territory with the threat of their arrest and sale on the auction block as slaves.[32]

Indeed, seamen did offer a common source for news about the happenings in other Atlantic world communities, and, like their counterparts in South Carolina, white Floridians thought Negro seamen laws would hamper black seamen and other sympathetic whites from passing on information about any revolutionary movements or events in the outside world and from stowing runaways onboard ships and vessels. When traveling on what Amon DeLaughter called the "Steamer Vixen," he became suspicious of the motives of several naval officers soon after the ship anchored at Apalachicola. He recorded the rather friendly relationship between seamen and blacks, penning that "they [are] very particular about Negroes." Regardless of law, the cordial relationship of white and black seamen toward bondpeople sometimes led the former to assist the latter with escape to freedom by sea. Once again, however, day-to-day reality managed to create ways and means that the law did not foresee. And, the Atlantic world nonetheless intruded into Florida slavery.[33]

With runaways seeking freedom in places on both sides of the Atlantic and in the Caribbean, law enforcement officials, indeed, faced the necessity of constant watch for bondservants who sought to stow away on ships and vessels in the various Florida port cities and towns. Leckstis and Ben, for example, were apprehended by the Duval County sheriff after they were discovered hidden away in the bowels of the ship *Seminole*. Tom's owner, meanwhile, believed that Tom would make his way to Port Leon "on a vessel." Enslaved Floridians knew well that, by secretly boarding ships or by securing the assistance of sympathetic seamen, they possibly could gain freedom on either side of the Atlantic.[34]

4. A Yearning for Freedom

Dey would beat him tel de blood run outen him.
—Margrett Nickerson in George P. Rawick, *Florida Slave Narratives*

Florida's enslaved men and women might take advantage of perceived weaknesses in masters and overseers in order to force a degree of flexibility into the institution of slavery sufficient to permit opportunities for lurking or even for more permanent escape; still, the enduring brutal reality of the institution could not be denied. The fact was that bondpersons constituted valuable property that most owners intended to preserve and exploit. In that endeavor, many, if not most, individuals who possessed human property were prepared to take whatever measures they found necessary. The resulting collision of wills sparked further resistance that, in turn, begat reprisal. In the end, the measures taken to undergird slavery proved unable to extinguish the greater desire embodied in the yearning for freedom.

Surviving evidence illustrates that enslaved workers often ran because of brutal treatment received from masters, overseers, and drivers, although it is less clear whether that brutal treatment arose as a cause or as a response to flight. In any event, bondmen and bondwomen were beaten, whipped, incarcerated, branded, collared, mutilated, and placed in stocks. More frequently, they were punished by whipping. Severe floggings, some slaveholders felt, would make the slaves stand in fear. The marks of whippings were suggestive of terrorism and brutality inflicted on the bondservants and a reason, no doubt, for many of them absconding. Individuals naturally ran away after barbaric whippings and to avoid floggings, although they ultimately faced submission to savage and inhumane punishment—or at least the possibility of such submission—upon their return to the farm or plantation.[1]

Margrett Nickerson recalled that some bondservants were mistreated for no apparent reason, a fact that offered further incentive for flight. Uncle George was one of them. According to Nickerson, "Dey useter jes take uncle George Bull and beat him fur nothing; dey would beat him and take him to the lake and put him on a log and shev him in de lake, but he always swimmed out. When dey didn' do dat dey would beat him tel de blood run outen him and den trow him in de ditch in de field." Nickerson related the result of this type of treatment:

> Some uv de slaves [would] run away, lots uv um. Some would be cot and when day ketched em dey put bells on em; fust dey would put a iron ban' round dey neck and anuder one 'round de waist and rivet um tegether down de back; de bell would hang on de ban' round de neck so dat it would ring when de slave walked and den dey wouln' git 'way. Some uv dem wore dese bells three and four mont'n and when dey time wuz up dey would take em off 'em.[2]

Sources clearly indicate that complaints of mistreatment by whites toward bondservants continued to increase from 1821 to 1865, with the 1850s constituting the worst decade of cruelty to bondservants in the territory or state, at least in Middle Florida. Of the 1,009 runaways detailed in newspaper accounts and the 1,403 probate records, diaries, and letters surviving from 1821 to 1860, 121 indicated scars, floggings, and other marks as a result of severe punishment inflicted upon the bodies of enslaved blacks by authority figures. Of that number, 61 (or 50 percent) were men and 31 (or 26 percent) were women from Middle Florida. In West and East Florida, 29 enslaved blacks wore scars of brutality during the same period; 12 percent of all rebels and runaways wore scars of mistreatment. By way of comparison, Freddie L. Parker's study of North Carolina runaways established that Florida's experience roughly coincided with that of the Tar Heel State (11.6 percent) during 1775–1840 and ran two times higher on the average than had been the case in Virginia, North Carolina, Tennessee, South Carolina, and Louisiana during what some historians have called the "late period," from 1838 to 1840. Seemingly, Florida slaveholders more frequently used inhumane methods to push and control their bondpeople than did masters in these nearby states.[3]

After Virginia's Nat Turner insurrection of 1831, change touched the nature of slavery in Florida as slaveholders began to view the institution increasingly as a necessary good instead of as a necessary evil. As this occurred, many began to change their attitudes about treatment of those whom they owned. Some manifested this dynamic by adopting a more paternalistic approach. For these individual masters, treating enslaved laborers more as human beings than as objects became the goal.

The majority of whites agreed on one basic thing: that Florida could not develop and prosper without an enslaved labor force kept under control. By 1860, the sentiments especially prevailed in Middle Florida where over half (58 percent) of the state's slave labor force lived and worked (see table 4).

Table 4. Middle Florida Population of Whites, Free Blacks, and Enslaved Blacks by 1860

County	Total	Whites	Percentage of whites	Free blacks	Percentage of free blacks	Enslaved blacks	Percentage of enslaved blacks
Gadsden	9,396	3,981	42.3	6	.06	5,409	57.5
Hamilton	4,154	2,734	65.8	23	.55	1,397	33.6
Jackson	10,209	5,263	51.5	43	.42	4,903	48.0
Jefferson	9,876	3,498	35.4	4	.04	6,374	64.5
Leon	12,343	3,194	25.8	60	.49	9,089	73.6
Madison	7,779	3,521	45.2	9	.12	4,249	54.6
Total	53,757	22,191	41.2	145	.27	31,421	58.4
Total for Florida	**77,746**			**932**		**61,745**	

Source: Joseph C. G. Kennedy, *Population of the United States in 1860*, 4 vols. (Washington, D.C., 1864), 1:50–54.

To succeed in their efforts to keep that workforce within bounds, Middle Florida slaveholders and counterparts in other areas found themselves forced to solicit the support of their countrymen and other non-slaveholding whites. Even with the legacy of the American Revolution and the Jeffersonian Republicans' vernacular of the common white man being equal to any other white man, Middle Florida planters, many of whom derived from the cavalier tradition of the Upper South, still found it difficult to concede political and social power to countrymen, yeoman farmers, and non-slaveholding whites. In a general sense, they treated members of these three groups only marginally better than they did their enslaved workers. This dynamic would change, however, after the mid-1830s in the wake of Nat Turner's insurrection, for the Middle Florida elite now needed the support and assistance of these groups. And, with the cooperation of small slaveholders and non-slaveholding whites, Middle Florida planters grew more persistent and successful in using the whip to clamp down on slave resistance than did their counterparts in West and East Florida, regions that had enjoyed a history of rugged individualism and that followed more relaxed race relations due to Spanish influences.[4]

Flight nonetheless continued as a major problem for the owners. Some individuals, it appears evident, did not even have specific reasons to run away except that they wanted to be free. Ellen McCormick, daughter of William Wirt, clearly understood that some bondpeople desired liberty and seized any opportunity they could to obtain it. In writing to her sister Catherine Wirt, she indicated as much concerning one particular slave on the Wirtland plantation. McCormick wrote that neither she nor her husband wanted to buy Charles from Wirtland. The wary buyer noted that she had "no confidence in his fidelity or attachment if the temptation to run away . . . were offered him." When advertising the sale of a slave woman, one owner warranted his bondservant "to be sound, sober and honest—an excellent Cook, Washer and Ironer, and the only fault she has is running away." This individual summed up what many slave owners probably knew about their bondservants—that many wanted their freedom and would flee if given the opportunity.[5]

As suggested by these and other accounts, some persons proved unrelenting in their desire for freedom. Many were the determined runaways who escaped, were captured, and ran again. Running away, the surviving documentation argues, emerged as a relatively common practice on some farms and plantations. A military officer attested to the habitual nature of one slave. As the officer informed his wife, this particular person had been "caught three or four times but had succeeded every time in getting to the woods again." He went on to relate:

> We left Pilatka on Monday morning early (7 A.M.) with seven inside passengers & a negro runaway slave in irons in front with the driver. This negro afforded quite a diversion since he got away ten minutes before we reached the place he was to [be] given to his master. You may think I pitied him but I must say that had I had a chance I would have shot him as he left the stage. He is a regular outlaw & ruffian and one of a gang of five infesting the pine barrens. As a matter of course these ruffians must live by plunder and make themselves very dangerous.[6]

Others also earned reputations as habitual and determined runaways. Of those with such a strong desire for freedom, Primus serves as a good example. He escaped from his owner a day before Christmas in 1839. After recapture, he fled from his new owner in September 1842. Following a brief sojourn, authorities apprehended him again. He ran away for the third time a month later. Primus may have succeeded in his third attempt since his name soon ceased to appear among advertisements for runaways. Much like Primus, George became a regular escapee from Augustus Lanier's plantation, having set out on his own over four times. As one advertisement noted, he wore the marks of terrorism inflicted by the whip to prove it.[7]

Women as well as men persisted in attempts to escape from bondage. Hannah became a chronic escapee, or so her master thought. The bondservant sought to gain her freedom three or more times. She disappeared around 1851. After a brief taste of freedom, authorities captured her. Within six months, Hannah fled again, only to be caught. On her third escape attempt, she stayed out for almost one year before being snared.[8]

Even individuals with long histories of life in their Florida homes, personal handicaps, or pending health concerns made repeated attempts to gain freedom. Newspaper accounts abounded with descriptions of bondmen who absconded with various physical impairments. Samuel Parkhill, another wealthy Middle Florida slaveholder who uprooted his captive laborers and brought them with him from Richmond, Virginia, around 1828, probably believed that his bondservants had settled in their homes and were making the best out of their situation. But, after years in their new area, some retained vivid memories of family members and friends left behind in the Upper South. This turned to be the case when Edmund and his wife, who was eight months pregnant, vanished from Parkhill's Lake Jackson plantation in April 1839.[9]

As stated, even physical challenges could not forestall some individuals from trying to seek freedom. A considerable number of fugitives actually were described as "cripples." Lewis's owner did not think that he would get far since he had a "crippled" left leg. Smart made his escape from the woodyard of St. Rosa Sound despite having a lame left leg. Described as having "a very lame walk," Kate did not let her malady hinder her from escaping. William B. McCall advertised the capture of Jesse, explaining that he had a scar on his left knee that caused "him to limp." William Tradwell described Ned as having to "limp somewhat when he walk." Favoring his "right leg while walking," Ben made his escape.[10]

Chimerical Yet Threatening Influences

Interestingly, more than a few Florida slaveholders found dark conspiracies behind the flight of their bondservants or else perceived individual flight as the precursor of widespread slave revolt. On several occasions, the evidence seemed to support their fears. Nat Turner's 1831 insurrection, for instance, set off waves of anxiety and apprehension, leading owners to sometimes draconian measures to control every movement not only of their bondservants but of free blacks as well. The eruption of the Second Seminole War in 1835 caused even more immediate fear. At that time, an ultimately futile attempt to curtail the movement of all slaves and free blacks appeared in the public press of Jacksonville in East Florida. The announcement declared:

> NOTICE
>
> Is hereby given to all persons, that the Commanding officers of the different Guard Stations, have strict orders to arrest and detain under guard, all slaves and free colored persons, found at large, except in the actual service and in company with their owner or overseer. Persons are therefore requested to govern themselves accordingly.
>
> John W. Warren
> Col. 4th Regt. F.M.[11]

Dark figures looming behind the fears often took on the form of abolitionists. Starting in the early 1830s, this perception took root on the heels of the

Nat Turner insurrection, as slaveholders grew alarmed over what they perceived as widespread northern abolitionist activities and materials sweeping into the South. Some of the owners knew that copies of David Walker's 1829 pamphlet *Walker's Appeal . . . to the Coloured Citizens of the World*, calling for slaves to rise up in rebellion, had reached the hands of bondservants and free blacks in Savannah, and it would become only a matter of time before copies would be found hidden away in the trunks of ships importing commodities to Florida's Atlantic port towns such as Jacksonville and St. Augustine. This constituted no small matter. As historian Merton Dillon noted, "Not for a moment did white southerners believe the abolitionists' repeated denials of insurrectionary intent."[12]

Many white Floridians came to live with dread of the possibility that this unwelcome group would incite rebellion among large numbers of slaves or else assist them in escaping to freedom. Reality, as Donorena Harris has noted, was that abolitionism never became a serious threat to Florida slaveholders. However, she would not have convinced many Floridians of the time. An Apalachicola paper warned citizens in 1844 to "wake from this lethargy in time to save themselves from a general massacre." It was against such a background that the editor went on to imply that abolitionists in the state were waiting for the day to incite "the slaves to discontent and disobedience." Specifically, large numbers of whites believed that abolitionists were encouraging bondservants to leave plantations and farms to join the Seminoles or outlaw groups in the peninsula.[13]

Middle Florida slaveholders possessed some concerns about abolitionism in their region, but they believed—rightly or wrongly—that they had their enslaved workers largely under control. Several reasons underscored these beliefs. The owners primarily, if not directly, controlled the political system and could pass laws or influence the passage of laws that maintained social order. Slaveholders were adept enough to afford countrymen, yeomen farmers, and non-slaveholders some political clout, hoping that they would buy into the political economy of slavery and protect it from outside influences. Plus, many non-slaveholders wanted to follow their well-heeled brothers by becoming slaveholders themselves one day. They, therefore, sought to protect the peculiar institution. And finally, slave owners appealed to racial solidarity. They sought to convince the majority of white non-slaveholders that it was in their best interest to support the overall economy of the region based squarely upon enslaved black labor. Many poor whites eventually served as patrollers in controlling the movements of slaves and thereby aided efforts to keep the Middle Florida region a largely closed society.[14]

Although Middle Florida whites did not exhibit extreme concerns about abolitionists in their region, a growing number of them believed that abolitionism would become a reality in East Florida, with its insidious Spanish influences and practices, if that area did not rid itself of antislavery activists. One newspaper expressed sentiments echoed elsewhere. "We shall have the germ of an Abolition State in east Florida, in less than five years," it insisted, "[and] it will be a receptacle for runaway slaves from the contiguous States, and more dangerous than the Seminole nation has been."[15]

Floridians up to the Civil War would continue to believe mistakenly in the abolitionists' power to aid slaves' escape. White Floridians certainly moved aggressively to rid themselves of the few actual abolitionists who were discovered. A sizable number of whites believed, for example, that Peter S. Smith, who allegedly had open ties with northern abolitionist organizations, should be run out of Florida. The brother of abolitionist Gerrit Smith had settled at St. Augustine around 1834 to speculate in land. To make matters worse, he had been accompanied by a cousin who was connected to women's rights advocate Elizabeth Cady Stanton.[16]

Slaveholders soon convinced themselves that these northerners entertained secret and nefarious plans. The problem only grew in intensity when additional northerners such as John C. Cleland, Thomas Douglass, David R. Dunham, and D. W. Whitehurst settled nearby. As reflected by the local newspaper, owners now knew—or at least thought they knew—that their "property" soon would be ushered off at the instigation of abolitionists. Accordingly, the community harassed Peter Smith until he departed. No evidence suggests that he or his compatriots abetted abolitionism other than by denouncing slavery publicly, and it appears that they gave no bondservants assistance in fleeing servitude. Even so, slaveholding Floridians wanted this disruptive influence out of the way.[17]

One celebrated case that touched on the subject of abolitionist activities involved something more, and it got the attention of virtually all white Floridians during the mid-1840s. That affair involved Jonathan Walker, a Boston abolitionist. This newly arrived West Florida immigrant actually assisted in the escape of seven Pensacola bondservants. Walker desired to usher them to another Atlantic world community in the Bahamas. Eventually, authorities seized the seven fugitives on the high seas and returned them to their masters. Walker faced trial on charges of "aiding and abetting" runaways. The court crafted its actions to send a clear message to others who assisted with slave escape. The judge ordered that Walker be placed in the pillory, be branded on the hand with the letters *SS* for "slave stealer," and be incarcerated for fifteen days and fined $150. Walker emerged as a celebrity of sorts in the North because of his Pensacola abolitionist activities.[18]

If public denunciations of slavery by abolitionists in East or West Florida concerned slaveholders, the Walker case troubled white Floridians much more than any other single example of antislavery activity. They believed that large plots to assist slaves in fleeing the peninsula would threaten the very foundation of slavery. Some West Florida residents feared additionally that agents of Great Britain and other foreign nations were plotting to aid hundreds, if not thousands, of bondservants in escaping. Many especially grew suspicious of Great Britain's motives after two letters from the British and Foreign Anti-slavery Society were found on Walker's person. The governor and legislative council subsequently demanded that the British stop "clandestinely co-operating with authorities of Massachusetts, in fiendish machinations against Florida's domestic [slave] institutions."[19]

Whites' beliefs that abolitionists had gained a strong foothold in the state intensified over time. As late as 1862, one Floridian declared to his son that "you must know, either by reading the newspapers, or from what you hear, that the abolitionists are determined at any hazard to let the slaves free, with out compensation for his loss, they are also determined to make the South, a wilderness and give the 'nigger' more privileges, than the white man for instance." During the same period, Robert Butler echoed Floridians' concerns about abolitionist influence. He believed that they had aided in the escape of his bondservant Julius Cezar from Leon County. To these men, abolitionists were awaiting any opportunity to incite workers to flee farms and plantations and to search for whites to kill. This never was the case. In Florida, abolitionists offered no outright organized resistance to slavery other than their formal protestations by written word and mouth.[20]

While large-scale abolitionist activity never touched the Sunshine State, individual whites acted to assist slaves to escape throughout the antebellum period. Former slave Shack Thomas encountered no trouble recalling what would happen when they were caught. Abolitionist-leaning individuals, he expressed, usually were run out of town or county.[21]

Slave Stealing and Enticement

More typically, simple slave stealing was involved when a white aided a black to depart. It would appear that the fear of recapture, severe punishment, and even death all helped runaways to overcome their apprehensions about trusting whites. Runaways figured out also that whites would be less suspicious when blacks were accompanied by other whites than when they were traveling alone. Moreover, in such circumstances, most slaves probably wanted to believe that the motives of whites who assisted them with their escape were genuine and good. Often, however, they were not. Bondservants enticed away likely were promised their freedom, but it was a promise seldom kept. A St.

Augustine advertisement run in 1829 articulated the point. It publicized the escape from jail of a white man named John Bryant for "negro stealing and sundry misdemeanors." In another of many such incidents, owner A. Danford, who advertised for several fugitives over the years, insisted that Titus had "no cause for absenting himself." Danford's advertisement declared, "Taking no clothes except such as he wore off, he may have been stolen." Celia's owner presumed that she had been "stolen by [a white man named] Jonathan H. Coolidge, a yankee." Slaveholders such as Danford obviously could not read the minds of their slaves, for—notwithstanding owners' presumptions—they had their own reasons for absconding.[22]

Details of many incidents of slave stealing have been preserved. One group of white men, by way of example, snatched one of Colonel Fleming's bondmen. They released him only when he pretended to be lame. Mary Roberts of Jackson County believed that Harry had been "carried off by some person." Her Middle Florida neighbors yearned to catch Stephen P. Yeoman, who reportedly stole both slaves and free blacks before selling them to unsuspecting buyers.[23]

Other whites enticed enslaved persons away to become partners in crime. This seemed to be the case with Pensacolan John B. Harden and a runaway in his company. Around 1851, Harden traveled to Geneva, Alabama, and stole five hundred dollars from West Florida native John R. Chapman. Authorities arrested Harden, but he soon broke out of jail. Free of that restraint, Harden subsequently took the sheriff's buggy, a lawyer's mare, and a double-barrel gun. The escapee returned briefly to Santa Rosa County and fled again with a runaway belonging to Joseph Forsyth. The two absconders did not remain at large for very long. They were caught with the stolen goods in southeast Mississippi and brought back to Santa Rosa County.[24]

Slave stealing as a serious problem beset Floridians, at least on an occasional basis, during much of the antebellum era. St. Augustine's city council even petitioned the US government in 1843 to protect the coastline better in order to reduce the amount of slave stealing and other related activities. The panel noted: "The coast of this Territory has been without any maritime protection—being a bare and exposed frontier, on which either smuggling, piracy, or the abduction of slaves, may be carried on with impunity—and as we have reason to believe have been perpetrated, both by the Indians and evil disposed white persons in connection with them."[25]

Punishments came quickly and often hard for whites convicted of stealing the human property of others. Although Florida laws made clear the dire consequences of "aiding and abiding runaways," the statutes usually specified or permitted a harsher penalty for those accused of confiscating enslaved blacks than for those charged with assisting bondservants in escaping. For aiding and abetting bondpeople with their escape, those caught might draw jail time. For example, Irwin Granger of Jefferson County, accused of assisting fugitives slaves, served his sentence in the local lockup. James Kelly of Leon County likewise landed in jail for sixty days for "aiding runaway slaves."[26]

A few slave stealers who snatched runaways were not so lucky. Recourse to hanging alleged stealers remained consistent over time. As noted earlier, Jonathan Walker received a harsh punishment for his "crime," but it did not call for a capital penalty. According to Tallahassee's *Florida Sentinel*, Stephen P. Yeoman was not so fortunate. When finally caught, the unlucky man in 1845 was hanged for "negro stealing." One year later in a celebrated case, four members of the Holloman gang stretched rope at Quincy for their temerity at ushering bondmen away from local plantations. Redding Evans of Jefferson County suffered the noose in 1850 for stealing a female slave. Two years later, a slave stealer got lucky. In 1852, Governor Thomas Brown pardoned him but only on condition "that he leave the state of Florida Never to Return." Florida officials remained persistent over time in bringing to justice those individuals accused of slave stealing, and the price often proved the ultimate one.[27]

Some owners were not above taking the law into their own hands and dispensing their brand of frontier justice in punishing slave stealers or others who assisted fugitives. While Florida law expressly proscribed slave stealing and specified penalties, many slaveholders knew that day-to-day realities of enforcement efforts ran slowly at best. So, individual initiative sometimes replaced official action. Some citizens even took the step of publishing what they would do to anyone caught aiding and abetting runaways. A. Watson believed, for instance, that persons unknown had helped his slave Ben to escape. Watson publicly announced that he would "apply the law of Judge Lynch to my own satisfaction, on those concerned in his concealment."[28]

Isolated incidents of blaming slave-stealing on other whites, by the way, appealed to the paternalistic sensibilities of some slaveholders. It afforded them justification for their desire to believe that their happy and obedient bondmen and bondwomen had been enticed away by other whites rather than that the laborers themselves had played the active agents in their flight. Many owners could not bear to think that their slaves would take the initiative in a search for freedom. Advertisements for runaways reflected as much, often referring to a mysterious third party as a "white scoundrel" or "thief." Among those who believed that his bondservants had been ushered off against their will was W. H. G. Saunders. He offered a reward of one hundred dollars for the "recovery of the three negroes [George, Joe, and Charles] and the thief." Like Saunders, George Willis claimed that Smart had "been enticed away by some worthless white man." Mary Forbes firmly believed that a white person had assisted her bondservant to escape. The enslaved black, the owner claimed, had been "decoyed off by someone."[29]

On rare occasions, an owner might acknowledge or be forced to acknowledge his or her error in crediting whites for an escape. W. H. G. Saunders, as mentioned, had thought his workers were stolen before he found out otherwise. His public, and likely embarrassing, confrontation with the truth came courtesy of an article that appeared in a Jacksonville newspaper about a month following their departure. It stated, "We understand that two of the missing negroes belonging to Mr. W. H. Saunders of this county, supposed to have been stolen have been recovered." The report continued, "[They had] concealed themselves on Fleming's Island." Florida slaves who stole themselves and fled to other places, as Saunders learned, did not always need the assistance of anyone.[30]

Enslaved blacks sometimes stole their fellow bondservants or enticed or aided them in escaping, and whites were not shy in accusing them of the crime. And what whites called slave stealing by other slaves usually boiled down, though, to bondservants assisting family members or kinfolk. Jenny's owner claimed that she had been "seduced away by a stout negro man." Martha H. Macon advertised that Dilsey disappeared from her estate with the assistance of another slave. "[The runaway may be] harbored," the slaveholder noted, "by a man by the name of Power." Another slaveholder believed that Jim had "decoyed off his wife."[31]

Free blacks—who never made up a large portion of Florida's population—rarely harbored or assisted their downtrodden brothers and sisters to escape servitude. Laws outlawing free blacks from entering Florida met with strict enforcement, although treaty rights from Florida's 1821 cession by Spain offered at least some protections to those whose presence predated the territorial era. However, the facts failed to convince whites. They saw only the potential power and influence of free blacks on those who were enslaved. Slaveholders' memories particularly held tight to the significant role played by free blacks in planning the uprising that began the Saint Domingue (Haitian) revolution in 1791, so close to Florida's shores and only forty years earlier. Two examples should suffice to illustrate white perceptions of the influence of free blacks on Florida slaves. One man implied that free blacks were harboring his slave Ben in "several places in St. Augustine." Similarly, whites in West Florida were so concerned about the influence that free blacks would exert on slaves that these whites pressured the free blacks to leave the state. By 1857, many of them had resettled in the relatively nearby Atlantic world community in the Bahamas.[32]

An exception to this general rule should be noted. As mentioned earlier, laws were enacted in 1832 to curtail the movement of free black seamen by placing them in jail upon their arrival at any Florida port. Whites feared the possibility that this group would assist their enslaved brothers and sisters by hiding them on outgoing vessels and ships. Their fears had merit. Sometimes, free black seamen living outside of Florida but working onboard vessels calling at various seaports along the Atlantic coast occasionally would assist in escapes. According to W. Jeffrey Bolster, black mariners contributed significantly to the antislavery movement. Dating back to the American Revolution and Crispus Attucks, a mulatto seaman, black seamen played an influential role in fighting slavery.[33]

A variety of incidents centered on such fears. Apalachicola seaport residents certainly believed them to be real. The city fathers grew very concerned about the influence that free blacks, especially sailors, were working on the local enslaved population. In 1849, the whites acted. To stem the problem, they restricted free black sailors from "coming ashore in Apalachicola." It must be assumed that the efforts met with limited and only temporary success. Other Floridians also held legitimate concerns about the activities of these men. One report noted an incident. "Two Leon County slaves," it revealed, "were discovered among the cotton on board the brig *Ocilla* bound for New York." After their discovery, the bondservants confessed that "Ambrose Taylor, a free man of color, acting as a cook and steward," had secured them onboard. For his crime, Taylor had "to spend his summer" in jail. Other consequences of his actions are not known.[34]

Also on the subject of free blacks, some escapees represented themselves as free either by presenting forged freedom papers or by claiming that they had been liberated by their former owners. Some runaways could read, write, and speak English relatively well, often representing themselves as skilled artisans. They had enough confidence in themselves to write their own passes to freedom. The very qualities that masters liked in their bondservants often assisted them in absconding. The owner of Jack suggested, for example, that the bondman had forged freedom papers and would present himself as a free man. As a skilled artisan, Jack may indeed have written his own freedom papers. One fact rings true: the owner never caught him. One master believed that a "stout Negro man [had] provided no doubt [his female slave] with forged passes." Jerry Smallwood passed himself off as a free black in the peninsula for three years. It seems that Robert James's runaway slave Sam did the same thing. According to the owner, Sam, who presented himself as a "bricklayer by trade," seemingly had "obtained free papers." Although Sam was assimilated, the owner could never conceive that he would write his own freedom papers. Nonetheless, with the exception of the Second Seminole War period and in a few other circumstances, not many fugitives, with or without manumission papers, succeeded at living as free blacks.[35]

One of those exceptions involved light-skinned blacks who tried to "pass" for whites in their escape to freedom. Some, indeed, were successful in this endeavor. John Butler's assimilated black displayed a confident demeanor as he attempted to pass himself off as a white man. The owner claimed that this fair-skinned slave would present himself as free. Describing his runaway as a "yellowish" mulatto, the owner also noted that the fugitive would try "passing as a white man." Thomas Ledwith claimed that his slave Ned or Edward Dixon, a "bright quadroon," would attempt to "pass for a white man" because of his straight hair. According to James Smith, his light-complexioned fugitive—whose mother was a mulatto and father a white man—likewise would attempt to "pass for a freeman." Based upon how masters described the character of their light-skinned blacks, the implication arises that these largely acculturated bondservants knew how to deal with whites.[36]

The ever-expanding United States had been successful by 1823 in pushing aside foreign nations, such as England and Spain, that stood in the way of its developing slave economy. However, such countries did aid runaways for several years after the United States came in possession of Florida in 1821. Fearing that their old allies ultimately would be hunted down by slave catchers, these nations allowed what likely amounted to hundreds of runaways to board their flagged vessels. The Spanish also assisted fugitives in escaping to other Atlantic world communities. One particular path aimed at Havana, Cuba. British wrecking vessels additionally picked up other fugitives in small boats and safely delivered them to Andros and New Providence Islands, which is to say Nassau, in the Bahamas. However, after 1823, the Spanish and the British publicly denounced slavery but did little else to assist runaways in the peninsula.[37]

5. Destinations of Runaways

Sylvia has been "lurking" about the head of the Wakulla River.
—*Tallahassee Floridian and Journal*, November 22, 1851

Questions related to where enslaved blacks fled have occupied historians of the southern experience for generations. Traditionally, the answers reached have pointed to the majority absconding to other southern states as opposed to the northern states. In that vein, John Hope Franklin and Loren Schweninger focused in one recent and respected study on fugitives who fled, primarily, from one place in the South to another in the same region. Florida's situation, however, offers a somewhat different view. Although considerable numbers of its fugitives replicated the traditional patterns noted by Franklin, Schweninger, and other historians, a significant number possessed or, at least, gained exposure to what could be described as an Atlantic worldview. This is to say that they sought freedom in various parts of the Atlantic and Caribbean regions, particularly in the Bahamas.[1]

An explanation of context will help to set the stage for an understanding of Florida's runaway story. Dating back to the Spanish era and its centuries of experience, Florida bondservants—especially those in East and West Florida—lived in a world often dependent upon and circumscribed by ocean travel, connections, and communications. Many of them had worked as artisans, longshoremen, and hirelings in and around ports and other locations up and down the Atlantic coastline, on the Gulf of Mexico, or on rivers or streams emptying into one or the other. Laboring in, and in proximity to, the maritime industry, they routinely came in contact with people coming in and departing from Florida in Atlantic and other oceangoing vessels. From this and other connections, these slaves knew or learned that freedom could become a reality beyond Florida's shores. Many particularly comprehended that the Bahamas and other islands in the Caribbean—especially after the early 1830s—offered freedom if they could get to them.[2]

By no means, of course, did the Atlantic world dominate as a geographical factor in flight. Florida itself took that honor. The colony, territory, and state covered an immense area. In fact, during the early statehood period that began in 1845, it claimed precedence as the second largest state east of the Mississippi River. After Virginia divided during the Civil War, Florida became the largest. It meanwhile possessed vast tracts of unpopulated or sparsely populated territory. If fugitives succeeded in fleeing their owners, havens almost without limitation awaited them in the panhandle and especially in the peninsula. They could run in any number of directions and remain undetected for months or, in some cases, for years.[3]

As Florida fugitives moved out from their domiciles toward freedom or some other object, wherever that might be, their destinations were many. Reasons and motivations for flight also varied significantly. One group, as mentioned earlier, consisted of truants who "lurked" around neighborhoods to be with loved ones and friends. Another comprised "disgruntled absconders" who fled from their venues to "cool off" or to seek temporary refuge from work routines, material conditions, or abuse. Some 90 percent of those who made up these groups stayed out for sporadic periods of time and typically returned to their homes voluntarily. Like lurking truants, disgruntled absconders stayed within relatively close proximity to those home places or else ventured only to adjacent counties.[4]

Some true fugitives, unlike the lurkers and disgruntled absconders, sought to break the chains of slavery completely by fleeing as far away from their venues as possible. Most of these persons held no intention of ever returning to their homes. The research data base referred to previously assists in drawing a true picture. By focusing on use of English, physical features, skin complexion, dress, and emotional state in 711 notices in newspapers and 1,403 probate records, journals, diaries, and other sources dating from 1821 to 1865, its outlines can be discerned. Slaveholders, in fact, revealed much about themselves in their characterizations of their bondservants. Of course, we also learn as well about the slaves they described.

Much like eighteenth-century masters, nineteenth-century slaveholders continued to praise their bondservants' physical features, skills, occupations, and character. Of the 1,009 runaways identified in the newspaper and documentary accounts from 1821 to 1865, 192 (19 percent) reportedly possessed one or more skills. This included 9 fugitives described as house servants, of which 7 were females. The percentage of skilled runaways was much lower than the

32 percent of skilled Virginia runaways from 1736 to 1801. But, the percentage of skilled runaways in Florida was higher than enslaved fugitive artisans from North Carolina (1775–1840) and South Carolina (1730–1878), with 13 and 14 percent, respectively. Generally speaking, a higher percentage of Florida runaways possessed more skills than the average 15 percent held by their counterparts in Virginia, North Carolina, Tennessee, South Carolina, and Louisiana during the periods 1790–1816 and 1838–1860. Owners from West and East Florida typically provided a description of the occupation or skill set of their fugitives more often than did owners in Middle Florida. Table 5 identifies the various types of occupation of Florida's runaways.

It is worthy of note that only five slaveholders mentioned that fugitives were African-born or wore African marks on their faces. Unlike some eighteenth-century African-born slaves who were in the process of acculturation, most African-born slaves who fled from Florida masters appear to have been largely assimilated. Some were artisans who could speak some English, as did an African-born bondservant who carried the name Congo.[5]

Yet, even with the degree of assimilation or acculturation possessed by individuals such as Congo, few African-born persons chose to break the shackles of slavery completely. Like other individuals referred to previously, they tended to lurk around various neighborhoods because of family ties. For example, M. DeFourgeres advertised in 1835 for his two runaways, noting that they had been out for "about two months." He described them as "two negro fellows—George and John. George, a South Carolinian born, is about 40 years old of the middle size, well built, he stammers so much that at times it is difficult to understand what he says. John, an African born, is about 28 years old, middle size, stout, fat, and of a very black complexion. Both jobbing carpenters. Those two negroes are probably lurking in the neighborhood of Whitesville, on Black Creek, [in] Duval County."[6]

Owners' Perceptions and Mentalities

African-born bondservants persisted in their usual mild form of resistance evidenced by "lurking around" through much of the 1840s, or, at least, so their masters wanted to believe. For example, John M. Pons paid the local newspaper to advertise for his several fugitives whom he believed were ushered away by another old African fugitive named Aleck or Ellick. Unlike Charles DuPont's Aleck, who fled alone, Pons claimed that his old African fugitive had taken Venus and her children with him and that they still were lurking around the Jacksonville area. But the master may not have known the fugitives' destination since they had disappeared from his place about four years prior to the

Table 5. Occupational Breakdown of Slave Runaways in Florida, 1821–1865

Occupation	Number	Occupation	Number
Apprentice (occupation unknown)	1	Gardener, hostler, wagoner	1
Baker	1	Glazer	1
Barber, house servant	1	Hostler	1
Blacksmith	12	Hostler, barber, millwright business	1
Blacksmith, carpenter	1	House and cabinet workman	1
Blacksmith, cooper	1	House servant	9
Blacksmith, cooper, shoemaker, carpenter	1	Military laborer	4
Blacksmith, fiddler	1	Musician (violin player and singer)	2
Blacksmith, shoemaker	1	Overseer	1
Boatman	5	Painter	1
Boot and shoemaker	1	Pilot	11
Bricklayer, plasterer	3	Plasterer	3
Brickmason	2	Plumber	1
Brickmason, plasterer	1	Preacher, singer	3
Brickyard worker	7	Railroad laborer	5
Butcher	1	Sailor	5
Carpenter	18	Sawyer	2
Carpenter, barber	1	Sawyer, carpenter	1
Carpenter, millwright business	2	Sawyer, shoemaker	2
Carpenter, painter, joiner	2	Sawyer, shoemaker, wagoner	1
Carpenter, shoemaker	1	Seamen	4
Carpenter, shoemaker, painter	1	Seamstress	1
Carpenter, wheelwright	2	Seamstress, weaver	1
Carriage driver	2	Ship carpenter	2
Caulker	1	Ship worker	8
Caulker, ship carpenter	1	Shoemaker	2
Cook	3	Shoemaker, tanner	1
Cook, drummer	1	Shoemaker, violin player	1
Cook, sailor	2	Steward, waiter	5
Cooper, carpenter	2	Tailor	2
Cooper, corker	2	Tailor, barber, horseman	1
Cooper, sawyer	1	Tanner	1
Cooper, sawyer, shoemaker	2	Wagoner	2
Cooper, shoemaker	2	Wagon and stage maker	2
Cowman	1	Waiter	9
Driver	2	Waiter, hostler	2
Fisherman	2	Waiting man, wagoner	1
		Total	**192**

Sources: Florida and Georgia extant newspapers, 1821–60, as well as other documentary accounts.

posting of the 1848 advertisement for their capture. Living in Jacksonville, both Aleck or Ellick and Venus may have known more about the seaport town and the Atlantic coastline than their master could credit. With four years out from their domicile, these fugitives may well have boarded a vessel in Jacksonville seeking a place of freedom across the water.[7]

If this method of flight in fact occurred, these escapees would have illustrated a dynamic that became more pronounced as the 1840s evolved through the next decade. Owners' perceptions often varied from slave reality. The masters desired to believe in the loyalty of their bondpeople and resisted comprehension of slaves' ability to conceive a larger picture. In the circumstances, some owners did not even want to incur the expense of advertising for their lurking fugitives, as did Pons and DeFourgeres. Often, that decision represented good business sense. Indeed, as Franklin and Schweninger aptly noted and has previously been underscored in this volume, "the most common form of absconding was not actually running away at all, but what might be termed 'truancy,' 'absenteeism,' and in some cases, 'lying out.'" Thus, Florida's absentee bondservants usually—but not always—followed a pattern seen elsewhere when they "lurked" around or simply "laid out" before returning to the places where they lived and worked.[8]

With the relatively high incidence of real flight, owners' mentalities thus could constitute a roadblock to recovering slaves, even though the roadblock was constructed upon a solid foundation. If Aleck and Venus were "lurking or "lying out," they typically did so very near the places where they lived and worked. Experience proved this to be the case time and again, and, at least in Middle Florida, many owners preferred to believe this was true all or virtually all of the time. One Franklin County planter, reflecting common belief, remained convinced that he knew his fugitive very well and also knew her whereabouts in 1840. J. D. Fisher described Dyce as a "mulatto woman . . . about 23 years of age, five feet high and cross-eyed. [She] is supposed to be in the neighborhood of Quincy." Dyce had at least one prior owner and came from out of state, yet her current owner still wanted to believe his bondservant remained nearby and that her destination was not Virginia.[9]

Given that enslaved laborers such as Dyce wore masks of deception, masters like Fisher could not have known her or other bondservants as well as they thought they did. Fisher could, in fact, only guess at the direction his fugitive might be going. Similarly, five years after Dyce fled, T. W. Bush thought in 1845 that he knew Jim well. He described the bondservant in these words: "a yellow negro fellow, about thirty years of age—with a scar over one of his eyes; weighs about one hundred and six pounds, a plausible villain, a tolerable carpenter formerly owned by a Mr. Yaughn, and then by Rueben Scott, his range is from about the Arsenal, Quincy, Major Coe's river place and Tallahassee." The owner missed an important factor. Despite Bush's perception, the facts that Jim was an assimilated carpenter with two prior owners may have given him the confidence to move far outside the plantation. Bush, like Fisher, could only guess where he might go.[10]

Interestingly, some bondservants who "lurked" close around home plantations and farms did so for long periods of time. John, a carpenter owned by Judge O'Neill of Fernandina, counted as one of numerous runaways who did not venture far from the estate. Amazingly, he stayed out for almost two years by concealing himself in the nearby woods. Sylvia laid out about the same length of time as did John, secreting herself near her master's plantation. As described by W. Skeine, the fugitive may have done so rather notoriously. These were his words used to describe her: "dark complexion, spare mode and red eyes. Supposed to be lurking around Tallahassee, and is no doubt often, in the city of evenings among the free negroes. Her husband when she left was R. Heyward's boy, Henry, on the Treadwell place, and it is supposed that she has got him yet."[11] The advertisement first appeared on October 27, 1849, and ran for almost two years until November 22, 1851. Yet, the owner still believed the bondservant had been "lurking around Tallahassee" only a few miles from his Lake Jackson plantation.[12]

Obviously, fugitives such as John and Sylvia could not have stayed out so long, if they actually remained near their home locales, without the assistance of members of the slave community. Put another way, truants such as those who "prowled around," "lurked around," or "laid out" near their owners' farms and plantations clearly required the help of other slaves in the quarters, and so owners typically preferred to believe that all runaways benefited from such assistance. One slaveholder, as was true of many of his contemporaries, strongly believed that his fugitive had received assistance from parties unknown but whom, he presumed, were fellow bondmen. In another instance, Jack—a slave belonging to planter John Finlayson of Jefferson County—had been out for twelve months. Finlayson also expressed his strong belief that some person or persons had been harboring and assisting his runaway.[13]

Other examples easily can be offered. Although his man had gone missing about four years earlier, W. H. Simmons of St. Augustine still believed, as he articulated in his September 10, 1835, advertisement, that someone had "probably harbored [him] in the city or its vicinity." Given that St. Augustine remained a small town and Simmons a prominent resident of it, his belief stretched credulity. Even with the bondservant absent for such a long period of time, the slaveholder could not fathom the possibility that his fugitive, who lived in an Atlantic port city, could have boarded a vessel to some free island in the Caribbean.[14]

Henry D. Holland of Jacksonville stated the point about people harboring escapees even more bluntly. While insisting that his house servant had "an air" about him, Holland speculated that the runaway had not gone far. The owner did more than imply that the bondman had received protection and food from the slave quarters. "The said negro has been seen frequently by other negroes on the place," he advertised, "and is no doubt prowling around the neighborhood." Again, like St. Augustine, Jacksonville became a busy port city by the 1850s and offered the potential for a fugitive of traveling by water. It was a fact that some owners simply refused to face.[15]

Havens and Intermediate Flight

Special havens for runaways are known to have been familiar destinations to many who chose to remain near their friends and loved ones. It appears, for instance, that Jefferson County fugitives who did not want to leave the area had a place to which they could go. John Byrd remembered his father, a former bondman, saying that a shelter existed "in a big section of the bush" in Jefferson County. It contained, he added, "pots and things . . . [and] could accommodate eighteen to twenty [runaways]." Byrd also recalled his father saying that this particular "den" served as a sanctuary for "tired" or "mistreated" bondservants. According to the *Tallahassee Sentinel*, Jackson County and the caves near the town of Marianna similarly became havens for "runaway negroes" who made them "their hiding place[s]."[16]

Even runaways who chose not to remain in the neighborhood of their former farm or plantation might travel only so far as a nearby county within the Middle Florida cotton belt, and this produced a curious result. When area slaveholders felt compelled to advertise runaways, the owners generally did not give detailed descriptions. Thomas M. Bush had a chronic problem with truants and seemed to be advertising for them quite often. He could not comprehend the case of Reuben and Willis since they took no clothes with them when they disappeared from his Jackson County plantation. But, some two months later they were discovered two counties away incarcerated in the local Leon County jail. Gabriel took off from Calhoun County and also ended up in the nearby Leon County jail. From reports he had received, one Magnolia planter firmly believed that his fugitive "may be lodged in [nearby] Tallahassee."[17]

Not all paths led to Tallahassee, and the trail easily might be reversed or else slaves might take another one altogether. After five months out, Leon County fugitive Levenia was seen in adjacent Gadsden County. Asa Munson also of Leon County believed that Dick had taken up residence in Gadsden County as well. From the same county, Laurence, described by his owners as "orderly and obedient," surprised them when he absconded to places unknown. And Franklin County slaveholder William Smith indicated that Willowby had been seen in the adjacent towns of Chattahoochee and Quincy in Gadsden County.[18]

Similar to the situation in Middle Florida, fugitives from within East Florida often sought refuge in other counties within its massive territory. Much as had been experienced in Jacksonville with respect to Jon M. Pons's Aleck or Ellick, John M. Payne's Alick obviously knew the geographical landscape of the region. He played games with his master as a habitual fugitive, traveling repeatedly between his master's plantation in Marion County and the Tampa Bay area ninety miles to the south. The owner nonetheless held his fugitive in high regard, asserting that he "has an intelligent look—is very quick spoken. He is one that would be classed as a No. 1 negro." The owner claimed that his bondservant "is supposed to be in the neighborhood of Tampa, in the company with one of Mr. James Turner's boys." With Alick so self-assured, his master could not know for sure but only guess as to where the fugitive might go.[19]

It goes without saying that, if runaways stayed out in their home areas too long, they could face serious challenges. In Middle Florida, the planter gentry had convinced the majority of white non-slaveholders as early as the late 1820s that it benefited them to support the social order and the economy by keeping the ever-growing slave population under control. By the mid-1830s, influential men even in West, East, Central, and South Florida had begun the slow process of convincing non-slaveholders about the utility of controlling the movements of the slave population. Thus, over time fugitives increasingly risked being spotted by whites who would report their whereabouts.[20]

Compounding this problem was the fact that, although some runaways received assistance, the majority did not, despite what the owners thought. With inadequate food, water, shelter, and clothing, fugitives confronted starvation, freezing weather, and other natural obstacles. On one occasion, for example, three very hungry runaways from the Fernandina area were caught "skinning a Beef" for food. Two were killed in the ensuing confrontation. Some six months later, the remaining escapee, John, paid the ultimate price as well. Once again, hunger likely drove him to slaughter another head of beef, and his luck ran out. A slave catcher ran across John engaged in that effort and killed him. The runaway already had survived two years of fugitive freedom. The likelihood that a dreadful price would be paid could grow if such a slave stayed out too long.[21]

Prices to Be Paid

As John's story illustrates, flight carried risks of privation, punishment, and even violent death. Especially the latter case could apply when fugitives avoided their masters for such long periods of time that the masters gave up on ever recapturing their property. In the circumstances, many owners designated the truants as outlaws. This gave slave catchers permission to kill the runaways if they could be located and appeared to resist seizure. In some instances, frustrated owners even chose to advertise for a runaway's capture, dead or alive. Chattahoochee's J. S. McDonnell, for one, placed such a notice. He offered "150 dollars . . . to any one killing the three [runaways] . . . or twenty dollars each for them if delivered alive at my plantation." Field F. Wynn, an executor of a Gadsden County farm estate, appeared defeated in his attempt to recapture two of twelve slaves belonging to the estate. On a receipt he noted, "[I have] paid $100 for the capture and return of two boys, dead or alive."[22]

Even individuals who returned voluntarily after short absences also took a chance that they would suffer serious punishment. Owners and their overseers particularly complained, frequently and bitterly, about either bondservants leaving their estates temporarily or truants coming onto the plantations or farms without permission. So, they often sought direct action to stem the tide. Madison County's DeLaughter plantation serves as an example. Overseer Amon DeLaughter, oldest son of owner Nancy DeLaughter, whipped Charles for riding a horse at night without permission after it became obvious that the bondservant was sneaking away to see a loved one or to participate in some other nighttime activity. Less drastically, DeLaughter also ran off with threats of punishment several of his neighbor's slaves whom he caught in the quarters without permission.[23]

Amon DeLaughter stood as only one among many owners and overseers when it came to beating bondservants who had vanished temporarily from their residences to visit nearby plantations and farms. Shack Thomas recalled that truants were subjected to "buck and gag" upon their return. "Sometimes the young men on the plantation would slip away to visit a girl on another plantation," Douglass Dorsey remembered. If they left the plantation without permission, he continued, they were "lashed on the bare backs." Charlotte Martin recollected that extreme forms of punishment could be imposed for such truancy. According to Martin, her eldest brother was whipped "to death."[24]

Somewhat to the contrary, individual masters, seeking to encourage the voluntary return of temporary runaways, might decline to punish those fugitives who stayed away only for a few days. Wanting to appear to be the magnanimous paternalist, Susan B. Eppes's father, at least according to her account, usually would not whip first offenders, nor did he allow anyone else to punish his laborers. Paul, owned by the Reverend A. J. Scott and a hireling in Pensacola, disappeared from the job site but reportedly remained in the city. Scott represented, in a sense, the larger number of Florida clergymen who owned slaves. He reportedly looked upon himself as different from most slaveholders in the region, however, as he considered himself to be a "Christian slaveholder" who treated his bondservants humanely. The minister did not advertise for the capture of his slave in the newspaper, although in a letter to a friend he claimed that he only wanted "to protect him [Paul] . . . [by placing] him in the country with a planter." Like most paternalistic masters, Scott did not ask Paul what he might want. And, obviously, Paul wanted his liberty, since he did not return willingly to his master.[25]

Freedom in the Peninsula

While most fugitives remained out only temporarily or else located in relatively close proximity to old homes, farms, and plantations, some true fugitives understandably sought to separate from slavery completely by securing freedom some place in the extreme expanses of the peninsula or, as will be discussed further in chapter 6, outside of it. They entertained no intention of returning to the control of their authority figures. Many of these real fugitives had been owned by more than one master and demonstrated enough confidence to break cleanly from their domiciles in search of freedom. Most had become acculturated or assimilated. Many were multilingual and possessed the wherewithal to hold their own when confronted by whites. These true or real runaways, unlike their eighteenth-century counterparts, usually were identified by owners as having carried away several changes of clothes.

As early as 1823, some two years after Spain ceded Florida to the United States, planters of the American era had begun to experience problems with real fugitives, just as had their counterparts in colonial La Florida. Eulalia, an Africa-born bondservant and a semiskilled seamstress in St. Augustine, became one of them. The owner described her in these words:

> [She is] about twenty-eight, of reddish complexion, middling size, stout and rather clumsey [*sic*], walking with a sort of difficulty as if lame of one foot, slight marked on the face with African marks which at first sight appear like pock marks, a hole in the middle of the upper lip made probably to wear a ring. She speaks French, English and Spanish. . . . She carried a large bundle of clothing of her own, consisting of some muslin, calico and checked homespun dresses, blankets, handkerchiefs &c. together with some blue Liverpool china. She always wears a coloured handkerchief round the head, and will probably wear on her way a cloak of fine grey bath coating.

Eulalia's owner did not know her exact destination but believed she possessed sufficient clothing and supplies to attempt leaving the territory of Florida. Still, he never envisioned the fugitive leaving the port of St. Augustine for an island in the Caribbean.[26]

The desire of such Africa-born fugitives to seek freedom—a dynamic itself reflecting a widespread desire within Florida's slave community generally—persisted as exemplified in 1829 by Maria's escape. Aged about thirty-five, she formerly had been the property of "Capt. Drummon" of Escambia. Maria stood approximately five feet ten and was "African by birth and her face tattooed." She absconded from her agent in Pensacola who believed she was heading to Alabama. Many bondpeople who lived in and about Pensacola knew the waterways leading into the Gulf of Mexico. Those, in turn, could take them out to the Atlantic in search of freedom. So, as noted previously with respect to other individuals and contexts, "Drummon" could only guess the fugitive's whereabouts and hope that Maria was, indeed, traveling to her former home in Alabama, where authorities might catch her.[27]

For those true runaways who sought freedom in the expanses of the peninsula, the Seminole nation also became an important destination. Blacks and Seminoles had established relationships and alliances dating back to the eighteenth century, when the Indians first established viable communities in the peninsula. Both races shared a desire to find refuges in its remote expanses. As a result, hundreds, if not thousands, of black runaways made their way over time to lands in the central and southern peninsula, as will be considered in greater detail in chapter 10.[28]

The existence of such peninsular havens for runaways had infuriated planters and politicians dating back to the mid-1500s and Pedro Menendez de Aviles's discovery that slaves he had imported to help build St. Augustine had decamped into the wilds. Planters and politicians from the emerging British colonies to the north and, later, the United States shared those frustrations in subsequent years as Spanish Florida emerged as a haven that promised not only safety but something greater. Congressman Joshua A. Giddings explained the situation from his vantage point in 1858. "Torn from their native land, their friends and homes, they were sold in the markets of Carolina and Georgia," he wrote. "Feeling the hand of oppression bearing heavily on them, they fled to Florida, and, under Spanish laws, became free."[29]

By the early 1800s, whites remained largely frustrated with their attempts to thwart fugitive travel to the Indian lands in La Florida. In 1816, US troops acting under orders from General Andrew Jackson unlawfully destroyed one concentration of blacks called the Negro Fort, which was located on the Apalachicola River a few dozen miles south of the colonial boundary with the United States. British agents had rewarded their War of 1812–era free black and runaway slave allies by handing over to them the keys to the well-planned fortification following the ill-fated British attempt to capture New Orleans in 1815. Many white settlers of newly opened lands in Georgia had viewed this fort as a magnet that would attract other runaways to freedom in the Spanish colony. Over two hundred black men, women, and children died within the post when, at least according to official reports, a lucky shot from a mortar exploded its gunpowder supply.[30]

By the early 1820s, Negro Fort survivors had joined other free blacks and runaways (or "maroons," as they sometimes were called) at several locations in the peninsula. While some fugitives lived with Seminoles who headquartered near the Suwannee River and also close to present-day Gainesville, most generally settled in their own villages near particular groups of Seminoles to which they were allied.[31]

Others, seeking a location both protected and remote, especially ventured close to Tampa Bay. The historian Canter Brown, who has pioneered studies of the subject, has noted the advantages offered by the bay area. They included a remote and difficult-to-approach location, an existing reputation as a safe haven, "rich hammock lands for farming," and "access to trade through contact with the Cuban fishermen at Charlotte Harbor and at Tampa Bay itself." Further key advantages, Brown explained, were that "the locale could be supplied easily by sea from the Bahamas and that the bay afforded ocean-going vessels a safe harbor." The same ocean connections, the historian stressed, could and would provide escape routes when necessary. Having such routes of escape particularly emerged as having the greatest of importance following Jackson's 1818 invasion of Florida and battle with the maroons and Black Seminoles that history has called the First Seminole War. By late that year, Jackson's aide James Gadsden had reported to his superior, "The bay of Tampa . . . is the last rallying spot of the disaffected negroes and Indians and the only favorable point from whence a communication can be had with Spanish and European emissaries."[32]

The maroon colony, located on the Manatee River at present-day Bradenton, was known to nearby Cuban fishermen as Angola, although one party of explorers referred to it in 1821 as the "Sarrazota, or Runaway Negro Plantations." By whatever name it went, General Jackson kept it closely in mind. As Spain prepared to transfer Florida to the United States in 1821, Jackson as provisional governor-designate saw Angola's destruction as a first step in plans to rid the peninsula of runaways. Denied official authority, he apparently dispatched Indian allies to do the work for him. "Within a matter of weeks, [Jackson's] Lower Creek ally Chief William McIntosh, whom Jackson had managed to commission a Brigadier General in the United States Army, ordered a Lower Creek war party into Florida," Brown detailed. "Led by McIntosh's man Colonel Charles Miller and Jackson's Red Stick Creek protégé William Weatherford, the raiders wreaked havoc as they progressed down the peninsula. At the Manatee River in late spring, they surprised Angolans and destroyed their settlement." This occurrence, tragic as it was, served to frustrate Jackson's ultimate purpose by bonding Indians and blacks more closely together, an outcome that soon would result, as Brown underscored, in a second and more deadly Seminole war.[33]

Jackson's move on Angola slowed but did not stop the movement of runaways into the peninsula, and after 1821, runaway slaves continued to reach Indians' reserved lands. New American settlers felt that they had to break the back of the longstanding alliance between runaways, Seminoles, and other Indian peoples in Florida if they were to build Florida's economy based upon enslaved labor. One newspaper reflected the sentiments of most whites, summing up the matter by stating, "If [the Indians are] located in Florida, all the runaway slaves will find refuge and protection with them."[34]

Indeed, several new villages in remote areas of Central and South Florida became sanctuaries of freedom for many fugitives. Peliklakaha, home of the leader Abraham, ranked as the most popular for a time and probably constituted the largest such settlement during the late 1820s and early 1830s. Other destinations for Florida runaways included places known as Suwannee Old Town, King Heijah's Town or Payne's Negro Settlement, Buckra Woman's Town, and Mulatto Girl's Town. Two other colonies also welcomed Florida runaways. Located near the headwaters of the Peace River in today's Polk County and inhabited partly by survivors of Angola's destruction, they were called Minatti and Tobasa (or Wahoo).[35]

As will be seen later, the alliance between runaways and Seminoles, as well as the viability of peninsular Florida as a refuge, would be tested by the US military in the late 1830s and early 1840s. Nonetheless, runaways would continue to rank the Indian lands as a destination and haven through the 1850s. According to one newspaper report, three runaways from the St. Augustine area were heading to the farthest extremes of the peninsula late in that decade to join the Indians. Some fugitives may even have clung to their South Florida homes into the 1870s and 1880s.[36]

A slave runaway haven for free blacks called Gracia Real de Santa Teresa de Mose was located two miles north of St. Augustine as late as the mid-1760s. Courtesy Florida Museum of Natural History, Fort Mose Exhibition.

This Tallahassee street scene dates to the 1830s and illustrates urban slavery then found in Middle Florida. Drawn by Francis Comte De Castelnau, courtesy Photographic Collection, Florida State Archives.

Tallahassee, the seat of government in Florida from the mid-1820s, also emerged as the center of slave-trading activities during the antebellum period. The town had not changed much from its appearance in the late antebellum days until this view was drawn. Courtesy Photographic Collection, Florida State Archives.

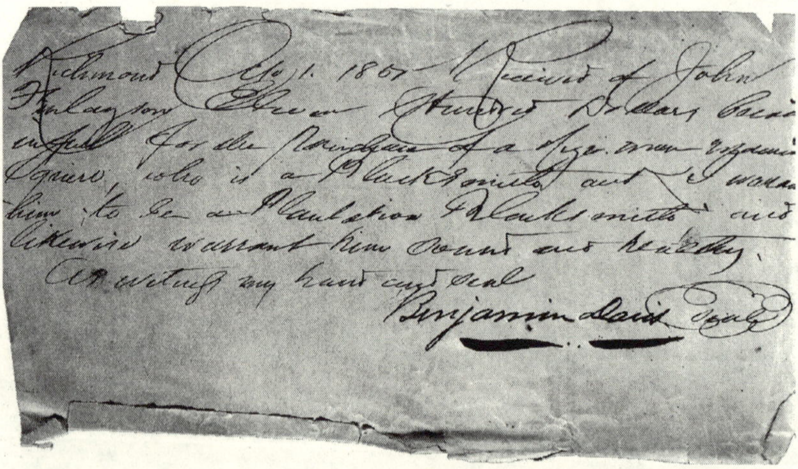

Richmond Oct 1. 1861 Received of John Finlayson Eleven Hundred Dollars [illegible] in full for the purchase of a Negro man Edward Squire, who is a Blacksmith and I warrant him to be a Plantation Blacksmith and likewise warrant him sound and healthy.
As witness my hand and seal
Benjamin Davis (Seal)

As late as the early 1860s, enslaved blacks still were being torn from family and friends in the Upper South to labor in frontier Florida. This is a receipt for blacksmith Edward Squire, purchased by Middle Florida slaveholder John Finlayson from Benjamin Davis of Richmond, Virginia, on October 1, 1861. Courtesy Photographic Collection, Florida State Archives.

After caring for the offspring of slave owners most of the day, enslaved women enjoyed little time for their own children and families. Aunt Jane cared for Sarah, the daughter of Doctor J. D. Palmer, during the 1850s. Courtesy Photographic Collection, Florida State Archives.

A typical Florida slave cabin during the antebellum period in the Middle Florida region. Here, members of a former slave family stand beside their cabin during the 1870s. Courtesy Photographic Collection, Florida State Archives.

"Words of Dissension." Florida bondwomen expressed words of defiance to authority figures more frequently than did enslaved men. Artist Ricky Callaway; collection of the author.

Some slave owners employed slave catchers to retrieve runaways. This artist's rendition portrays slave catchers encountering defiant runaways. Slave catchers commonly used a whip to subdue fugitives in frontier Florida. Artist Ricky Callaway; collection of the author.

Whipping enslaved blacks with a paddle constituted one form of punishment. Other common implements used to punish rebels and runaways included whips and leather straps. Courtesy Photographic Collection, Florida State Archives.

Rebels and runaways sometimes were punished by standing in the stocks. This practice continued for blacks well after freedom came. Courtesy Photographic Collection, Florida State Archives.

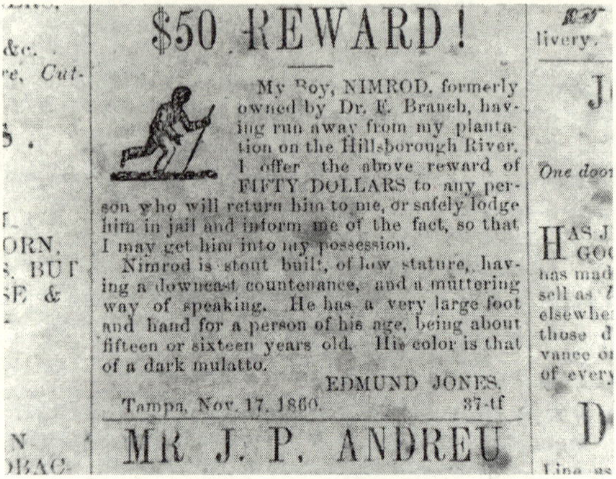

$50 REWARD!

My Boy, NIMROD, formerly owned by Dr. E. Branch, having run away from my plantation on the Hillsborough River, I offer the above reward of FIFTY DOLLARS to any person who will return him to me, or safely lodge him in jail and inform me of the fact, so that I may get him into my possession.

Nimrod is stout built, of low stature, having a downcast countenance, and a muttering way of speaking. He has a very large foot and hand for a person of his age, being about fifteen or sixteen years old. His color is that of a dark mulatto.

EDMUND JONES.

Tampa, Nov. 17, 1860. 37-tf

MR. J. P. ANDREU

A typical runaway slave notice from the *Tampa Florida Peninsular*, November 17, 1860. Collection of the author.

A portion of the Duval County estate of Zephaniah Kingsley. As an astute Atlantic trader who brought enslaved blacks from Africa, Cuba, and various parts of the Caribbean, Kingsley learned that keeping bondservants grouped in families, use of the task system, and adequate material conditions kept dissension and rebellion to a minimum on his plantation. Courtesy Photographic Collection, Florida State Archives.

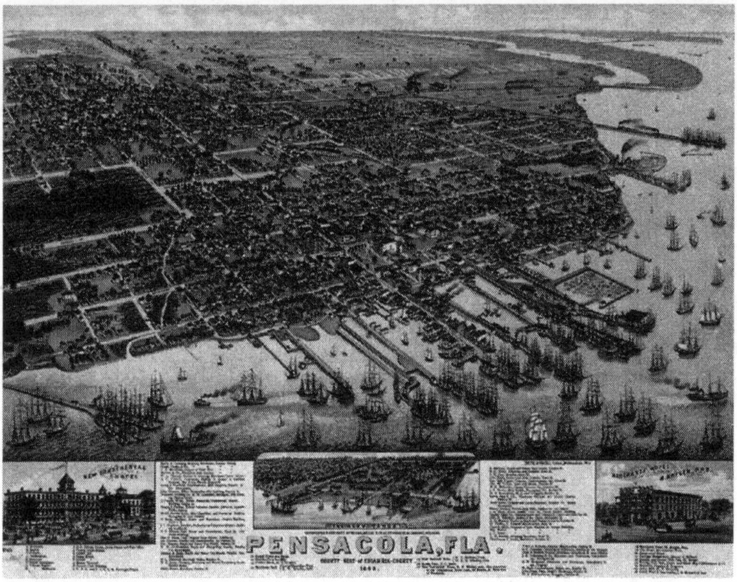

"Pensacola Birds Eye View Map, 1885—Florida Escambia County, Pensacola, Fla., County seat, 1885." This view of Pensacola following slavery days represents the town's busy port and waterfronts that sometimes offered access to free communities across or along the byway of the Gulf of Mexico or the Atlantic Ocean for seafaring runaways. Collection of the author.

"Jacksonville Birds Eye View Map," 1893 Florida Duval County, Jacksonville, Florida, drawn by August Koch, 1893. Although this bird's-eye view of Jacksonville and adjacent waterways is pictured here at a time following slavery's demise, it affords an excellent sense of the town's busy port and teeming waterfront when it opened paths of opportunity for escapees seeking freedom, whether in the isolated reaches of the peninsula or in the greater Atlantic world. Collection of the author.

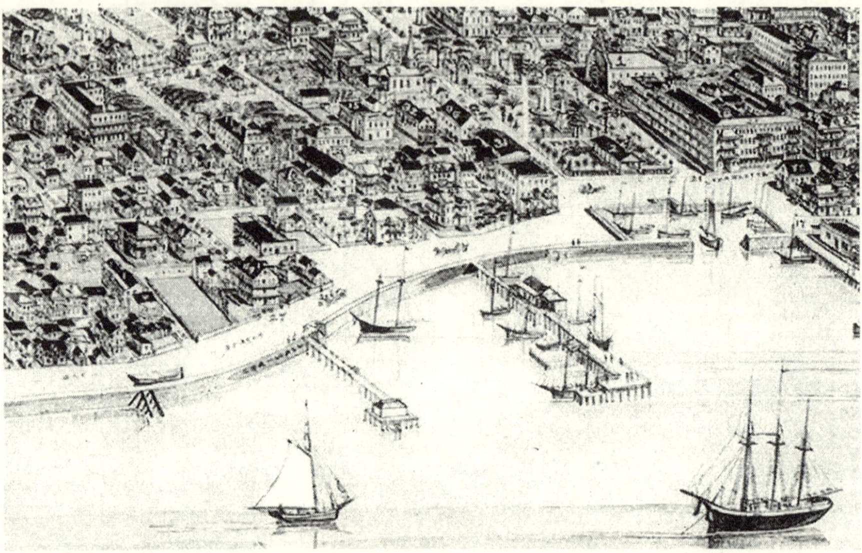

"Birds Eye view of St. Augustine, 1885, drawn by H. Wellge, published by Norris, Wellge & Swift, Brockton, Mass." This view of the country's oldest port town of St. Augustine suggests the relative ease with which runaways could have boarded ships or boats in search of freedom in other Atlantic world communities. Collection of the author.

"Panoramic View of Key West," c. 1855, Lithograph by Chandler & Co., Boston. Runaways endeavored to reach port towns such as Key West in their quest to secure freedom in an Atlantic world community. Collection of the author.

Some fugitives attempted to frustrate slave catchers by boarding outgoing ships or boats in various port towns. This artist's sketch shows fugitives trying to reach a ship as it sails away from the shoreline. Artist Ricky Callaway; collection of the author.

The distant appearance of a sailing vessel off remote Florida shores could conjure hopes of better days for captive men, women, and children. 1871 engraving, courtesy University of Tampa Press.

Some black seamen assisted Florida fugitives by stowing them away on vessels headed to a free community on either side of the Atlantic Ocean. Artist Ricky Callaway; collection of the author.

The author confined in the pillory.

Abolitionist Jonathan Walker suffered branding and was confined to a stock or pillory at Pensacola during the 1840s. Courtesy Photographic Collection, Florida State Archives.

Florida served as a runaway slave haven from the 1500s to the Civil War's end. Fugitives often joined other runaways and Seminole Indians who lived in maroon communities spread out over the sparsely populated peninsula. Courtesy Photographic Collection, Florida State Archives.

Interaction of blacks and Seminoles constituted an everyday experience in Florida well into the 1840s. Courtesy Photographic Collection, Florida State Archives.

An artist's depiction of the Second Seminole War as what General Thomas Jesup called a "negro war." Courtesy Photographic Collection, Florida State Archives.

Abraham escaped from slavery as a small boy to become one of the most trusted advisors of the Seminole chief Micanopy while playing a critical role in starting the Black/Indian Rebellion known as the Second Seminole War. Courtesy Photographic Collection, Florida State Archives.

John Horse, also called John Cavallo or Gopher John, became a principal leader of the Black Seminoles and plantation runaways during the Second Seminole War. Courtesy Photographic Collection, Florida State Archives.

Ben Bruno became an interpreter for the US Army after serving as private counsel to Seminole leader Billy Bowlegs. Courtesy Photographic Collection, Florida State Archives.

Black women lived and worked among the Seminoles as nurses, cooks, seamstresses, farmers, and general laborers. Selina Rollins seemingly served as a cook or nurse during the Black/Indian Rebellion. Courtesy Photographic Collection, Florida State Archives.

Some enslaved black women, whether willingly or unwillingly, labored for either the Confederate or the Union forces during the Civil War. Charity Stewart made soap for the Confederacy. Courtesy Photographic Collection, Florida State Archives.

Enslaved black men willingly joined the Union army to fight for their freedom and that of loved ones. Here, an artist has represented a black Union infantryman who fought in Florida as well as in other theaters of the South. Courtesy Library of Congress.

Runaway Thomas Warren Long, as was true for over one thousand of his brethren from Florida, fought on the side of the Union for his freedom from slavery. Courtesy Photographic Collection, Florida State Archives.

Black Union soldiers fighting in Florida at the Battle of Olustee, 1864. Courtesy Photographic Collection, Florida State Archives.

Some runaways used Florida waterways in efforts to reach Union boats to escape from slavery during the Civil War. Courtesy Photographic Collection, Florida State Archives.

1. West, Middle, East, Central, and South Florida during the antebellum period. Collection of the author.

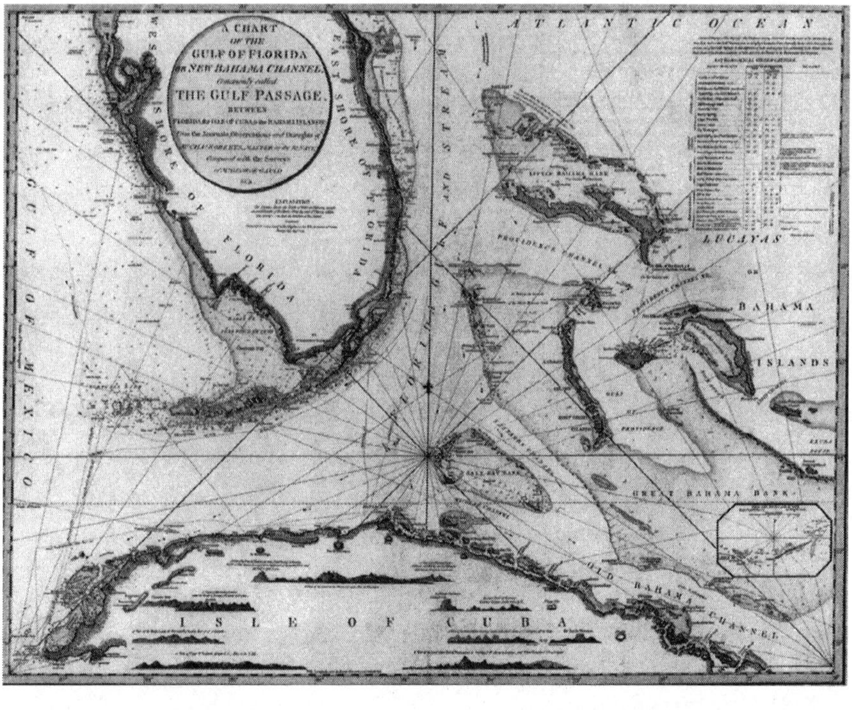

2. "A Chart of the Gulf of Florida or New Bahama Channel, Commonly called the Gulf Passage, etc., Cartographer: George Gauld, 1794." Florida in proximity to the Atlantic world. Collection of the author.

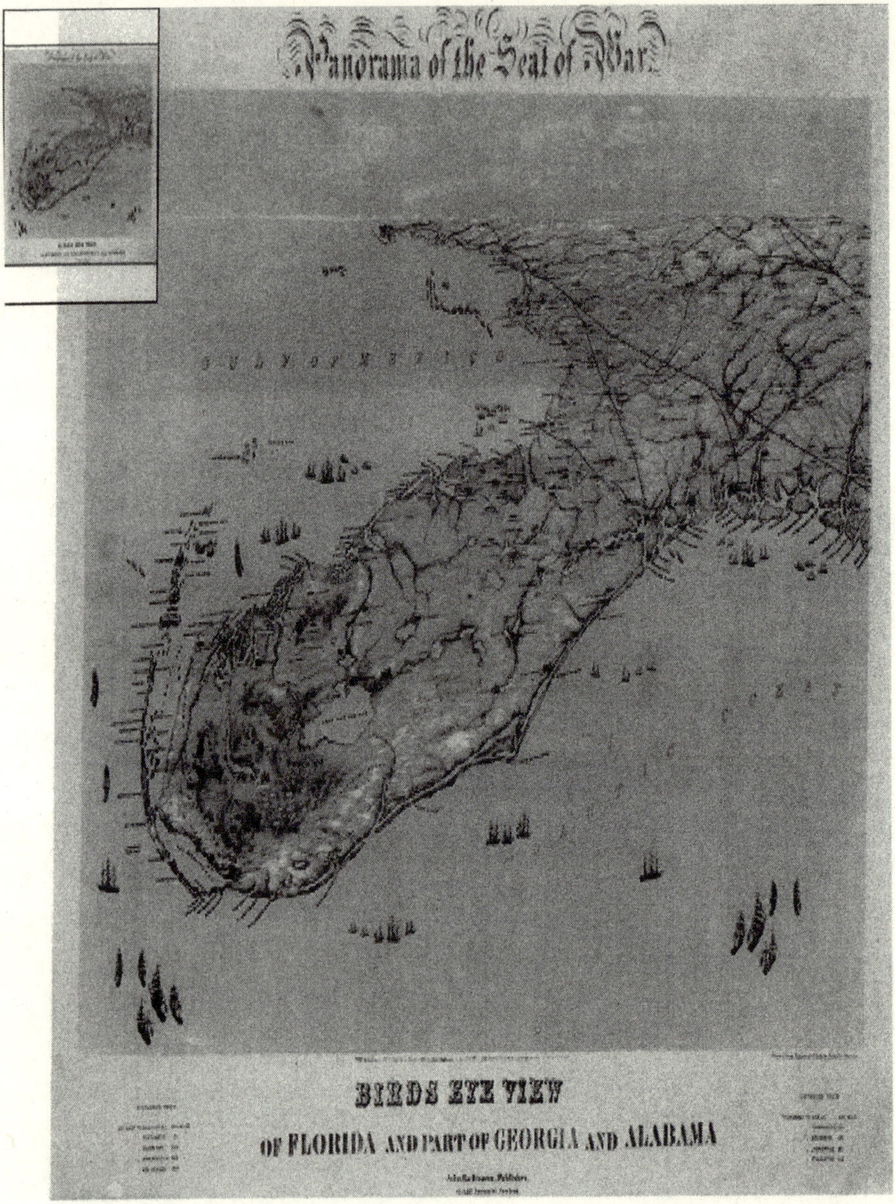

3. "Birds Eye View of Florida and Part of Georgia and Alabama," drawn from nature and lith. by John Bachmann, 1861. Florida shown with the Gulf of Mexico, the Atlantic Ocean, and part of Georgia and Alabama. Collection of the author.

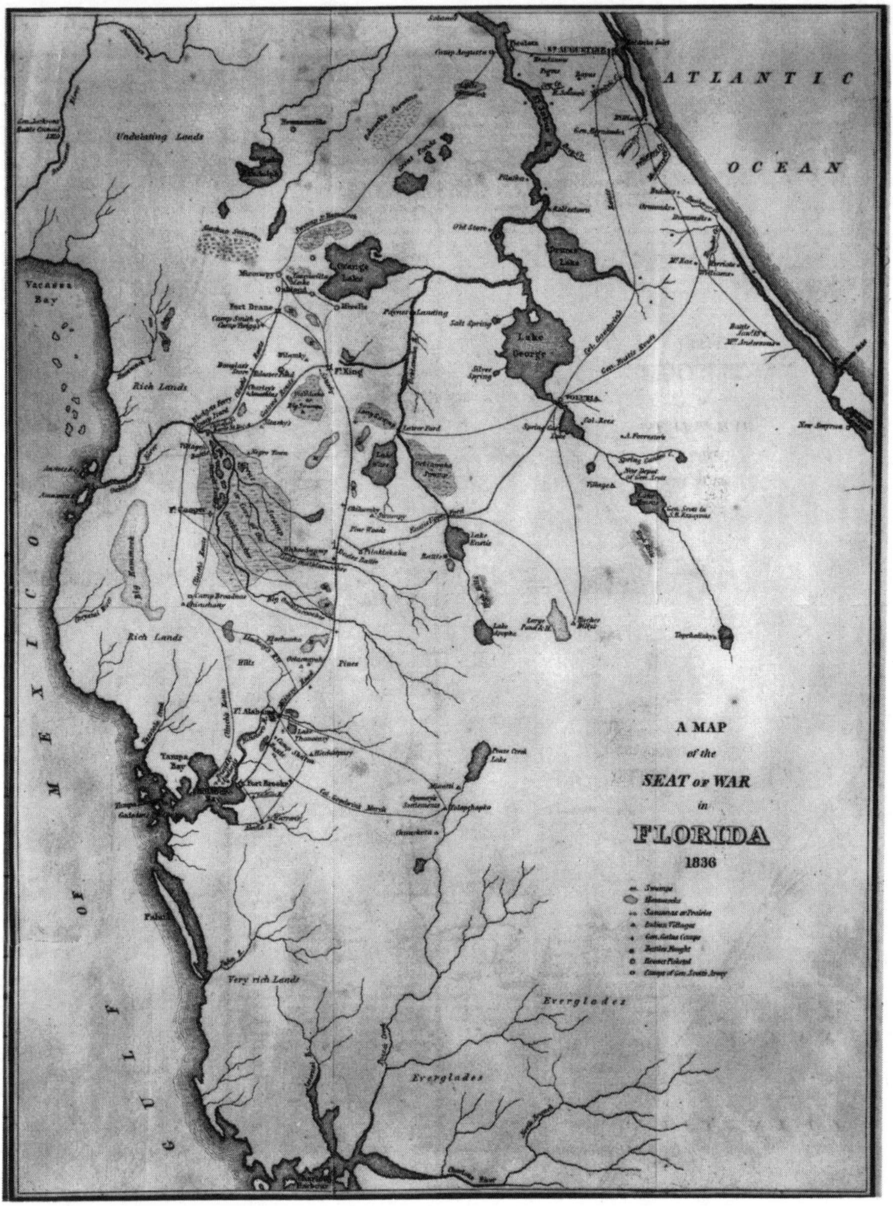

4. "A Map of the Seat of War in Florida, 1836." House Document No. 78, 25th Congress, 2d sess., ser. 323, p. 768. The main concentration or seat of the Black/Indian Rebellion or Second Seminole War in northeast and Central Florida. Collection of the author.

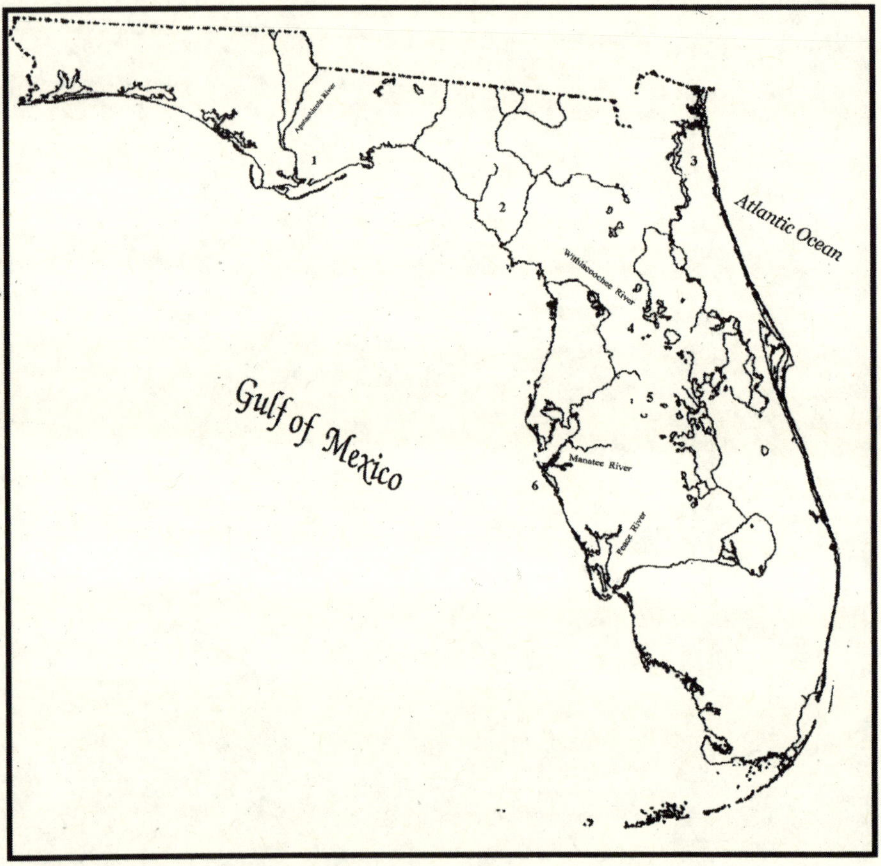

5. Principal Florida Maroon (Runaway Slave) Havens from 1738–1836. Collection of the author.

1. Negro Fort (1815–1816)
2. Suwannee Negro Towns (1816–1818)
3. Gracia Real de Santa Teresa de Mose (Fort Mose) (1738–1763)
4. Peliklakaha (c. 1803–1836)
5. Minatti (c. 1818–1836)
6. Angola (c. 1812–1821)

6. Flight Away from Florida

The slaves had steered right over to Nassau.
—*Tallahassee Floridian*, February 20, 1858

As promised early on, this survey intends to emphasize the complexities inherent in Florida's slave resistance experience, and it must be stated that those complexities applied to flight just as they did to other facets of the subject. To this point in the narrative, temporary flight, flight within the immediate vicinity, flight within the immediate region, flight to area havens, and flight into the wilds of the peninsula have received close attention. Those discussions do not begin to cover the topic of the present chapter. However, highly relevant to any examination of this kind are additional factors, including flight away from Florida. Relevant, as well, is consideration of the methods of flight that suggest how escapees eased their passages through the state and to other places, including ones within the Atlantic world and the associated Caribbean basin.

It may be helpful to recapitulate that, in West and East Florida, bondservants typically possessed more of an Atlantic world perspective than did slaves living in Middle Florida. For hundreds of years by the time of the Civil War, enslaved persons had been employed in or around the maritime industries in those regions. Many times they and those whom they influenced had taken recourse to the use of their skills as pilots, mariners, coopers, sailmakers, boatmen, lightermen, shipwrights, caulkers, and riggers—as well as their knowledge of coastal port towns—in efforts to secure everlasting freedom.[1]

While knowledge of, or residence in, coastal ports was not a prerequisite for flight across the ocean, such familiarity usually served as an extremely helpful resource. Such ports as St. Augustine and, later, Pensacola stood out as towns (*presidio* in Spanish) during the greater part of the Spanish era, although the outpost at St. Marks on the Gulf of Mexico, south of the future site of Tallahassee, eventually did indicate the Spanish presence in what would come to be called Middle Florida. The last decades of Spanish rule also saw Fernandina begin to thrive, in good part because it offered a base for slave smuggling into the United States following the banning of the international slave trade as of January 1, 1808. Meanwhile, at the crossing of the King's Road on the St. Johns River (the Cowford), the outpost of San Nicholas presaged future development of Jacksonville on the stream's opposite shore.[2]

The scene had not changed all that much by the Civil War's eve in that it more closely resembled the Spanish picture than the one familiar to modern Floridians. The state's largest towns then included Pensacola and Key West, nearly tied for first place with fewer than three thousand residents, followed by Jacksonville, Tallahassee, St. Augustine, and Apalachicola. Fernandina came ninth. Smaller port towns operating during this period included St. Marks, Magnolia, Newport, and Alligator Point in Middle Florida; Milton and Blackwater (Bagdad) in West Florida; and Cedar Keys, Tampa, and Manatee (Bradenton) in the East Florida peninsula. These places became, as would be expected, favored destinations for runaways. Why so? Many true fugitives probably believed that they could remain largely undetected and free if they mixed with both the slave and free black populations roaming about in most of these busy places. Others felt they could use their skills to board ships sailing to Atlantic communities in the northern states or to various islands in the Atlantic and Caribbean.[3]

In fact, two out of every ten Florida fugitives used waterways leading to or including the Atlantic or the Gulf of Mexico in attempts to secure freedom from 1821 to 1865. Some of them likely were descendants of bondpeople and free blacks who had lived under Spanish rule and retained memories of the massive departure of relatives and friends to Cuba when the British took over control of Florida for two decades in 1763. Even under US rule in and after 1821, the desire for complete liberty continued to reverberate for fugitives who still knew they were connected to the outer world thanks to the Atlantic Ocean, the Gulf, and the Caribbean. Some fugitives knew if they could secure passage on a ship leaving any of the aforementioned ports, they might secure for all time that chance for freedom.[4]

Through the Civil War and subsequent years, there lived in Florida any number of enslaved blacks and former bondservants who held personal memories of the Atlantic world and a long-ago home in Africa. East Floridians Corporal Jaudon and Dolly met that qualification. Daddy Corporal, as he was better known, lived to the age of 117, according to surviving reports, and informed listeners that he had belonged to the Esco Gullah Tribe in Africa. He had traveled across the Atlantic to Charleston, South Carolina, as a boy and later was purchased by E. C. Jaudon, who eventually brought him to Jacksonville to live and work. Daddy Corporal remained in that port city until his death on May 22, 1877. Unlike Daddy, Dolly died in bondage, seemingly at the age of 116 in June 1851. An African native, she clung to her African traditions; her funeral consisted of "bestowing those particular rites which among Southern slaves is singularly superstitious; but amid incantations, prayers, and day and night watching." Such rites connected Dolly to her ancestors and her African homeland, however peculiar or suspicious whites might have found them.[5]

Thanks to Patricia C. Griffin's excellent work, students of Florida's experience recently have been afforded a detailed example of another enslaved African who possessed an Atlantic worldview and who settled in East Florida. Remarkably, much of his story appears to be told in his own words. As an uprooted native of West Africa, Sitiki held memories of his forced emigration from his homeland and the long voyage he endured across the Atlantic—what was called the Middle Passage. The captive landed in North America at Charleston, South Carolina, although he later was taken to Savannah, Georgia. There, Josiah Smith purchased him and renamed him Jack Smith. Shortly afterward, Jack moved with the Smith family to Watertown, Connecticut, before relocating one year later to St. Marys, Georgia. Ultimately he reached St. Augustine in 1817. As his narrative details, Sitiki then lived through the Spanish, territorial, antebellum, Civil War, and Reconstruction eras in Florida before passing away in 1882. Through those years, the one-time African exerted significant influence on the slaves and other blacks with whom he came into contact, whether as an ordained clergyman, teacher, neighbor, or friend. If one knew him, the world outside Florida became much less of a mystery.[6]

Port Towns as Points of Departure

Perhaps Sitiki's presence in St. Augustine offered a partial explanation for why that town became a destination for so many runaways who wanted to escape farther down the peninsula or to some place across the ocean, such as the Bahamas. Added to his presence, the town enjoyed legacies of Spanish traditions that resulted in the relatively free movement of slaves there. In providing an example of the town's allure, Jim's experience may prove helpful. In 1840, St. Augustine authorities boarded the vessel *William Gaston* and found the fugitive preparing for a voyage. The Alachua County absconder, they reported, had been "concealed among the cargo." Jim's destination was not known with certainty, but his desire for freedom outside of Florida rang clear.[7]

Three years later, seven fugitives are known to have departed St. Augustine for the Bahamas, where emancipation had gained the force of law on August 1, 1834. According to various accounts, two of the escapees had been employed as sailors onboard the schooner *Walter*, a vessel in the service of the United States. They had planned their escape well, taking with them "seven stand of muskets, a compass, and sufficient quantity of provisions to last them" for some time. As they traveled in a stolen pilot boat up and down the coastline near present-day Miami, the fugitives picked up two additional fugitives before landing briefly at Key Biscayne. The *St. Augustine News* reported, "[They] have been committing murder and plundering the settlers on the coast." On October 7, 1843, the same newspaper informed readers, "Should these negroes succeed in reaching the Bahamas Islands, they should immediately be demanded by our Government." Five weeks passed before the newspaper noticed that they "have arrived at Nassau." Repeated attempts by Florida authorities to extradite the fugitives, it should be noted, ended without success. Interestingly, seven members of this group had numbered among at least three other groups of seven to abscond from their owners during this general period.[8]

Much like St. Augustine, Jacksonville also became a favorite stop for Florida fugitives and for many of the same reasons, plus a few more. The town and vicinity, where maritime jobs were plentiful, contained a large black population. Its thriving port, meanwhile, offered a variety of possibilities for escape, especially after improved roads and railroad construction began to open northeast Florida during the 1850s to major development in the timber and lumber industries. Fugitives in the circumstances naturally aimed at the port town as their departure point to freedom. When two fugitives were found hidden away on an outbound ship during that decade, the capture merely punctuated many previous and future successes.[9]

The desire of fugitives to continue using the waterways of Florida to secure freedom in some Atlantic world community persisted over time. As late as 1858, over one dozen Key West bondservants fled their masters with "all of their clothing and possessions." The efficiency of their escape suggested the months of careful planning that had preceded the event. "The slaves," a notice read, "made their escape in a boat owned by the tender keeper of the Sand Key Light House which had been supplied with provisions the previous day from that establishment." The newspaper noted also, "The slaves had [probably] steered right over to Nassau as the wind was fair." A newspaper editor speculated nonetheless that, if the fugitives had not been successful in reaching the Bahamas, then perhaps they might be carried by a British ship to Boston. No available evidence suggests that the fugitives ever were recaptured.[10]

Pensacolans, too, lived amid strong Spanish traditions and heritage, and their town and port also offered at least some avenues for escape. As noted earlier, a noticeable free black community resided there until around 1857, plus the community maintained a relatively tolerant racial atmosphere. The vast distances through virtually uninhabited territory that challenged Middle Florida runaways who found it necessary to make their way through the panhandle all the way to Pensacola posed a problem, however. As a result, few of that region's escapees made it to the old Spanish outpost. One who did, at least according to surviving documentation, lived to regret it. The man's name was Henry, and he absconded from John Williamson of Tallahassee. Unfortunately for the fugitive, a "welcoming party" picked him up in Pensacola upon his arrival at the old West Florida capital.[11]

Given these facts and West Florida's sparse settlement patterns, it may not seem so surprising that more slaves ran away from Pensacola than to the town during much of the antebellum period. Prior to the mid-1840s, only a few slaves managed to flee the area. By the early 1850s, though, over 90 percent of fugitive advertisements carried by the *Pensacola Gazette* testified to the fact that bondpeople had disappeared from, rather than appeared in, the city. Most of the escapees—the total numbers were relatively small as the town also was small—typically sought refuge in different parts of Alabama, with a few heading to Georgia. A partial explanation may lie in the fact that many bondservants were brought from Alabama to Pensacola as hirelings to work at the military establishment or in the large Pensacola brickyard. Most probably were trying to return to their former homes to be with kinfolk and friends. Numbers of Alabama fugitives were caught and jailed in Pensacola, which might further suggest a strong kinship network between the two places.[12]

Again, exceptions exist, as the cases of Pensacola fugitives Aaron and James illustrate. As early as 1822, these fugitives sought to make Pensacola their destination. Owner John Seater proudly pointed out on that occasion that James had been apprehended but that Aaron had out-finessed the slave catchers. Seater went on to advise, "[The runaway] has changed his name and calls himself Zear Mankin; his left thumb has been split and is stiff." Some eighteen years later, John Betton similarly made his escape to Pensacola. Like James, the artisan used his skills and arts of deception in planning his escape after he had been hired out to work at the Pensacola brickyard. The owner implied that his fugitive was a crafty fellow who would change his name if it fit his purpose. In the neighborhood around Pensacola, he became known as John Flaps, described as "black complexion, 22, 5'7" large mouth and ears, and was at times a rather guilty countenance. It is expected he will make his way to the [port] of Pensacola with a view of making his escape in some vessel." Given that John knew the people and geography of Pensacola, his success in boarding a ship for some Atlantic coastline community or the Caribbean became a distinct possibility.[13]

Although a smaller place than the Florida port towns previously addressed, St. Marks served as a terminus for Middle Florida slaveholders who shipped their cotton and other commodities to the North and, as a result, became a destination within the Middle Florida region for slaves who wanted to travel to some Atlantic or Gulf community. Thirty-year-old Rebecca, described as "short and stout in form, of a dark copper color with freckles—and with long straight black hair," was one. The owner claimed the fugitive had been seen in St. Marks. He also believed that she "probably would remain in that town until she figured out how to get back to South Carolina where she had been purchased." Given that St. Marks had become such a busy locale during the territorial and statehood periods, the likelihood of Rebecca and other fugitives boarding vessels for places outside of Florida appears high.[14]

The small town of Apalachicola played a role, as well, as a destination and as a seaport town where bondservants could secure passage on a vessel for freedom from slavery. The citizens, as noted earlier, knew of the possibility of sailors stowing away fugitives and sought at times to jail black sailors until their ships departed the port town. R. K. West believed as much. His published notice specified that Cain might be there, since he "is well known at Apalachicola" and previously had traveled up and down the coastline on Apalachicola River steamboats. With the confident bondservant used to working around whites and familiar with the comings and goings of boats at Apalachicola, the owner could not say with certainty whether the fugitive would remain in the town or would board a ship in his attempts to secure freedom. While Cain may well have made his escape, Tallahassee slave Eaton Thompson's efforts met a more unfortunate end. In 1838, he was captured at Apalachicola as a runaway and incarcerated. Another escapee who reached Apalachicola met a worse fate than did Thompson. Not only was he captured and jailed, but the sheriff sold the bondservant when no owner came forth to claim him.[15]

Paths to the North

Of those who aimed to depart Florida permanently, relatively few attempted to make their way to the North and Midwest, a fact that reflects the conclusions reached by John Hope Franklin and Loren Schweninger in their 1999 study, *Runaway Slaves*. Still, some bondservants with a larger worldview used waterways leading to northern destinations in their quests for freedom. Isaac's owner did believe such to be the case with his fugitive bondman. He claimed that the escapee from Duval County would be "traveling to the North by St. Marks, Apalachicola, Mobile, or some seaport [town]." He postulated that his bondservant was "used to the sea . . . [and will] attempt to ship as a free man." Albert's owner also insisted that the fugitive would make another attempt to escape to the "North by hiding away on a ship at St. Marks." Dick's master similarly speculated that the well-assimilated fugitive had procured papers to enable him to get to a "free state." As a stowaway about the ship *Franklin* at Jacksonville, Edinbur Randall, a runaway mulatto, utilized Atlantic waterways to make good his escape to Boston in 1854. Also taking advantage of the water routes, another fugitive successfully made his way to Dayton, Ohio. Both these men reached their destinations in the North and there became the concern of abolitionists who, in light of passage of the 1850 Fugitive Slave Act, aided them in resisting their extradition to Florida.[16]

Given some such exceptions, table 6 indicates that a total of 179 runaways, or 18 percent of Florida fugitives, sought to leave the peninsula from 1821 to 1860. This statistic was higher than the 14 percent of North Carolina runaways who attempted to leave the state from 1775 to 1840. Over a twelve-year period (1775–87), a higher percentage of fugitives left Virginia (24 percent) and South Carolina (28 percent) than did their counterparts from Florida. As in years past, the territory and state remained the destination of fugitives from Virginia, North Carolina, South Carolina, and Georgia.[17]

The large majority of fugitives who left Florida journeyed no farther north than to Georgia, Alabama, South Carolina, and North Carolina. As the state closest to most enslaved Floridians, Georgia understandably appeared as the destination for the larger number of those who fled on foot. Several of Augustus H. Lanier's laborers absconded during the 1830s and 1840s. He described one Georgia-bound escapee as follows: "34, 5'3", very well built, between copper and black color, talks a little fine and tolerable quick when spoken to—has a scar on two areas of his arms up in a line with his thumb, and I think same scars on the breast. He has a large scar on his back near, I think, the left shoulder blade, with other marks by the whip for fighting. Good field hand and a rough carpenter." The owner went on to say that the fugitive, named Adam, might try to make his way back to Savannah, where he had been purchased "16 years ago." With so many scars and marks on his person, it must be said, it appears

Table 6. Destinations of Runaways Leaving Florida, 1821–1860

State	Number	State	Number
Alabama	28	Pennsylvania	1
Georgia	62	North Carolina	11
Louisiana	2	South Carolina	16
Maryland	3	Tennessee	4
Massachusetts	1	Virginia	6
Mississippi	4	Bahamas/Cuba/Caribbean	33
Ohio	1	North or to a free state	4
New York	3	**Total**	**179**

Sources: Florida and Georgia extant newspapers, 1821–60, as well as other documentary accounts.

more than likely that one important reason for Adam absconding grew out of abusive treatment inflicted by the whip.[18]

Luke also vanished from Florida with Georgia on his mind. Departing the little port town of Magnolia in 1829, he took, as often appeared the case with such runaways, "a variety of clothing with him including a good fur hat and new brogans." Luke seemingly understood many of the waterways of the peninsula, "having been employed for sometime as a boat hand on the river." The owner thought his bondservant might partially use the Atlantic coastal waterways to get back to either Macon or Tifton. On the other hand, it is entirely possible that Luke, with all his provisions, also might have headed to other Atlantic world communities in the Caribbean or elsewhere.[19]

The small stream of Florida fugitives that emptied into Georgia continued to flow over the years, as the 1838 experiences of Isaac and Jack illustrated. Owner D. A. Gillard believed that the two fugitives were headed for Columbus and outlined their character and personality in a newspaper ad. Notably, Jack appeared to Gillard the more confident of the two, at least when it came to dealing with whites when confronted. The owner described the bondservants with clarity: "Isaac is a yellow boy, about 19 years old, about 5 feet 7 or 8 inches high, slow when spoken to and has a very awkward appearance when walking, his feet turning much out. Jack, or Blaud, as he has once been called, is a very black fellow, about 21 years old, 6 feet high and a bold and impudent expression when addressed."[20]

A decade later, Tom—incidentally, that was perhaps the most popular name for absconders from Florida—reportedly was making his way to Georgia. As a clever and self-assured eighteen-year-old, the slave managed to elude the grasp of his owner for three years. Kermit Moore of Middle Florida's Jefferson County did not know the exact destination of his fugitive, but a slave informer had told him that the bondservant would probably head back to his former home in Augusta.[21]

Thomasville apparently attracted more Florida fugitives than any other single place in Georgia—at least as a stopover point—because of its proximity to the state line and the Middle Florida plantation belt. Leon County fugitive Tom, for instance, fled across the line to the Thomas County seat in 1835. Some eleven years later, the town served as the destination for yet another Tom. He was, according to the advertisement, "very dark, [with a] perched forehead and intelligent countenance, a noted mark in the forehead extending down between the eye-brows, about 5'8" between 25 and 30." Apprehended in the Peach State, the smart fugitive broke out of the Thomasville jail. Recaptured and incarcerated at the small Florida port community of Alligator Point, the bondservant took to calling himself John as well as Tom. Displaying vibrant ingenuity, the fugitive then escaped again. At that point, the owner did not know where his slave would head next. The master, of course, should not have disregarded the possibility that Tom or John, like other fugitives, may have boarded a vessel to some other Atlantic world community.[22]

Other than for Georgia, more Florida fugitives fled to Alabama than to any other southern state from 1821 to 1865. Sam may have been one of the first. He departed his Pensacola home for Mobile shortly after Florida was ceded to the United States by the Spanish. Specifically, on August 17, 1822, the highly skilled bricklayer left his master Robert James. Sam, a highly assimilated artisan, could read and write, and the owner conjectured that he may have possessed "free papers" as he made his way. Orrin also decided to separate completely from a Pensacola master by taking off for Alabama. The fugitive had been held by two previous owners—the second being Isom Robinson of Alabama—before being sold to Tallahassee's Byrd C. Willis. The new owner believed that the escapee, who was described as six feet two and "28 or 30," would endeavor to get back to his previous home.[23]

Such patterns persisted over the years as runaways here and there continued to head for Alabama. Take the 1828 cases of Mary Lewis, Tom, Jacob, and Peter. Owner Richard Dealy of Pensacola described them. Mary, he began, "[is] a bright negress, about 30 years old, speaks French and English, Tom, 7 years a mulatto, Jacob, an infant of 6 months, and Peter, age 45 years." Dealy noted additionally that they were well provisioned for their escape, having stolen from him ten dollars in government notes, a plate of considerable value, and valuable clothing. He "presumed said negroes are gone for the direction of Mobile."[24]

A noticeable portion of the runaway population that made its way north from Florida fled to South Carolina. This should not surprise students of the state's history, since a respectable percentage of Florida's captive laborers came with their owners from South Carolina during the 1840s and 1850s. This was true, for instance, of the Nancy and Amon DeLaughter family. It would be expected that some of the men, women, and children they brought to Madison County would seek to return to the Palmetto State and that the same would apply to other former South Carolina slaves elsewhere who also had been led to Florida. Harry, for instance, took leave of Tallahassee for South Carolina. His owner described his self-assured fugitive as well dressed, "coal black, his front teeth decayed, his head well combed, . . . with gray . . . forward in speaking and not timid."[25]

Another incident of South Carolina–bound flight underscores the point that fugitives sometimes sought to pass as white if they had light complexions and that owners typically made sure to describe fugitives who qualified as light-skinned mulattoes. Cornelius Beazley (also spelled Beasely) of St. Augustine certainly did so. The slaveholder took great care to alert others that his bondservant Harrison was "a bright mulatto . . . 25 years old." Beazley also informed newspaper readers that he thought Harrison would make his way back to South Carolina. Ned's master in a similar vein advertised that his fugitive would "probably . . . make for Columbia, S.C."[26]

More than a few fugitives sought to reach North Carolina. One illustration of such, concerning the cases of George and William, also permits reinforcement of the facts that, unlike eighteenth-century escapees, over half of nineteenth-century acculturated slaves took more than the clothes on their backs and about a third of them could read and write. Owner R. K. West, who had lost several other absconding slaves, thought these two fugitives were making North Carolina their destination. The master described George as "about 22 years of age, stout made, rather a downcast look when spoken to, fiddles with his left hand, and once belong to Mr. Harvey, and had plenty of clothes." William, he added, was "about 25 years of age, six feet high, his knees rather bend back when standing erect, has a pleasant countenance, and reads and writes well."[27]

Few Florida fugitives fled to Virginia or Tennessee, but that does not mean that individuals did not occasionally make the effort. Billy's owner thought that he—"[a] very black fellow, tall, thin face, thick lips and inclined to knock knee—[who] had on a black broad cloth coat, a small black cloth cap, and cotton Pantaloons"—had Virginia in mind as his destination. The owner averred that the fugitive possessed an understanding of the geography involved and ultimately would "get back to Virginia, by the way of the Flint River and Hawkinsville." Charles Lavalette, a brickyard owner, meanwhile considered his fourteen-year-old bondservant to be a very daring and confident fellow. At least, such seemed to be the case since Lavalette accused the fugitive of "having no knowledge of the country" while still attempting to get back to Norfolk where he had been purchased. Possibly, the bondman remembered the lakes and towns on his journey to Florida and may have known far more about getting back to Virginia than his owner was willing to credit. The same may have applied to William and Maria, both "black; man middle sized; woman large, both about forty years of age." Their master believed they would try to make their way to their "original home of Tennessee." Some fugitives obviously did not let long distances hinder them from trying to get back to a previous home.[28]

Very few fugitives departed Florida for Mississippi or Louisiana. As to the former, surviving accounts suggest that runaways more typically were apprehended in Florida after fleeing from Mississippi rather than that they were caught running toward that state. Those runaways who headed to Louisiana usually did so in hopes of reaching New Orleans. Some wanted to use the waterways as opposed to traveling on foot, as in the case of Ben Owens and Essex. Owner Celestino Gazales believed these rebels would use the Gulf of Mexico from Pensacola to get to their destination. He noted: "Essex, a light mulatto, about 5 feet 10 or 11 inches high, 28 or 30 years old, & Ben is a mulatto, about 6 feet 2 inches high and about 40 years of age, [had supposedly] gone towards N. Orleans in a boat."[29]

The ability to make a successful getaway necessarily involved a mixture of luck, persistence, and cunning. The owner's insights could make a difference, as well. While some masters confidently believed that they comprehended the locations and intentions of their fugitives, others made no pretense of such knowledge, indicating they possessed little or no idea of the direction in which their runaways might travel. This lack of insight could benefit a runaway enormously. Thus, Pompey's chances of escape from Gadsden County in 1845 rose greatly when his owner felt compelled to acknowledge his ignorance of the slave's whereabouts. A year later, Moses's master advertised his disappearance but, again to the slave's advantage, held no opinion concerning his destination. The strategy of runaways keeping their owners guessing as to their destination, to the extent that a strategy prevailed, seems apparent from scattered evidence to have been maintained or pursued over time.[30]

Not all slaveholders found themselves befuddled, and those who took the time to get to know their bondmen usually came to understand that their runaways could display remarkable cunning and intelligence in masking their intentions and the direction of their escape. By the same token, some fugitives carefully and craftily attempted to confuse their owners as to their whereabouts. Runaways' attempts to deceive sometimes even could rise to the level of ingenious. Tom's possible itinerary for flight seemed to qualify him in that regard. Owner John Rhodes could only guess at the direction he would travel. "I suppose," Rhodes volunteered, "he will endeavor to make his way to Mobile, Columbus, Griffin, or Atlanta." Augustus H. Lanier warned that his fugitive George, as also had been true of Tom, might try to deceive slave catchers by saying that "he belongs to some one else, as he has already played this game once."[31]

One final factor that played a key role in escapes, especially with respect to those fugitives who sought to travel long distances, related to literacy. Florida's laws, like those throughout the South, forbade bondpeople to learn to read and write. Individuals who were caught teaching bondservants theoretically were to be punished to the law's full extent. Generally, this did not happen. Some persons learned at least the rudiments of reading and writing. On the average, two out of nine pertinent newspaper advertisements for runaways noted that the slave could read or write or both. Slaveholders in Middle Florida, such as

John Parkhill and Achille Murat, openly taught selected and trusted bondservants basic skills. Such abilities could prove indispensable when a slave was assigned to conduct plantation affairs or work in business establishments.[32]

By the same token, many a planter father of a slave child, especially a son, prepared his progeny by arranging for the child to become literate. Historian Canter Brown Jr. reported, for instance, that Reconstruction-era leader and minister Robert Meacham actually was dispatched in the late 1840s or early 1850s by his planter and politician father, Banks Meacham, to study in classes at Quincy's elite school for white children. Resistance from other parents led quickly in Meacham's case to private lessons at home.[33]

That those same skills could prove indispensable or, at the very least, extremely helpful to runaways in their escapes to freedom appears evident. A literate or skilled bondservant simply enjoyed a better chance of reaching his or her destination than did an individual without those skills. Some, for instance, wrote passes for themselves or others, and this allowed movement with relative ease. When Madison County's J. D. Reid advertised for his runaway, he acknowledged the bondservant's acumen. Considered by Reid as "very intelligent," the slaveholder postulated, "It is very probable that he has an instrument of writing, by which I think he will attempt to escape." As Dic's frustrated owner proclaimed, that fugitive had "procured papers to enable him to get to a free state." Wade's owner stated that he could "read and write and will probably forge passes for himself." Jerry's Duval County master noted that he could read and write and might try to use a written "pass" to acquire his liberty.[34]

Where most fugitives eventually returned to their domiciles in hopes of receiving concessions from authority figures, real or true runaways tended to be more self-assured; many were skilled laborers who had experience with several previous owners, and some had knowledge of the world outside their domiciles, which in turn gave them the confidence to take off for freedom. This group consisted of intrastate, interstate, and international travelers. Some traveled northward to Georgia, Alabama, North Carolina, and South Carolina, while others made the Indian lands in Central and South Florida their destination.

Significantly, though, one in five fugitives advertised in various newspapers and other documents used the many waterways of coastal Florida to get to various communities that touched upon the Atlantic Ocean, Gulf of Mexico, or Caribbean. Comparisons are difficult to make, however, because the percentages of fugitives from Virginia, North Carolina, South Carolina, Tennessee, and Louisiana who used the waterways in making escapes remain uncertain. In any event, the fact was that, where runaways from states north of Florida might avail themselves of the underground railroad to reach a free state farther north,

Florida runaways more often utilized an underground railroad to head south to protected maroon settlements and various Atlantic world communities. Some succeeded in reaching their goals. Familiar with the maritime industries, others sought refuge in Florida's relatively busy and cosmopolitan port towns. Here, they tried to blend in with the free black population or board vessels leaving the peninsula for other Atlantic world communities, particularly the Bahama Islands or a location in the Caribbean. Whatever form slave flight took, it nonetheless presented real and profound problems for slaveholders throughout Florida's territorial and antebellum periods.

7. In Search of Kinfolk and Loved Ones

Harrison [fled] in pursuit of his wife.
—*Tallahassee Star of Florida*, May 5, 1838

The direction that escapees traveled when running away might have varied, but the knowledge of where does not necessarily offer an explanation as to why. The answer to that question, in good part, involved one of slavery's most unfortunate aspects, the separation of family and kinfolk. In their dream to regain what they had lost in the Upper South, elite planter families and considerably greater numbers of less well-to-do farmers sought honor, independence, and wealth by forcibly uprooting their bondservants and moving them to the Lower South (or Deep South), where cheap, fertile land could be found in which to grow cotton and other cash crops. Quite a few of these families settled in Florida. Its lands, especially in Middle Florida, generally proved ideal for this purpose. By separating family members and destroying the slave family in order to realize their own dreams and hopes, however, Florida slaveholders set the stage for bondservant flight aimed at reunion with kinfolk and loved ones.[1]

It is worth noting at the outset that relocation involving separation of loved ones and kinfolk did not touch enslaved Floridians only at the outset of the territorial era in 1821 and the years immediately following. Although Ira Berlin has observed correctly that a great migration of white slaveholding settlers from the Upper South poured into the uninhabited lands of the Lower South and Old Southwest during the 1820s and 1830s, historian Edward E. Baptist has assured us that this dynamic process repeated itself in Florida until the 1860s. As a result, fresh emotional pain regularly and continually supplemented older memories within Florida's slave community, thereby providing at all times prior to emancipation urgent cause to flee bonds and shackles that held individuals to Florida homeplaces.[2]

Many individuals, it seems highly likely, perceived the profound contradictions in their forced removal to Florida as compared to the experiences of the owners. On the one hand, they saw complete white family units and webs of kinfolk moving together in support of each other with the goal of securing a better life and greater economic opportunities. Yet, to achieve power, honor, influence, and independence, slaveholders had to destroy within the slave community the very thing they sought for themselves. Where was the honor in destroying the slave family—particularly when many a white family evidenced little or no regard for the destruction left in its wake? The choices made were cruelly practical ones, even though the price paid was human. The owners typically preferred, for example, to take the young, those who could work best and could be expected to work longest in a disease-ridden, raw cotton frontier such as Middle Florida presented. Older parents and the elderly, meanwhile, often remained behind.[3]

Florida's surviving documentation provides many examples. From 1826 to 1830, Middle Florida migrant planters such as Samuel Parkhill, Robert Ricks, and Peter W. Gautier Sr. and Jr.—all Virginians—brought with them slaves mostly aged between twenty-five and thirty-six. Gautier Sr. owned twenty-seven of thirty-four men who were under the age of twenty-four. Twenty-three of the thirty-seven women brought by Gautier Jr. basically reflected the same age categories. Ricks owned twenty females of forty-one slaves who were under twenty-four years old. Parkhill owned during the early period twenty-one enslaved blacks, with seventeen of them being male under the age of thirty-six and four females in the same group. Coming from kinship-conscious Virginia, how could men such as Parkhill, Ricks, and the Gautiers not know the pain experienced by bondservants upon separation from their kinfolk? They then acted to place further obstacles in the path of slave family reformation by mandating at least an initial imbalance between males and females. No wonder slaves absconded from their new homes.[4]

The example of the one-time French aristocrat Achille Murat offers further insight. Just as with Parkhill, Ricks, and the Gautiers, he gave little thought to the impact of leaving slave family members behind as he forcibly removed his bondpeople to Middle Florida. Murat represented what some historians have called a "planter-borne" slave trader, by which is meant a planter who sought to purchase slaves for cash resale in the domestic market. In a single trip to Maryland, Virginia, and South Carolina, he sought to invest "from $10[,000] to $12,000 in negroes." By the 1840s, the émigré possessed over sixty-five slaves. That they felt the pressures derived from their involuntary removal from their homes—and that Murat was aware or should have been aware of those pressures compelling slave flight—can be witnessed in the case of Chester. That bondman required, in Murat's estimate, only two months after arrival to flee. As the owner noted in a runaway advertisement, his fugitive was "a mulatto, 24–25, stout and muscular." Murat acknowledged that Chester was "trying to make his way back to either Hanson County, North Carolina or [Virginia]."[5]

Of course, planters proved quite capable of separating slaves from family and other loved ones in many circumstances beyond relocation. Daniel Campbell and John Branch reflected such attitudes as they then prevailed among slaveholders who arrived in the frontier territory during the 1820s and 1830s. Campbell chose his will as a tool to split families. He stipulated that his son Archibald would inherit a Negro woman but not her children or future increase. Campbell noted that Archibald also would inherit Isabel "with the exception of her increase so far as her next two children, as well as one now at her breast." Daughters Nancy Webster and Sarah Patterson were to receive, the owner specified, Isabel's increase "so far as to extend to two children one for each and no further." John Branch meanwhile bequeathed to one of his daughters "Ann & her children, with the exception of Ann's oldest," which he gave to another daughter.[6]

Separations of slave families may have constituted somewhat less a problem for bondservants in West and East Florida than in Middle Florida because of ameliorated conditions based upon Spanish traditions. Still, in all regions it became fairly common during the period 1821 to the late 1840s for Florida owners to separate family members without much thought to the matter. Given that Middle Florida men such as Campbell and Branch were sons of fathers who lived or even might have fought during the Revolutionary era, they had to have learned about the ideological principles announced in the Declaration of Independence. Yet, for perpetual financial gain, they ignored the principles inherit in the document that focused on equality and liberty when it came to their bondservants.[7]

The profound impact of separation and accompanying emotional pain merits added emphasis. As John Hope Franklin and Loren Schweninger have noted, "The separation of families was an inherent part of the South's peculiar institution." Slaveholders did not mask their lack of paternalistic concern for enslaved laborers if cash was to be made. When it suited their purposes, most slaveholders separated slave families without remorse on the owners' parts; yet, they did so despite having at least some sense of the consequent agony to be endured by their slaves.[8]

Indeed, forced migration and separations damaged or destroyed over 75 percent of all slave family units in Middle Florida during the period from 1821 to 1840. This level of incidence lessened somewhat over time as the slave family began slowly to achieve stability with an increase in abroad marriages during the period from 1841 to 1865. Still, in order for bondservants to reconfigure the slave family after arrival to Florida, they lived at the mercy of slaveholders who could allow or refuse to allow abroad marriages. As masquerading paternalists, some owners such as Robert and John Gamble, Thomas Randall, William Wirt, and George Noble Jones did start allowing slaves to marry away from their domiciles by the 1840s. Caring paternalists they may or may not have been, but these men also knew that a stable slave community built upon stable slave families meant a better chance for peace and prosperity on their farms and plantations.[9]

Available documentary evidence supports such conclusions. The primary research base utilized for this study referenced 103 newspaper-reported sales of slaves, and further information on the selling of slaves was derived from 1,403 probate records, diaries, and letters pertaining to the period 1821 to 1860. Of these sources, a total of 489 had "slave families" listed in groups. Of that number, 123 covered the period from 1821 to 1840. Of those, 93 (76 percent) advised that a slave or slaves could be separated for sale if that meant closing the deal. Bondservants also were separated from family members due to marriage arrangements, debts, trades, and, as seen, estate arrangements. Of the 366 slave families listed from 1841 to 1865, 161 individuals (or 44 percent) could be separated from family members and sold as solitaries if a transaction so required. More slaves could have been separated from 1841 to 1865 if cash and other emergencies became a part of the equation. For both periods, slightly over 81 percent of slave families were listed with a female as head of household. As Florida's slave society expanded and settled, it appeared that Middle Florida slaveholders made more of an effort, at least in written word, to keep the families of the enslaved together, for peaceful slaves usually were profitable workers.[10]

As also was true in other slave states and territories, Florida bondpeople nonetheless lived in fear that they and their families at any time might be separated due to the topsy-turvy economic situations of their masters. One or more family members might be sold for cash at a moment's notice to satisfy owners' debts. In 1840, for instance, the *Quincy Sentinel* carried notice of a private sale of "40 negroes and families." The advertisement related, "They have resided for six years in the territory [and] any person wanting to purchase [them] will apply to . . . Haywood and Austin, or me, Thomas T. Withers." Two years later, the *Tallahassee Florida Sentinel* ran similar notices suggesting that persons could buy slaves in families or as individuals. To satisfy a debt, the Duval County sheriff sold John, a twelve-year-old boy, to satisfy the owner's obligations. Another Tallahassee newspaper published an advertisement for "Negro" boys between the ages of six and ten and/or "Negro" girls between the ages of ten and fourteen. The ad carried no mention of parents.[11]

Middle Florida slaveholders' desire for profits grew over time. If slaveholders were not making as much money as they thought possible in a particular enterprise, they often disbanded it. This was the case with William D. Moseley. In June 1850, he believed a steam mill "to be more expensive than profitable." So, he turned his enslaved workers to the production of cotton. Sometimes bondservants and family members suffered consequences from the actions of frustrated slaveholders such as Moseley. It is clear in his case that three years later he wanted to know the "price" he could get for all his "land and negroes." Six days later he "wrote to John Unse about [selling all of his] land and negroes." Much like Moseley, other slave owners sold their slaves if they could not foresee making a profit through their labor. Former bondservant Mary Ann Murray, better known as Mary Gomez, told of her experience in servitude during a 1934 interview, when she was eighty years old. As she related, her master, believing he would ultimately lose money on her, sold Mary at the slave market for "one dollar because she was so sickly and small that everyone was sure [she] would die within a year." Mary considered herself lucky since her new owner decided to purchase her mother as well.[12]

Entrepreneurial-minded men such as Moseley and Mary Gomez's first master demonstrated that making profits from the labor or the sale of enslaved blacks often became the first order of business. By operating as they did, their actions could disrupt the stability of the enslaved family in a very particular way. Separation of individual family members or whole families could, in fact, become routine business. In such cases, a slave-trading firm might obtain a group of slaves, some in families and some not, with the simple intent of hiring them out as individuals or in family groups. As one advertisement advised, "To be hired—about 40 negroes, consisting of men, women, and children." Understandably, slave-trading firms received a full measure of blame for tearing slave families apart. Many deserved it. But, planter-borne slave traders such as Achille Murat and Leon County's William Croom were just as much at fault for separating slave families as were professional slave traders.[13]

Even tender age did not protect a person from separation. Babies and young children could be, and sometimes were, sold away from their parents. No evidence has come to light, fortunately, to suggest that Florida slave babies were traded for horses, as was reported in the case of a Kentucky woman. Yet, Douglas Dorsey remembered his master dealing in an eight-month-old baby on the Mattair plantation. The former slave recalled the master sold the child "to the highest bidder." Charlotte Martin recollected that her master profited from selling young male and female slaves. She recorded, "The huskiest babies were given the best of attention in order that they might grow into sturdy youths, for it was those who brought the highest prices at the slave markets." As already mentioned, a number of wills left by slaveholders clearly provided that babies and young children were to be separated from their families and given to heirs or sold to pay off debts. And during the late 1830s, when the disastrous failure of Tallahassee's Union Bank came at a time of economic depression brought on by wild speculation, slaveholders found it even more desirable to sell and separate slave families in order to save themselves and their other properties.[14]

Circumstances Compelling Flight

To some extent, and as has been discussed in previous chapters, Florida varied from the norm when in came to the dynamics of flight. This variation applied as well to the trade in children. Wilma King has noted that, as far as the larger picture was concerned, "The nineteenth-century domestic slave trade was age-specific." Many slave children under ten, she found, were sold in family units, usually with their mothers. This did not seem to be the case with children under ten in Middle Florida, though, at least from 1821 to 1840. Given a world where their children could be snatched from them even before age ten, parents understandably fled farms and plantations in search of these young human beings. Most of the time, their efforts to locate offspring proved an exercise in futility. Similar to the plight of fugitives in other parts of the South, Florida fathers and mothers fleeing to find children usually were captured within a few days and returned to the farm or plantation.[15]

Attempts to locate other loved ones competed as reasons for flight. With bondservants routinely being sold, hired out, and otherwise separated, many fled from new owners in search of familiar surroundings and friends. For example, Jupiter, "age 45—5 feet 10 or 11 inches in height, hair slightly grey," traveled far and wide to be with friends. His ability to accomplish that feat derived in part from special talents and a finely honed ability to deceive. As his owner stated, "[He] pretends to be a preacher." In fact, Jupiter's self-assured disposition seemingly allowed him to travel with ease between Glynn County, Georgia, and his home in Jacksonville, Florida, some sixty miles away. Thus, he managed to visit many acquaintances and friends.[16]

Much like parents fleeing in search of their offspring, children fled in search of their mothers. Children who absconded stood less of a chance, however, of finding kinfolk than did older fugitives. Still, they kept trying through the antebellum era. In 1851, a *Jacksonville Courier* notice offered a two hundred dollar reward for the return of "two children; probably seeking freed mother." In a similar vein, Joseph ran away from Black Creek in Duval County for St.

Augustine. At least the advertisement indicated as much, since it mentioned that his "mother lives" in that town. "A small Negro girl" belonging to a Leon County man probably fled in search of her parents. After she had been out for about one day, the bondservant was returned to her master.[17]

The research base utilized for this study provides a helpful overview of the incidence of child flight. Of the 711 advertisements for runaways, nine of fourteen children under the age of ten were reported as fleeing during the period stretching from 1821 to 1840. Only five were reported in the same age group from 1841 to 1860. Overall, about 2 percent of the children under ten were reported as runaways. Contributing to the occurrence of child flight, Florida—unlike Alabama and Louisiana—enacted no law restricting the sale of young children from their mothers. But, assuming that the mentioned newspaper advertisements reflected the attitudes of Florida slaveholders, more of them beginning in the 1840s seemingly tried to follow the custom of not separating young children from their parents. By the same token, the changing attitudes of slaveholders as caring paternalists once slavery began to be seen as a positive good in the era following the Nat Turner insurrection in 1831 may have played a part.[18]

The age of a son or daughter sometimes made no difference in terms of his or her desire to reunite with a parent. As illustrated by the story of London, even an adult could seek reunion. The young man, who had been raised in Liberty County, Georgia, was described as "27 or 28 years of age, black complexion, about five feet 4 or 5 inches [in] height, [and] rather bowl legged." Owner Robert W. Alston, upon his flight, "presume[d] he will make his attempt to go [to Liberty County], as his mother resides their [*sic*]."[19]

Flight could anticipate an act of separation or else come within its immediate aftermath. For instance, family members who had become accustomed to living in urban areas might abscond when they learned that they were to be sold to a farmer or planter. Much as was experienced by their counterparts in other regions of the South, Florida's urban bondpeople enjoyed flexibility of movement within the community as masters generally grew complacent when it came to restricting their local travel. Or, they might turn around almost as soon as they had arrived in a new location to return to old homes.

Surviving records identify fugitives from Key West, St. Augustine, Jacksonville, and Pensacola—Florida's four largest towns—who absconded under such circumstances. Robert James, who had recently purchased Sam for his farm, concluded that Sam would try to make it back to Pensacola or beyond. William B. Hammack of Crawford County, Georgia, discovered that Charles, whom he had purchased, soon disappeared. Hammack believed that the bondservant would try to get back to East Florida. Seemingly, this meant that the fugitive would work his way back either to Jacksonville or St. Augustine to be among family and friends. William T. Hopkins, a transplanted Georgian who settled in Jefferson County, lost two slaves whom he had purchased in East Florida. Much like Hammack, he believed that his two fugitives would return to East Florida, since they "were well known upon the St. Johns River."[20]

On numerous occasions, bondservants acted, not always with success, to forestall the necessity of flight when rumors surfaced that masters were moving to new locations. Particularly, they requested that they be sold and left behind to remain with loved ones. Some masters honored their bondservants' requests out of compassion or else from an understanding that the slaves might flee as an alternative to relocation. One of them, William Croom, initially imported slaves from North Carolina to Florida and later exported them from Florida to Alabama. He also formed plans to move another group from Florida to Mississippi. With the knowledge of what such a relocation might entail, Manuel adamantly argued that his family be sold in order that it might remain in Florida. The owner, faced with the objections, obliged the bondservants by selling Manuel, his wife, and their children as a group for $3,800. The family remained in Florida, and the pragmatic owner quite possibly avoided a runaway problem. Croom, like any good businessman, looked at his bottom line and comprehended that keeping the slave family together could leave him better off than having to face the possibility of paying to have the runaways captured or, worse, losing them altogether. Admittedly, this planter-borne trader also clearly understood that keeping slaves families together permitted him a more reliable form of social control.[21]

Distance, as with tender age, posed no absolute obstacle to flight. Most of the time, the efforts unfortunately resulted in the bondmen and bondwomen being brought back to their owners in neck and leg irons. Still, this dire possibility did not stop the attempts, including one by a fourteen-year-old boy. He had been purchased by a Marion County man but quickly tried to make his way back to loved ones in South Carolina before being captured and jailed at Jacksonville. Another slaveholder noted that three of his fugitives would more than likely make their way back to North Carolina, having been in Florida for only six months. Given the extensive river system and other waterways that bound Florida to Georgia, the Carolinas, and the Atlantic market, some fugitives may well have made it successfully to destinations in North and South Carolina.[22]

Further examples easily come to hand of slaves escaping to return to a distant place where they previously had lived among family and kinfolk. Hector, twenty-two, and Simon, sixteen, fled soon after their arrival in Middle Florida. Owner Joshua Croom believed that they probably were "making for" the Muscle Shoals area of Alabama. Abraham Brown, George, and William Isaacs absconded together one week after reaching the St. Augustine area. "These Negroes were brought from Charleston, S. C., last week," an advertisement advised, "where it is expected they are now trying to make their way."[23]

Although men typically traveled alone in their escapes, brothers and male companions sometimes combined efforts in flight. When Brass and his brothers March and Monday left their Palatka home together, trusted companions Tom and Frank joined them. Skilled carpenters George and John absconded from St. Augustine. Brothers Tom and Dave, with their friend Jesse, similarly departed together, perhaps for North Carolina. Meanwhile, A. H. Cole insisted that Charles, George, and Jacob, having escaped from Fernandina, were traveling along the Atlantic coastline in "a leaky boat" with South Carolina as their destination.[24]

Men fled plantations and farms in search of their wives more often than for any other reason. According to Cornelius Beazley of St. Augustine, "Harrison . . . a bright mulatto . . . 25 years old" fled to South Carolina "in pursuit of his wife [who is] in possession of [her new owner] Captain Bird." Bill parted company with his Putnam County owner in search of his spouse, whom he believed lived in Nassau County, while V. R. Dupont advised that Tim "has a wife at Arthur Gwin's at Fort Reed in Orange County and was seen since in that neighborhood." And John—who feared that he would be shipped west by the US Army in 1835—absconded in order to be with his wife, who lived on an East Florida plantation.[25]

As evidenced by the case of Prince, male bondservants' desire to reunite with their wives remained a cause of flight through the territorial period and until late in the antebellum period. Prince had worked and lived along the Manatee River in the Tampa Bay area, but after his wife was sold in 1858 by master Josiah Gates, the twenty-six-year-old escaped so that he could "get to Columbus, Ga., where his wife recently went."[26]

More men absconded by numerical count, but women also ran away to reunite with loved ones. Martha H. Macon believed that Dilsey fled to be with her mate. Levenia disappeared from Leon County in search of her husband, who now lived over thirty miles away in Gadsden County, near Quincy. By the same token, Sally and July—from Gadsden and Wakulla Counties, respectively—attempted to run away together to search for loved ones. They sadly met with no success. During the period 1821–40, of 353 fugitives identified in various newspapers and documentary accounts, 20 percent consisted of females, as table 7 indicates, with 69 percent of that number ranging from thirteen to forty-two years of age. During the same period, 80 percent were male. Of those male runaways, 72 percent ranged between the ages of thirteen and thirty-four. Of 656 sampled runaway notices and other documents published from 1841 to 1860, 23 percent involved females, with 70 percent of that number consisting of females aged thirteen to forty-two. Males made up 77 percent of all fugitives for the same period, with 72 percent of that number aged thirteen to thirty-four. So, a somewhat higher percentage of women ran away during the second period.[27]

Moreover, these statistics suggest that more women attempted to flee as slavery developed and expanded in Florida during the late 1840s and 1850s. Overall, for the period 1821–60, 23 percent of all Florida fugitives were women. This compares exactly with the 23 percent of women who fled their domiciles in South Carolina from 1730 to 1787 but is much higher than the 13 percent of female runaways from Virginia during the same period. When focusing on North Carolina from 1775 to 1840, approximately 13 percent of females left their homes compared to Florida's higher percentage of female runaways.

Interestingly, when contrasting the overall Florida period under study with the late period (1838–60), a higher percentage of females left their domiciles than in Virginia (9 percent), North Carolina (14 percent), Tennessee (12 percent), and South Carolina (19 percent). For the period 1838–60, Louisiana had more enslaved female absconders, with 29 percent. Clearly, a higher percentage of Florida enslaved females took flight than did their counterparts from most of the other states mentioned, likely due to brutal treatment and the violent nature of frontier Florida. As one historian appropriately noted, slavery in Florida was "harsher than the labor that [the prior] two centuries of captivity had extracted from its victims."[28]

It should be noted that—as Deborah Gray White has informed us—women enjoyed less of a chance to run away than did men because of their immediate responsibilities to children. Naturally, one virtually irresistible answer to the dilemma was for women to carry off their children with them. A small percentage even succeeded in making it to freedom. This seems to have been the case with an unnamed woman who escaped with her child from St. Augustine to

Table 7. Gender of Florida Runaways

	1821–40 number	Percentage	1841–60 number	Percentage
Females	71	20.0	151	23.0
Males	282	80.0	505	77.0
Total	**353**	**100.0**	**656**	**100.0**

Source: Florida and Georgia extant newspapers, 1821–60, as well as other documentary accounts.

peninsular Indian lands. When Mr. R. Sanchez caught up with these runaways, Indians protected them and ushered them off to safe havens. It seems highly probable that they lived among the Indians for many years, since the owner apparently never sought to advertise for their capture and return.[29]

Some escaped as couples. Shortly after their Florida arrival in 1829, William and Maria, both about forty, took flight. The owner, who advertised for over three months to no avail, believed they would aim for their former home in Tennessee to be among family and friends. Charles and his wife, Mary, who had disappeared from Jekyll Island, Georgia, were said to be heading to "Musketo where they formerly lived." Another Charles and his companion, Dorcas, departed from Jacksonville. While owner Henry W. Maxey did not know where they were going, he accepted that they had disappeared together.[30]

The flight of couples could take several forms. Husbands and wives sometimes figured, to note one alternative, that they stood a better chance of reaching their destination if they escaped separately as part of a coordinated plan. Typically, they would agree to rendezvous at some designated place. By way illustration, Clara disappeared first from R. H. Crowell's estate. Some three weeks later, her husband, Isaac, absconded. The owner asserted in a frustrated tone that "from his [Isaac's] threats, made sometime back, I am apprehensive they are making their way back to North Carolina." Unlike the experience of most bondservants, Clara and Isaac may have been successful in reaching their destination, since the owner never again advertised for their capture.[31]

Curiously, as paternalists who believed they treated their people well, some slaveholders did not or could not acknowledge that wives willingly absconded with their husbands or partners. These owners preferred that the public believe these happy and contented women either were "decoyed off" or "seduced" away by these men. At least, Thomas J. Green propounded such a scenario. The owner asserted that Ime probably had "decoyed off" Martha, his wife. Such assertions, of course, did not change the fact that many slave wives possessed strong feelings for their husbands. No matter how well they were treated by authority figures, they still might flee with their spouses.[32]

Although few examples have come to light, some fled in family groups. The three-generational family of George, his wife, Lettus, and their children, Adam, Beny, Liz, and Susan, plus Susan's one-year-old son, fled Monticello. Dick, along with wife Margaret and a five-year-old son, likewise absconded together. One factor especially limited the number of such flights. Bondpeople knew that traveling in family groups increased their chances of being captured. Yet, that strong possibility notwithstanding, family flight occurred and reoccurred.[33]

More ran away from East Florida in large family groups than from any other place in the territory and state. In 1850, one slaveholder believed that his seven runaways had found refuge in Jacksonville, if not permanently then for a period of time. He noted that Hampton, Nanny, and their five children had disappeared "very mysteriously" and that they had "a large connection in Jacksonville." A skilled craftsman, Hampton possessed a pass for one night's leave, which the slaveholder believed he would use to aid his flight. The master acknowledged, meanwhile, that some north Atlantic seaport town or an island in the Caribbean might be their goal. "They may have been secreted," he admitted, "on board some outward bound vessel." Marion County's Lloyd Hill, who recently had purchased Dick, Margaret, and their five-year-old son, mentioned earlier, expressed that they were "making their way to New Orleans." One family escaping from the area faced immense challenges in that it numbered seven individuals. They included Davy, sons Edmund and Henry, and daughters Silla (with one small child), Lucy, and Lizzy. Ages ranged from fifty-five or sixty down to two.[34]

Sometimes, a large group of unrelated but highly skilled artisans possessed sufficient confidence to travel together in search of loved ones. Thus, in 1847, "Sy, 50, Jacob 35, rather intelligent, Maurice 35, long hair . . . neatly arranged, deep blue eyes, pleasant countenance, good barber, raised as a house servant, unusually intelligent; Alfred, intelligent, good blacksmith, 25; and Larry 18" absconded from Joseph Vaught. The owner claimed that the fugitives "took with them three or four hundred dollars in the bills of Charleston SC." He believed they would use the waterways along the Atlantic coastline by boarding a vessel headed to South Carolina.[35]

Schemes, Stratagems, and Circumstances

Whether choosing to escape alone, with a spouse or relative, in a family, or in a larger group, fugitives often displayed craft and intelligence while carefully taking advantage of prevailing conditions and circumstances. At least a few families managed, for instance, to get away thanks to shrewd manipulation of events when Indian war threatened. Jane Murray particularly remembered the escape of a large group when husband John Dwight Sheldon served as overseer in East Florida of the Cruger and DePyster estate. The large plantation held many slaves. Among them were two-parent and single-parent family units, as well as solitaires. With the 1835 eruption of the Second Seminole War, most of the slaves deceived Murray and her husband into thinking that Indians were about to attack. Murray's recollections are revealing: "A large number of negroes were captured [by the Indians, but] it came to light that the negroes had been in sympathy & aided the Indians from the first. Among the darkies I recognized a number of the Cruger & DePyster slaves. I learned from that that they had concealed many of the Indians about the plantation until the main body came up [to rescue them]."[36]

Other bondservants devised similar schemes that also took advantage of fears of Indians. On one occasion, the aim was to persuade an owner to allow a newly arrived slave to return to her original home. The woman was named Mandy, and her plan played out in 1835. Years later, Orange County's W. B. Watson recalled the following concerning Mandy's plot:

> Dr. [A. S.] Spear owned a mulatto girl by the name of "Mandy" who had become tired and disgusted with Florida and a deprivation of the comforts of the "old plantation" up Georgia. One day the people were startled and alarmed with the most frightful screams down by the bay or swamp at whose edge the negroes did the washing for all hands. Five or six men quickly grabbed their guns and looked at the priming as they ran toward the swamp. They went from tree to tree and when within about seventy-five yards of the place out jumped that yellow girl.... As she ran she uttered the most terrorizing, blood freezing screams—"Run for your lives! Indians! Indians! run! For God's sake run!" ... Mandy immediately became the center of attraction, screaming: "Oh Lawdy, oh, Lawdy! Dey like to kill me, but tank God I got away!" ... Like most liars "Mandy" overacted her part and on a close cross-examination her statement was made to appear shaky.

Mandy may not have tricked her owners into returning to Georgia, but she clearly attempted to do so in a shrewd manner.[37]

As noted previously, stratagems utilized in flight many times took advantage of available waterways, including the Gulf of Mexico, the Atlantic Ocean, and the Caribbean Sea. In fact, as early as 1823, a group of self-assured fugitives had used the port of St. Augustine in furtherance of their plan to escape to another Atlantic world community. An owner involved in a later incident specifically credited the shrewd planning involved. This occurred when Tomasa, Ben, and an unnamed person sought to make their way from St. Augustine to Havana, Cuba. The runaways were owned by different masters, one of whom subsequently advertised that they had planned well their escape together. If someone found one of them, he acknowledged, he probably would find them all.[38]

Recognition of careful planning continued to be accorded over time. Some twenty-four years after the St. Augustine fugitives made their way successfully to Havana, a group of seven tried to reach an island in the Atlantic from Key West. The men had been hired out to work on fort construction in the Dry Tortugas. There, they schemed escape. According to one military officer, "Their plans were well arranged and well executed. They took all of the boats, with the exception of my bateau so as to cut off pursuit." The officer went on to assert: "My impressions are that this thing has been maturing for some time

[and] they would have made a general robbery of everything which could prove useful . . . and go to the Bahamas. Jack, English, and Ephraim, were the active spirits—Jerry and others but subordinates." The seven unfortunately were picked up at sea after two days.[39]

It might be expected, given the long distances many bondpeople were compelled to travel during relocations, that opportunities for escape would arise. Mostly, this did not prove the case even after credit is accorded to slaves for intelligence and ingenuity. Especially when slave traders transported their charges, they secured the men, women, and sometimes children with shackles, chains, and irons that made successful escape virtually impossible. In the event an escape did occur, traders cooperating with slave patrols usually captured the runaways. As J. Benwell, an Englishman who visited Tallahassee in 1835, noted: "[I] saw in the streets . . . two negroes with heavy iron collars around their necks. These were captured run-away[s]; the collars which must have weighed seven or ten pounds had spikes projecting on either side. One of the poor creatures had hold of the spikes as he walked along to ease the load that press[ed] painfully on his shoulders." Thus, although scholars as respected as Franklin and Schweninger suggested otherwise for the southern experiences as a whole, few escaped from slave traders en route to Florida.[40]

Some did, however, make their escape shortly after being purchased from a trader. For example, within a three-month period, owners John W. Hale and Cornelius Beazley both advertised for the return of their newly acquired property purchased from Tallahassee's Patterson and Hughes. Nelson, his wife, Jenny, and their son, Jody, and daughter, Mary, fled their new home in Jefferson County after being purchased from, as Beazley noted, these "well known . . . Negro traders." Jacob Stroman, like Hale, lost another slave shortly after purchasing his property from Patterson and Hughes. Robert Butler also lost his slave to elopement after purchasing him from the slave trader C. C. Williams of Tallahassee, "who brought them from Tennessee."[41]

As opposed to relocation travel under the supervision of slave traders, travel through the peninsula could offer special advantages to bondservants who were determined to reunite with loved ones. One owner advertised for the return of his newly purchased laborer who had escaped from him "while on his way in moving from Leon County to South Florida." The master believed he had returned to be with family and friends, since he had "been seen several times in Tallahassee."[42]

Looking at the same dynamic from a different viewpoint, slaveholding settlers newly arrived in Florida—particularly to the peninsula—faced a constant threat of bondservants absconding. Men, chafing at separation from kinfolk, took off with some small degree of regularity shortly after arriving at their new homes. William, at Enterprise on the St. Johns River, fled his new master for South Carolina. Ned left his owner after two weeks. "It is probable," the advertisement noted, "he will make for Columbia, S.C." The St. Augustine area's Edward T. Jenkes had "recently purchased [a Negro boy] in Charleston" before he disappeared.[43]

Smart owners naturally attempted to frustrate desires for flight, or else to compel return of runaways, by encouraging and manipulating relationships between husbands and wives. George Noble Jones's overseer D. N. Moxley tried to control Dealier, who had run off but returned, by not allowing her husband, Tom Blackledge of Tallahassee, visitation privileges on the El Destino plantation. Eventually, the owner chose to take a different tack. During the time of Dealier's sojourn, Jones had experienced several problems with other runaways from his two plantations. Probably fearing that Dealier ultimately would run off with Tom, the master vetoed the overseer's policy and allowed Tom to visit his wife.[44]

Jones's neighbors struggled, as well, to find the right mix of reward and punishment. Mention has been made earlier that, as Middle Florida society began to stabilize financially during the late 1840s and 1850s, the paternalistic expressions of men such as John Gamble, William Wirt, and Thomas Randall became more evident in terms of the slave community in that they agreed to allow bondservants to marry off the plantation and in granting liberal visitation privileges. One important aspect of such policies involved the fact that, by allowing bondmen to visit wives on other plantations, the owners knew where to start looking for a male fugitive. And knowledge of a wife's location could be of key importance. Of the 711 runaway slave advertisements from 1821 to 1865, 135 owners (or 19 percent) believed that their runaways were trying to find wives. Phrases such as "he may be on his way to find his wife" or "his wife lives in that town" were often used to pinpoint the possible whereabouts of the male and female fugitives.[45]

As throughout the South, most of Florida's enslaved laborers never ran away from the places where they lived and worked, at least not in the sense of seeking permanent freedom. Those who did usually were captured and returned to owners. But, there always were those who successfully achieved their goal, especially when the aim involved reunion with a spouse, family member, or other loved ones. Evidence suggests that, in pursuit of such ends, slaves absconded as individuals and in family groups; children fled in search of parents; and women took flight even though they did so less often than did men because of the special difficulties of taking children with them. Although the slave family tried to reconfigure itself, it did so within the context of a white frontier culture underlain with violence, abuse, separation of loved ones, and risky business practices that affected the lives of all bondservants in the slave community. Some enslaved persons simply refused to accept such circumstances and showed their determination through flight; some successfully absconded, while others would be caught again and again.

8. Catch the Runaway

"Paderollers" . . . roved the country to molest a slave.
—Mary Minus Biddle in *Florida Slave Narratives*

Florida by the 1820s had long stood out as a runaway slave haven. The origins and evolution of this status will receive closer attention in chapter 10. Suffice it for now to assert that slave owners and persons desiring to own slaves who moved to Florida during that decade and afterward demanded that lawmakers take firm steps to control and eventually stop the flow of freedom-seeking slaves coming into the territory. As the years passed, these and individuals like them found greater and greater need to regulate all movement of human property, not simply of runaways bound for freedom in the remote places of the peninsula. Their influence produced not only laws but also certain degrees of unity of purpose on behalf of whites, at least at certain times and in certain places, to enforce law and custom by group action. Slave patrolling resulted, but the effort of patrollers overall in regulating the movement of enslaved blacks was, at best, only a theoretical success.[1]

Territorial Florida's leaders sought to address the problem of runaways. In one early example, an 1824 statute provided: "If a slave shall absent him or herself, a greater distance than five miles from his or her usual place of residence, or owner's service, without the leave of his or her owner, overseer or master, such slave shall be deemed to be a runaway, and may be apprehended by any one without a warrant." The statute provided further that, upon confining a fugitive, the sheriff should notify the "owner, overseer, or master, if known, by a letter by the public mail, and if unknown, by advertisement in the nearest newspaper."[2]

As suggested by this example, Florida lawmakers spent considerable time designing and enacting laws to deal with what they perceived as two great potential problems—rebellious slaves and runaways. The solons passed slave codes addressing the life and movement of bondservants in 1822, 1823, 1824,

1827, 1828, 1836, 1840, and 1850. Based upon the evolutionary development of these laws, a variety of officers and persons, including traders, sheriffs, constables, jailers, justices of the peace, slave catchers, and patrollers, would play critical roles in assisting slave owners to recover their lost property.[3]

When it came to runaways, Florida's laws both differed somewhat from and partially echoed those of other slave states. For one thing, the territory, being chronically short of funds, could assure a person or persons who captured a runaway only six dollars in reward. Other states generally paid from thirty dollars to a high of fifty dollars per capture. As was true of the other slave states, the sheriff had to advertise the incarceration of a runaway for six months. If no one came forward within one year of the first newspaper advertisement, the runaway would be sold at public auction thirty days later. In a typical case, the Escambia County sheriff advertised in the *Pensacola Gazette* in 1839 for the owners to come forth and claim Jacob and Edward. How long the runaways had already been confined in the makeshift jail is not known, since the notice did not specify that information. When the owner failed to claim them in a timely manner, the fugitives were sold at auction for $1,800, the proceeds going to build "a substantial jail."[4]

Most southern states moved to create or enhance patrol systems to monitor and capture fugitives during the late eighteenth and nineteenth centuries, and Florida followed this pattern. Specifically, it established such a system in 1833. The code declared: "It shall be the duty of the several justices of the peace within this Territory to cause their respective districts to be divided into convenient patrol districts which division shall not be altered unless by the justices or a majority of them in said district and in case the said justices of the peace of any district, within this Territory, shall neglect to perform the duty herein before required by him or them, he or they, shall forfeit and pay the sum of fifty dollars to be recovered before any justice of the peace in said district."[5]

The patrol statute contained numerous additional provisions of significance. It required all free white male inhabitants of the territory from ages eighteen to forty-five, for instance, to serve a three-month term in the patrol. Unlike the pattern in some states, the Florida patrols did not operate like military units. They consisted simply of white males led by a "prudent and discreet person as commander." No privates, sergeants, lieutenants, or captains exercised authority, nor did the code specify the number of men that made up a patrol.[6]

The law was designed to be self-executing. Patrols were authorized to form immediately upon the threat of a slave uprising or the disappearance of bondservants. These men could enter any plantation or farm, disorderly house, vessel, or boat suspected of "harboring, trafficking or dealing with slaves." They possessed authority to destroy property by breaking open "doors, gates or windows" where runaways might be hiding. Patrollers were permitted to administer "moderate whipping, with a switch or cowskin commonly called a cowhide, not exceeding thirty nine lashes." If a runaway resisted, he or she could be shot on sight.[7]

Slave patrols in some places and at some times policed the countryside and towns of Middle Florida for runaways even in the absence of a threat or notice of a specific flight. At least, former slave Shack Thomas recalled as much. He recorded that the "pu-trols" would give "him a lot of trouble every time he didn't have a pass to leave" the plantation.[8]

Douglas Dorsey vividly remembered male slaves being caught by the slave patrols and the consequences for not having a pass to be away from the plantation. Although he gave no direct indication, Dorsey may have been one of those males caught away without permission. "Sometimes the young men on the plantation would slip away to visit a girl on another plantation," he recalled. "If they were caught by the 'Patrols' while on these visits they would be lashed on the bare backs as a penalty for this offense."[9]

Other former bondservants retained their own vivid memories of experiences with slave patrols. "The various plantations had white men employed as 'patrols,'" Louis Napoleon claimed, "whose duties were to see that the slaves remained on their own plantations." Much as the Florida law specified, these absconders were "whipped with a 'raw hide.'" Mary Minus Biddle summed up what she thought of slave patrols by recording that "any slave caught without [a pass] while off the plantation was subject to be caught by the 'paderollers' (a low class of whites who roved the country to molest a slave at the least opportunity)." Biddle concluded by insisting that the patrollers would whip runaways "unmercifully." Thomas McKnight echoed Biddle's sentiments by acknowledging that he received "four balls from a double-barreled gun" when he failed to stop running at the command of patrollers.[10]

Although some former slaves remembered patrols that policed farm and plantation areas routinely, these organized groups of unpaid slave hunters operated sporadically at best. The lack of enthusiasm of some white males to participate in such drafted work became increasingly evident over time. Plus, pursuing runaways could be a dangerous business, and some residents did not want to put their lives on the line to catch another man's slave. Accordingly, in the absence of a crisis, the patrols seldom operated through most of the territorial and antebellum periods. By way of illustration, mention has been made in chapter 6 of the incident involving nine fugitives from St. Augustine who made their way to the Miami River and then on to the Bahamas. According to law, a slave patrol should have formed immediately to pursue the fugitives. That did not occur. "The settlers . . . excused themselves for not arresting the murderers," the local newspaper reported, "by saying they 'were not strong enough.'"[11]

Slave patrols were put on special alert during what became known as the Second Seminole War, which lasted from 1835 to 1842 and which will be discussed at length in chapter 10. Governor Robert Raymond Reid proclaimed in a typical manner at one point in the conflict, "All Justices of the Peace throughout the territory [are] strictly to carry into full effect the act concerning Patrols, approved February 11th, 1833." Such efforts proved practically worthless. The US Army, Navy, and Marine Corps required almost seven years to subdue the Seminoles, Creeks, and their black allies. Through the early 1840s—despite patrols, militias, and regular military units—the combatants regularly raided deep into Middle Florida, occasionally almost to Tallahassee.[12]

Whether the times involved crisis or peace, slave patrols did little to curtail the runaway problem, and citizens continued to complain about the unauthorized movement of slaves through the territorial and statehood periods. Often whites came together to voice their concerns as one. An instance of such action occurred, for example, when Jacksonville citizens—alarmed on the verge of the Second Seminole War's outbreak about the possibility of large numbers of bondpeople absconding from the area and the potential of slave unrest—held several public meetings to require that the "patrols do their duty strictly, and to call public meetings whenever in their opinion public safety shall require it." As usually proved the case, little resulted from such efforts.[13]

Overseer Amon DeLaughter's personal journal permits an inside glimpse at the operation of one Middle Florida slave patrol or, at least, attempts to mount a patrol. Even in plantation-oriented Madison County, it appears from DeLaughter's writings, the monitoring of the movement of slaves did not appeal to the majority of the vicinity's white males. In a six-year period, DeLaughter recorded his attendance at a patrol or regulator meeting only once. His brothers Jasper and Pickens each attended only one or two over the same period of time. DeLaughter never recorded the formation of a patrol party to hunt for specific runaways. The DeLaughters' experience with slave patrols reflected the general trend throughout Florida.[14]

Slave Catchers

Individuals who pursued fugitives seemingly succeeded more often at catching their prey than did slave patrols. These men often were hired by owners or else made it known that they were in the business of catching runaways. Typically, a slaveholder might publish a notice to alert slave catchers of his desire to have his runaways retrieved. One advertisement of this sort commented, "A reward will be paid to any person catching the said negro wench, and all expenses for sending or going after her and returning her to the subscriber, will be cheerfully compensated." Since pursuing runaways could prove extremely dangerous, these men offered their services for a set fee for capturing the fugitive, typically ranging from six to ten dollars, plus expenses. Given that, eventually, most slaves seemingly returned—or were returned—to their owners, many slave catchers apparently did their job well.[15]

Most slave catchers were not professionals but men who occasionally accepted the risks inherent to the task in order to cash in on the rewards. Leon County's Thomas Footman was one such man, and he learned firsthand in 1860 of the dangers of the trade. On that occasion, a slave shot and "very severely wounded" Footman as he pursued the suspect. A man named Pratt nearly suffered the same fate. His story concerned a slave called John, who belonged to Judge O'Neill of Fernandina and had successfully eluded capture for almost two years. At that point, Pratt set out after him. The slave catcher tracked John for many miles before he found him near St. Mary's, Georgia, close to that state's boundary with Florida. When Pratt ordered the fugitive to surrender, the bondservant went for his gun. Pratt thereupon shot and killed the runaway.[16]

Sometimes slave catchers used highly trained dogs to track runaways. Frederick Law Olmsted observed that dogs ranging from bloodhounds to Scot staghounds effectively pursued fugitives in other slave states. These animals were trained to follow scents for miles. The Florida record suggests that highly trained bloodhounds stood out as the tracking dogs of choice. The *Pensacola Gazette*, for instance, regularly advertised the sale of bloodhounds. One such ad declared:

> Blood Hounds
>
> A healthy pair (dog and slut) black, Cuba BLOOD HOUND PUPPIES, three months old, for sale. These dogs are very valuable on the trail of runaway slaves, which, they can trace thirty hours after. Inquire at this office.

Army general and future president Zachary Taylor had ratified the choice during the Second Seminole War. He, too, had sought to capture runaways with bloodhounds imported from Cuba, believing they could track scents throughout the large expanse of Florida's peninsular landscape.[17]

It remains unclear exactly how many hunters used bloodhounds to catch runaways. As most of these canines were imported from the Caribbean, though, they were known widely to be excellent hunters and quite vicious attack dogs. The Florida slave codes did not mention the use of bloodhounds to track runaways nor the consequences, if any, that slave catchers might face if such a dog killed a runaway.[18]

Oftentimes, the services of such semiprofessional slave catchers, if such a term can be used, were neither sought after nor secured. Instead, local men—particularly including overseers—more or less voluntarily hunted many runaways. Madison County's Amon DeLaughter recorded his pursuit of runaways. He noted, for instance, that he unsuccessfully chased Jump, who got away. Usually DeLaughter, like most whites, succeeded in the hunt. On several occasions he apprehended a neighbor's slave at the DeLaughter slave quarters and returned him or her to the home plantation. He also joined others in pursuit of runaways in the general area. In April 1858, to cite an example, he "help[ed] Joe Hampton hunt for a negroe." Another overseer named Bonsel Cochran also tracked runaways for the DeLaughters. When the manager came upon several runaways who obviously did not heed his command to stop, he shot them.[19]

Civilians and relations of slaveholders such as Jasper and Pickens DeLaughter might hunt for runaways, as well. The latter caught Charlotte, one of his mother's slaves, in the fodder loft of O. E. Sullivan's barn. The former seized a runaway owned by a man named Sever, a Madison County neighbor and planter. C. Dougherty, another Middle Florida civilian, caught a slave "in the woods near Tallahassee" and placed him in the city jail. Although a reward had not been posted for this particular runaway, Dougherty probably felt confident that he would receive one of some kind.[20]

Although most did not, some slaveholders took the time to pursue their runaways or even those owned by other masters. This disrupted the work routine on plantations and farms, but some masters believed that they had no other choice than to act given the value of their potential loss. They could not wait to hire slave catchers in fear that runaways would be long gone from the area. Nor could some afford to hire slave catchers or pay them for capturing and returning their property to them. A Madison County slave master named Sanders may have been one such owner. In pursuit of his runaway, Sanders came to the DeLaughter plantation during the night "to hunt his negro." William D. Moseley, a prominent planter and future governor of Florida, apprehended and received a reward of twenty-five dollars for returning a runaway to J. F. Higgs. About one year later, he captured and returned "a small negro girl belonging to Robert Hayward," his neighbor in Jefferson County.[21]

On occasion, Native Americans, particularly the Seminoles, served as slave catchers. There were several reasons for this. Particularly, it appears that, following the Second Seminole War's conclusion, Seminoles found themselves vulnerable to government pressures and also resentful of their former black allies who had worked out suitable arrangements for their migration from Florida. By that point, most Black Seminole leaders had switched from the role of aiding Indians to supporting the US military. In the circumstances, Seminoles sometimes helped to track, capture, and return runaways to US authorities.[22]

The Fugitive Slave Law of 1850 and monetary rewards to slave catchers for enforcing it also motivated some Florida Indians to hunt runaways. The Upper Creek Indian Cotsa Fixico Chopko served as a slave catcher in South Florida. On at least one occasion in 1853, he received a reward of twenty-five dollars for the capture of a runaway. A report that recorded the details of an encounter with other runaways the same year near Fort Myers offers interesting insight to the situation:

> Three nights ago, a light was seen across the river—a boat was sent over & returned with three negro men who "all tattered & torn" said they belonged to [Chief Billy] Bowlegs, had been out hunting & were out of ammunition! They had rifles & shot guns—*hats & pants*—jabbered "e-cho," "suc-cos-che" and talked good english. They were taken to the Com[mandin]g officer & ordered to the guard house, but ran from the Sergeant & made their escape, dropping a bundle of meat. They were yelling all night, endeavoring to get together, which they accomplished & no doubt made their way into the interior. They were undoubtedly runaway slaves, & we will probably hear of them from the indians, who will execute the Fugitive Slave law, especially for a reward.[23]

The monetary rewards mattered to Florida's poor Indians in the 1850s, prompting them sometimes to argue about the amount of money paid for runaways by US authorities. In 1853, a year for which good records are available, the Indians protested that the small rewards did not justify their efforts. Late in the year, Seminole chief Billy Bowlegs urged his followers not to give up runaways since whites were not willing to pay $150 each for the fugitives. An officer reported, "Billy says, 'the Crackers stopped the trade, let them come and catch their own niggers.'"[24]

Advertisements and Rewards

When self-help failed, slaveholders often advertised for the return of their property, perhaps hoping for a little good luck that might aid them even more than the attention of a professional slave catcher. Depending on how long the runaway had remained at large, written and printed handbills offering rewards could vary from a few lines to lengthy and detailed paragraphs. Owners tried to be as accurate as possible in describing the character, abilities, background, demeanor, dress, speech, and possible destination of runaways. Others went so far as to specify any unique features of their runaways such as color, gender, age, intellectual qualities, speech characteristics, facial expressions, body piercing, or distinguishing marks. Obviously, accurate and comprehensive data allowed slave catchers a better chance of apprehending the runaways.[25]

Many of the advertisements also contained references to racial stereotypes as part of the descriptions. Since only a fraction of slaves ever ran away, it remains difficult to determine whether the perceptions of whites concerning these runaways properly reflected all or any part of the larger slave community, not to mention the slave to which reference was made. Some owners advertised, for example, that their runaways had a "rather downcast look" or that fugitives had "a rather guilty countenance." One master claimed that his runaway "hesitates and hems, when spoken to." Leon County planter John Braden characterized Levi as having a "down look and when spoken to his features put on an expression of wildness." A St. Joseph owner, offering a perception similar to Braden's, claimed that Scipio had an "unmarkable wild look when alarmed." Some males were "loud spoken," while others had "a rather feminine voice." Simon's master portrayed him as having "thick lips" with a "dark sneaking look." H. P. Armestead described Andrew as being "generally sluggish in his appearance." Owners repeatedly depicted their runaways as "artful and cunning scoundrels" or words to similar effect.[26]

Many other owners declined use of stereotypes in favor of more objective descriptions. Henry Bond probably described Matthew accurately when he noted that he "can read and write, and no doubt has a regular pass." Augustus Steele wanted Lewis captured and returned to him, giving slave catchers a better chance of apprehending him by providing them with detailed information. Steele portrayed Lewis as having a "dark complexion, short neck and full face, with a pleasing expression of countenance, of stout, athletic and muscular frame and 5 feet, 4 or 5 inches high, a carpenter by trade, and a quick and ready workman." Michael Ledwith knew his runaway well and obviously respected him to a degree. He characterized Caution as a "bright mulatto, about five feet nine or ten inches . . . [a]nd is a little knock-kneed." Ledwith added, "When he left, he was well dressed, and will no doubt attempt to pass himself off as a free man."[27]

Not too unusually, as the Ledwith example hints, the advertisements—not always begrudgingly—expressed slaveholder admiration for runaways. One Gadsden County owner described George as a "healthy and well looking" man. Robert Butler admired Sandy's looks and skills. He explained that the runaway was "low stature[d], good looking, with whiskers, mustache and perhaps a goatee, 27, plays the fiddle and dances well." Butler added, "[He is] an experienced body servant and has been enjoyed among the blacks as an exhorter." Henry Mash of Sopchoppy admired at least one facet of Prince's appearance, noting also that the runaway had a "round face [and] remarkably beautiful white teeth."[28]

Slaveholders at times recognized and specifically commented on the intelligence of their runaways. The Madison County slave George "speaks quick when spoken to, and is a smart sensible fellow," or so his owner declared. W. C. Smith and R. J. Roberts knew another George, who had absconded with his family, to be an intelligent bondservant. They observed, "He has always had charge of his master[']s affairs, is rather an intelligent fellow, can read well and most probably write." William Alsop described Wade as "very intelligent" and a bondservant who "can read and write and will probably forge passes for himself." Five slaves disappeared from Mrs. P. U. Bryant's Madison County plantation. Most were described as intelligent, skilled bondservants. John Butler's owner considered him to be very smart, saying that he usually changed his name when he ran away and "can read and is quite intelligent." Like Butler, Jerry was considered by his owner to be a skilled bondman who could "read and write and is very intelligent otherwise."[29]

Masters offered substantial rewards for the return of runaways with special skills. Notices normally offered payments that ranged from $5 on the low side to around $25. But, for those slaves who were considered literate, physically strong, young, articulate, handsome, or clever, owners offered considerably more for their capture. Considering him a "tolerable carpenter," Jim's Jackson County owner advertised a reward of $50 for his capture and delivery. H. H. Chapman of Apalachicola also offered $50 for Hall, "a well made [bondservant], bow-legged, his hair is shimmering black, when combed is pretty straight." Chapman noted, as well, "He plays [a] little on the violin [and] is by trade a tailor." Described as "healthy and well looking [and a] carpenter by trade," Augustus Lanier's slave merited a $50 payment. John Parish offered a $100 reward for the capture of Hunter or Sam Jones, whom he described as having a "pass to hire his own time." Meanwhile, Leon County's Hamilton Hudson advertised a $100 reward for the return of Lewis, a young man of eighteen. One slave owner promised to pay a $200 reward for two children.[30]

The highest rewards offered during the 1830s and 1840s came when slave owners presumed a white person had "stolen" or "inticed" away their runaways. They usually pledged one amount for the slave and a larger sum for persons caught with the runaway. Thomas M. Bush concluded that his six runaways were ushered off by some white person. He offered a $675 reward for the capture of his fugitives and "proof that will connect any white person or persons who caused them to leave." Like Bush, Leon County slaveholder Jacob Stroman theorized that his slave had "been enticed away by some white man." He agreed to pay $25 for the runaway in the territory and $50 if he was captured outside of Florida. Stroman made it clear that a $100 reward would be given to the individual who could prove that a person assisted his slave in "absconding." W. H. G. Saunders offered $30 (or $10 each) for runaways George, Joe, and Charles. He vowed to pay $100 for the "recovery of the three negroes and the thief" who took them.[31]

Reflecting the general prosperity of the 1850s, slaveholders paid substantially more for runaways they considered stolen by whites than they had during the previous two decades. W. J. Scott offered $200 for the return of his escapee and the "white man claiming him as his property." Another slave owner promised to pay the same $200 reward for the capture of his runaway, whom he believed "to have been stolen by a white man." Guaranteeing $250, A. A. Fisher also wanted his man and the person who stole him.[32]

Owners paid a little more than the average of $15 to $20 dollars for runaways when they considered their bondmen to be "harbored" or "hidden" by other slaves or whites. Slaveholders apparently differentiated between "stolen" and "harbored" fugitives, since their rewards for the latter reflected as much. Martha H. Macon, for one, guaranteed to pay $50 for the return of Dilsey, whom she surmised had been harbored for several weeks by a slave named Power. Madison County's James Osmond vowed to pay $25 for his slave and another $75 "for proof to connect his being harbored by a white person."[33]

Some masters showed less confidence that out-of-county or out-of-Florida fugitives would be apprehended by offering even higher rewards. Robert W. Alston promised to pay $40 for London's return in Florida but $100 "if taken in Georgia." Qua's master feared that he had disappeared from Escambia County and guaranteed $100 for his capture and return. John Hunt had lost confidence that Perry would be captured after he, too, left Escambia County. Like the reward on Qua's head, Perry's master pledged $100 for his return. Hypothesizing that his runaway would head to South Carolina, Cornelius Beazley also vowed to pay $100 for capture and return of his fugitive. As a general matter, slaveholders usually offered at least $100 when they feared their runaways had left the county or state.[34]

The converse also was true. Masters who concluded that their runaways had not gone far offered smaller rewards. J. D. Fisher, owner of the Florida Works in Gadsden County, guaranteed only $5 for capture of his mulatto Dyce. Fisher speculated that she would appear in Quincy, only a few miles from his business. Likewise, Francisco Moreno held out only $5 for capture of his runaway, believing him to have stayed in the Pensacola area. Slaveholders Henry Carr and George Fisher offered $5 each for the return of their runaways, who they believed were "lurking" around their plantations. Tallahassee's John R. Lloyd vowed to pay only $10 for an "African Negro named Aleck" since he postulated that Aleck had traveled only a few miles west of the master's plantation to Quincy.[35]

Slave owners often took pains in runaway notices to make it clear to slave catchers that subduing or apprehending their runaway could be dangerous. When Jackson County's Mary Roberts advertised her "muscular" runaway, she suggested that Harry might put up some resistance given that he already had had one ear bitten off "close to his head." Madison County's A. H. Lanier warned would-be pursuers about his fugitive, as well. The owner commented that George "is a smart sensible fellow who ran off after an attempt to murder my manager and one or two of my negroes." Lanier further commented, "George was shot some years back while on a runaway trip and received 8 or 9 shots in, I think, his left leg and thigh and has some small marks of the whip on his back." Adam, another of Lanier's runaways, possessed a reputation for meanness. The owner described him as having a "large scar on his back near . . . the left shoulder blade, with other marks by the whip for fighting." From the advertisement, it appears that slave catchers and others who might pursue one of Governor Richard K. Call's slaves had their hands full. The fugitive had stabbed the overseer in the back when he tried to apprehend him.[36]

Especially high rewards were offered for the capture of runaways accused of murdering a white person. A large payment, for example, was offered for the capture of two slaves accused of killing James Roundtree. The two men, who lived and worked in Gadsden County, had been sold to Roundtree. As they made their way from Gadsden to Lowndes County, Georgia, the slaves killed their new owner in "Leon County, near the line between Georgia and Florida." Citizens of Tallahassee increased the original reward of $100 each for the capture of these runaways to a total of $405. Newspaper accounts do not indicate whether the fugitives ever were caught.[37]

After Capture

The processing of captured runaways followed certain patterns. For one thing, a person who refused to give his or her name or that of the master was housed in the nearest jail. Most counties in Florida had at least a rudimentary jailhouse located near the county courthouse. Few descriptions of Florida jailhouses that existed during the territorial or antebellum period have been preserved. If they were anything like the poorly ventilated cabins that housed slaves and poor whites, which were hot in the summer and cold in the winter and had only a dirt floor, they easily constituted a health hazard for incarcerated runaways. Runaways who did not want to give the jailer or sheriff any information about themselves remained in these unhealthy places for months or possibly years before they were sold at public auction to defray various expenses incurred by the county.[38]

Some imprisoned fugitives obviously preferred to remain in jail until they could plan their escape. Since most jails were rather flimsy and poorly constructed affairs, numerous runaways managed to make successful getaways. Two of Leon County planter Samuel Parkhill's slaves were caught and confined in the Hawkinsville, Georgia, jail, which probably differed little from those of Middle Florida. "Edmund fired the jail," a report noted, "and subsequently broke out." The owner speculated that the bondservant and his wife thereafter persisted in their attempt to get back to Hamburg, South Carolina, where they once had lived. Six Madison County runaways accused of killing overseer Matthew D. Griffin were captured and confined to the county jail. Biding their time, they broke out two weeks later. They eventually were recaptured. Leon County runaway Tom made it to Thomasville, Georgia, before his capture. He refused to divulge his real identity and that of his master, while offering several misleading assertions. Creating enough confusion to permit him some time to plan, Tom took a mere five days to make his break for freedom.[39]

In sum, Florida attempted to address the problem of runaways but achieved mixed success at best. The legislative council and legislature passed numerous laws. Many reflected those of other southern states, although Florida offered lower rewards for the capture of runaways. The same laws anticipated that most white male Floridians would play a role in catching runaways. Private citizens, professional slave catchers, and others pursued and apprehended fugitives. Sometimes they used bloodhounds; many times they did not. Few owners and overseers pursued runaways personally because of the time involved away from plantations and farms. Slave patrols sometimes operated during times of crisis but proved, for the most part, ineffective in capturing runaways. Privately posted rewards generally brought better results, especially when combined with published notices that provided accurate information.

PART THREE

Violent Resistance

9. Slave Violence

[He] . . . split in twain the head of his master.
—*Tampa Florida Peninsular*, December 15, 1856

Without doubt, many more of Florida's enslaved blacks absconded from 1821 to 1860 than committed physical violence against whites, but acts of physical violence remained nonetheless the ultimate demonstration of discontent with the institution of slavery. Violence could result in the destruction of human lives but might simply entail destroying property. Large-scale rebellion certainly constituted the ultimate in violence against whites; yet with a major exception to be discussed in chapter 10 and not unlike the southern experience generally, individual acts of violence perpetrated by slaves against whites represented the typical and most frequent such action in Florida.[1]

Acts of physical violence perpetrated on whites by captive laborers may have been seen less frequently than nonviolent forms of resistance in Florida, but the possibility of slave-perpetrated violence persistently sent chills through and often wreaked panic in Florida's white community during the territorial and early statehood periods. Offering context, the peninsula had enjoyed a reputation as a haven for armed runaways from the Chesapeake region and Carolina Lowcountry dating back at least to the establishment of the free black community of Gracia Real de Santa Teresa de Mose (Fort Mose) near St. Augustine in 1738. Whites had learned from firsthand experience in the years subsequent to that event that blacks could and would fight. When whites streamed into frontier Florida after 1821, Fort Mose had ceased to exist, but still they found themselves dealing time and again with armed free blacks and runaways who were well prepared to defend their right to be free.[2]

Ironically, the tradition of fighting to defend home and family that struck so fundamentally at white psyches when demonstrated or threatened by black Floridians formed a core element of the culture many whites brought with them to the territory and state. Based upon traditions dating back to the seventeenth century, Virginia migrants and others who settled in Florida also stood ready to defend their honor and that of their families with violent reprisals. Those actions could include fighting and dueling, although sometimes they encompassed outright murder. The proclivity to defend one's rights and space thus pervaded Florida society and made for a volatile climate. Slaves, of course, could not defend their families in the same manner as whites because, if they did so, they faced the reality that such acts risked instant death for themselves and perhaps their loved ones as well.[3]

Acts of violence committed by blacks against whites concerned Floridians so much that their councilmen and legislators time and again enacted measures designed to protect the public from bondservants and runaways. Plus, owners and their agents took care to ensure that enslaved blacks, as well as runaways, generally knew of the potential consequences of assaulting or killing a white person. In order that enslaved blacks not turn the slaveholder's world upside down, laws clearly delineated prescribed, strict punishments. A statute enacted in 1824, only three years after the United States accepted Florida from Spain, plainly declared: "Be it further enacted that if any slave shall consult, advise, or conspire to rebel, or make insurrection against the white inhabitants of this territory, or against the laws of the government thereof, or shall plot or conspire the murder of any white person, or shall commit an assault and battery, on any white person with an intention to kill, he or she shall, on conviction of either of the said crimes, suffer death."[4]

Other legislative acts followed the 1824 statute. Three years after its enactment, for instance, the territorial council specified that a slave convicted of murder would not even be allowed assistance to save his mortal soul. That is, the law clearly articulated that "if any Negro should make an attempt to kill a white person, or aid or abet such attack," he was to suffer death without benefit of clergy. Historian Julia Floyd Smith aptly summed up other punishments that eventually were to be imposed on enslaved blacks convicted of physically touching a white man or woman. As she summarized, they were subject to "having his [or her] hands burned with a heated iron, his [or her] ears nailed to a post, or a certain number of lashes by the whip." As would be expected, Smith added, "a felony [was] punishable by death."[5]

Whites' fears were not without some foundation in fact. The real potential and threat of a large-scale uprising by runaways and bondservants did exist and, given that fact, never ceased to be a concern to whites. In the year of the Nat Turner revolt in Virginia, 1831, Pensacola mayor Peter Alba, for one, insisted that runaways, slaves, and free blacks in his town were about to rebel. He pleaded with Governor William P. DuVal to raise a voluntary army to control

Pensacola's black population. No rebellion occurred in the city as Alba thought would happen, but the incident nonetheless helps to make the point. The same fears circulated especially during times of crisis prompted by events such as the Mexican War, suspected abolitionist plots, and the heightened national conflict over slavery during the 1850s. Florida newspapers routinely portrayed whites during such periods as firmly believing that blacks and runaways could and would rise up in rebellion.[6]

Physical Attacks

Physical assault on whites by enslaved laborers occurred relatively frequently, and, as in the case of Cato, murder typically loomed far from the original intent. On his part, Cato rebelled against his master by striking him in 1848. Instead of taking off after this outward act of violence, the bondservant interestingly stayed on the plantation to face the painful and potentially self-destructive consequences of his actions. Indeed, he received 150 lashes for his behavior. In a separate incident, Adam's confrontational behavior became increasingly masochistic because he continued to wear the scars of "the whip for fighting" by authority figures. An unnamed bondservant also attacked Leon County planter and two-time governor Richard K. Call's overseer before fleeing for the nearby woods. He remained in the area before eventually getting caught, and he, too, suffered a whipping for his actions.[7]

As common sense would suggest, many physical attacks on whites came when a person believed he, she, or a loved one was being mistreated. Even some whites acknowledged the fact of such behavior by other whites or even themselves, if not the legitimacy of the reaction to it. Douglass Dorsey, for one, recalled whites admitting to slave mistreatment. On the Pine Hill plantation, J. L. Taylor, the estate's overseer, acknowledged that Rachel, a white domestic servant with some authority, had been whipping Frances "unnecessarily." The manager or overseer reassigned Frances to another domestic servant's supervision. George Noble Jones challenged overseer D. N. Moxley about a letter he had received from a neighbor concerning mistreatment. John Evans, overseer of Jones's other plantation, acknowledged that Moxley at times could lay on a "genteel" whipping. Evans was not one to judge, given his reputation for laying the cowhide on the backs of enslaved blacks in a rather severe manner.[8]

As has been well established, Florida claimed its share of owners and overseers noted for cruelty to their enslaved laborers. They, like their counterparts throughout the antebellum South, made bondservants stand in fear. Former slaves Harriet Jacobs and Charles Ball attested to the cruelty of authority figures toward enslaved laborers. Jacobs, from North Carolina, sadly remembered that bondservants who ran away or crossed an owner or overseer could suffer while "the blood flows at his feet; and his stiffened limbs are put in chains." Ball, who had lived and worked in Maryland, Georgia, and South Carolina, recalled in his autobiography that an overseer "gave . . . [two bondservants] a hundred lashes more than a dozen times" for running away. Men such as John Evans and D. N. Moxley, mentioned earlier, did not spare the use of the whip. Middle Florida planter Charles Bannerman's manager Christopher C. Bryant probably fell into the same category as the overseers cited above—or at least one bondwoman on his plantation thought that when she guarded against the blow of Bryant's whip. In doing so, the hoe she held flew up, killing the manager. Interestingly, she suffered no consequences for her actions. She was initially charged with murder, but the court acquitted her "because of the belief that the blow which caused his death was accidental."[9]

Less frequently than in cases of simple battery, incidents and courses of conduct nonetheless occasionally drove individuals to the point of murdering owners or overseers. Such was the case with Jesse Watts's bondservants in Madison County. Here, long-term resentments due to treatment compelled action to alleviate frustration. The slaves had long held grievances concerning food rations and living conditions. Hauled into court several times regarding his standards for feeding and clothing his bondservants, Watts and his overseer nonetheless had ignored the subtle and not-so-subtle criticisms of the court and the larger community. Over a two-year period, conditions worsened for the bondpeople. Six of them retaliated by killing the overseer. They escaped from jail and were recaptured. Death became the ultimate form of violent punishment inflicted by whites on recalcitrant rebels. Subsequently, three individuals were hanged, and the fates of the remaining three remain uncertain.[10]

Despite the capture and punishment of the murderers of Watts's overseer, this and similar incidents created tensions and spread terror on many remote farms and plantations. Any such event rekindled anxieties anew. Among others, they included the killing of Liberty County's Duncan A. McPhaul by Ned. The sense of terror sometimes reverberated even more greatly following occurrences subsequent to actual killings. On one such occasion, a runaway—who was awaiting trial for the murder of a local white man—broke out of Jacksonville's jail. He sought friends, a hiding place, and—whites feared—other victims in the countryside.[11]

In an unusual twist on the issue of homicide by slaves, Hamp seemingly murdered his master not because of some apparent abuse but because he was to be paid for his deadly deed. A Tampa newspaper described the circumstances surrounding this October 1860 incident: "We learned that citizens of Hernando County of Saturday last, hung Hamp, a slave belong to the estate of Albert Clarke, for being the immediate cause of the death of his master. The negro confessed that he was promised $200 by James Boyd (a step-son of the deceased) and Mrs. Clarke (decedent's wife) $100." Careful note should be taken that the available evidence does not prove conclusively that Hamp actually committed the murder. He may have been forced into falsely confessing that he did. James Boyd, in any event, ended up in jail as a co-conspirator. Whether Mrs. Clarke was found guilty or innocent and the exact type and degree of punishment Boyd received for his role in this deadly plot are not known.[12]

Bondservants at times pursued quiet forms of violence against authority figures, which permitted them to rebel outwardly while (they hoped) not being detected and thereby avoid the punitive consequences of their actions. One such assault particularly feared by whites involved murder by poisoning. As Deborah Gray White has commented, "No one will ever know how many slave owners and members of their families were poisoned." In Florida, some slaves likely succeeded in this endeavor, while others attempted it but failed. Others certainly dreamed of or pondered such action but did not act. Among those who did act were Florida's lawmakers. In 1829, they specified: "*Be it further enacted that*, if any slave or free negro or mulatto shall prepare, exhibit or administer any poison or medicine whatever, within intent to kill any person or persons, he or she so offending shall be adjudged guilty of felony, and shall suffer death."[13]

Quite a number of examples of poisonings can be found. In one of them, three bondwomen owned by Thomas Randall attempted to poison their overseer. It remains unclear how their plans were discovered, and fortunately for the white man, they failed. This form of quiet outward rebellion resulted in the three women ultimately being sold to new owners. Two went to an Alachua County buyer. The other, Sally, was a second-generation house servant. She first was banished from the house but was not sold immediately because of the high regard Thomas Randall had for her parents. At his wife's urging, however, Randall sold the bondservant one year later.[14]

Surviving documentation fails to explain why Sally and her compatriots tried to kill the overseer, but as John Hope Franklin and Loren Schweninger have noted, many reasons could have compelled the women's actions, ranging from anger at punishment of some kind to arguments over work assignments. It is clear, though, why one former slave wanted to kill his master's wife. As Charles Joyner has observed, "Cruel plantation mistresses . . . often turned their ire upon female slaves." This seemed to have been the case with Douglas Dorsey. He chafed at the mistreatment suffered by his mother when the mistress, Mrs. Mattair, slashed the slave woman's arm with a butcher knife. Further, as the freedman remembered, the master's wife was "a very mean cruel woman [who] would whip the slaves herself for any misdemeanor." As a result, Dorsey decided to put strychnine, which was used on the place to kill rats, in her coffee. "Fortunately freedom came," an interviewer recorded, "and saved him of this act which would have resulted in his death." Madison County planter J. Pearce's luck did not prove as felicitous as did Mrs. Mattair's. Several of his bondmen killed Pearce by poison when he tried to whip them for attempting to poison him.[15]

While it never occurred with the frequency that whites feared and perhaps believed was the case, some bondservants occasionally molested or raped white women. Whites considered this to be one of the most violent acts that a slave could commit and a heinous crime. Most rapes or alleged rapes were committed against lower-class white women, and the possibility of consensual sexual relations should not be disregarded in many cases. At least eight slaves were prosecuted to the law's full extent for rape during the antebellum period, although it should be understood that bumping or touching a white woman in any way appeared tantamount to rape for some whites. Of the eight, six were convicted and hanged. A jury acquitted one, and another panel could not reach a verdict in the final case. Dick, a Leon County slave indicted and convicted of rape in 1840, unfortunately died at the hands of a lynch mob while his case was being reviewed on a writ of error by the territorial court of appeals. At basis, many whites feared that, if the power relationship had been different, black bondservants would abuse their wives, daughters, and other white women in the same manner that whites had manifested for generations toward the wives and daughters of enslaved black men. To those whites, the situation and threat had to be dealt with severely and swiftly in order to maintain social control.[16]

Premeditated or Spontaneous

Any understanding of the nature of violent resistance requires an appreciation for whether the act had been premeditated or resulted from sudden impulse. For instance, Ben rebelled against what he perceived as the overseer's unreasonable work demands on the Leon County plantation of Isaac Mitchell. When pushed by Irvin Kent to pick more cotton at a pace other than what the bondservant had established, Ben simply refused to accommodate his supervisor. His rebellion, had it occurred then, probably would have meant that hot blood had overcome good sense. That was not what happened, however. At the end of the work day in the field, Kent conveyed to Ben that he could expect a whipping the next morning for his intransigence. In the cabin that evening, Ben thought about his impending situation and made his choice. Not waiting until the next morning, Ben went to Kent's cabin and pounded on the door. When the overseer opened it, the slave clubbed him to death. The bondservant did not attempt to run away. He simply went back to his cabin to suffer the consequences of his action, a premeditated but courageous act.[17]

As in Ben's case, most individual acts of violence were premeditated, but some obviously were spontaneous. The case of one bondservant can serve as an example. George Noble Jones owned two large Middle Florida plantations. He had hired very strict disciplinarians to run his operations. One of Jones's slaves, Aberdeen, knew that overseer D. N. Moxley could and would whip slaves unmercifully for various transgressions. When the overseer went to whip Aberdeen's sister for not picking her cotton allotment, the sibling tried to kill the white man with an ax, but "the driver [Prince] kept him from it."[18]

Weapons and Results

As Aberdeen's attempt illustrates, fugitives and other blacks might use axes and a variety of other weapons during an act of physical rebellion against whites. Hatchets, guns, knives, clubs, and shovels numbered among them. For instance, Adam, a mulatto who had hired himself out, was charged with killing his Tampa-area employer Luke Moore. An account of the murder stated that Moore had been "killed by a blow with the butt of a hatchet [that] took effect in the upper part of the forehead, literally mashing the skull, and penetrating the brain." Tampa lawyer Ossian B. Hart, a future founder of the state Republican Party and Reconstruction-era governor, served as counsel for the slave. Because of the trial's sensational nature and a prejudicial environment, Hart convinced the state supreme court to overturn a guilty verdict and order a new trial despite the inflammatory nature of the evidence and testimony. Unfortunately for Adam, he never got another day in court. The bondservant's life ended when a mob overpowered the sheriff and lynched the accused. Hart's biographer Canter Brown Jr. believed that at least some good resulted from the tragedy, in that Adam's fate afforded Hart a level of sensitivity "to the role of law in society" that underscored his activist stances in preservation of the peace during his later tenure as governor.[19]

As seen with Luke Moore's demise, axes enjoyed a certain popularity when bondservants opted to murder their masters. These implements were utilized commonly by whites and blacks on the farms and plantations of Florida and could be purchased readily from most general stores. As Ray Granade described, "The razor or axe was most liable to drip with the master's blood in an individual act." A news report detailed how one bondservant killed his owner with such an instrument and then fled the premises:

HORRIBLE TRAGEDY!
A Man Murdered by his own Negro!!
The Murderer Escaped

> We . . . record one of the most heartrending tragedies that ever occurred in this State: On Tuesday night, the 30th ultimo, Mr. WILLIAM PEARCE, residing about five miles from this place [Madison] whilst he was eating supper, told one of his negro men, who had been guilty of some misdemeanor, that so soon as he was through he would give him a flogging. According, when he got up from the table, he went out into the backyard and called the fellow out of the kitchen, and told him to come to him. Manifesting a great deal of submission, he obeyed; but so soon as he got within striking distance, drew an axe, which he had concealed and split in twain the head of his master—scattering the brains in every direction.

As had occurred to Tampa's Adam, this fugitive was hanged by a mob after his capture.[20]

Even when axes were used and the assault committed up close, slaves' attempts to kill whites failed on many occasions. One frustrated attempt came in the Jacksonville area during 1835. On that occasion, Mrs. Thornton's slave approached her bed one night with "an uplifted axe." One can only imagine that Mrs. Thornton's blood-curdling screams upon discovering her assailant looming over her turned the tables in her favor. In any event, the slave failed in his attempt to kill her.[21]

Washington first attempted to use an ax and, after that failed, eventually took up a gun to kill Marianna's H. O. Bassett. According to the news account, the ax attack proceeded as follows:

> A most daring attempt was made in this place Tuesday night last, by a Negro, to take the life of one of our citizens, Mr. H. O. Bassett. Mr. B. had retired about 9 o'clock and was lying in bed, preparing to read before going to sleep, and hearing a noise of some one in the room, asked who it was.—On turning around, he discovered a Negro man named Washington, belonging to Col. C. C. Young, of this place, standing at the bed with an axe upraised, in the act of striking him. Mr. Bassett rolled out of the bed in time to prevent the blow and grappled with the Negro. They scuffled for a while and the boy finding that Mr. B. was too strong for him let go the axe, and Mr. B. struck him; the boy dodged the blow and the axe stuck in the floor, making a deep indention.

Authorities apprehended Washington a day later, he having stolen a horse in his attempt to flee the area.[22]

Knives offered another effective weapon in taking white lives. One was used by a bondman in 1860 to kill Dr. W. J. Keitt, a state senator and Marion County planter. According to one account, many people thought at first that he had "died suddenly, from an affliction of the heart." Soon, though, the details of the murder became clear. "On visiting his house," the report read, "his body was found bathed in blood, and his throat cut from ear to ear." Upon further investigation, an inquest concluded that the murder, in fact, had been at the hands of one of the doctor's own slaves.[23]

Easily available farm tools permitted a few slaves to dispatch their masters. Celia, a mulatto, killed her white father and master, Jacob Bryant of Jacksonville, with a hoe. An argument or disagreement between the bondservant and her mother seemingly drew in the elder Bryant. Celia subsequently blamed her mother for her action. According to the newspaper report, the slave split open Bryant's head by striking him with a hoe. A jury found her guilty of murder, and she subsequently hanged for her deeds.[24]

Knives, axes, or poisons may have been fairly easily obtainable, but firearms figured in slave violence as well. A gun was the weapon of choice for St. Augustine runaway Randall, for instance, who took the life of Christopher S. Thompson. Unlike most individuals who undertook a violent assault in Florida, Randall endeavored mightily to make his way to freedom. Authorities pursued and caught him, though, shortly after the crime had been committed. Randall confessed, although as the local newspaper observed, "How he came to be armed, or for what purpose, is not known." Such an unanswered question deeply concerned local citizens, who endeavored as well as they could—but apparently unsuccessfully—to convince the defendant to give up his source.[25]

There were times when aggrieved individuals required no specific weapons in order to vent their fatal wrath on an owner. The three men originally charged in 1840 with the death of Jefferson County's Richard B. Cole did not use any of the previously mentioned weapons to kill him. According to the trial record, Ellick and Poor Boy won not guilty verdicts as the court judged Simon the guilty one. The bondservant had pushed his master "against the ground [and then] did strike, beat and kick, and choke him." Simon finished off his deadly deed by suffocating and "drowning" his master in a stream. As Florida law prescribed, Simon was hanged for his crime.[26]

Violence against authority figures by fugitives could prompt terrible consequences after a perpetrator was secured, and that was assuming the alleged attacker lived. Margrett Nickerson recalled with a former slave's perspective how belligerent bondservants and captured fugitives would be dealt with on the plantation where she once lived. She commented that, once slaves were caught, the owners would "put bells on em; fust dey would put a iron ban' round dey neck and anuder one 'round de waist and rivet um tegether down de back; de bell would hang on de ban' round de neck so dat it would ring when de slave walked and den dey wouln' git 'way." Nickerson vividly remembered such bondmen as Jake Overstreet, George Bull, John Croen, Ruben Golder, Jim Bradley, and others who "wore dem bells." Shack Thomas reminisced about one overseer who "used to 'buck and gag' us." This particularly applied, the former slave noted, to runaways who were sometimes "gagged and tied in a squatting position and left in the sun for hours." Some even were suspended by their thumbs for long periods of time, he concluded. Douglas Dorsey recalled that some black men knew they could face violence from authority figures if caught visiting "a girl on another plantation." If discovered, he claimed, they would be "lashed on the bare backs." Indeed, some enslaved blacks appeared prepared to face such potential violence from whites if it meant controlling some aspects of their lives.[27]

No doubt infuriated by the treatment or well aware of what lay in store for them, detainees often became violent upon their incarceration and understandably endeavored by every available means to break out of jail. One example comes courtesy of Leon County sheriff William Cameron, who advertised for the capture and safe delivery of Sandy, "who broke [out of] Jail." When six fugitives—who had been accused of the murder of planter Jesse Watts's overseer—were captured and incarcerated, they broke out of jail a few days later. Moreover, twenty-four-year-old Harry and eighteen-year-old John both escaped confinement in Palatka to continue their journey to freedom.[28]

Despite all of these and many other accounts of actual violence, most fugitives during the antebellum period probably did not attempt to fight their would-be captors or to break out of jail. Many times, they were outnumbered and possessed little in the way of guns or other weapons with which to wage a successful fight. Yet, exceptions to the general rule obviously occurred. Of the few who had guns, some were prepared to use them to maintain their freedom. The experience of John, a man owned by Judge O'Neill of Fernandina, offers a case in point. He had eluded his captors for almost two years by hiding in the nearby woods. Ultimately, his haven had been discovered. According to the newspaper report, a white man who found John shot him when the slave allegedly went for his gun. A jury of inquest cleared a Mr. Pratt of killing the slave, finding the act to have happened in self-defense.[29]

10. The Second Seminole War

This, you may be assured, is a negro, not an Indian war.
—Thomas Jesup to J. R. Poinsett, June 7, 1837

Florida's experience with slavery from 1821 to 1865 evolved within an environment that, from beginning to end, was filled by the threat of race war, the actuality of race war, or the legacies of race war. Patterns of resistance that developed in the territory and state during that period also derived from that environment. In fact, it can be argued with credibility that the nation's largest slave rebellion marked the midpoint of that era, an event so profound that no Floridian could have escaped its impact in one way or another. Known to history as the Second Seminole War, this significant but often neglected conflict came about through the leadership of maroons and was supported by hundreds, if not over a thousand, rebelling slaves. And, unlike some other nineteenth-century rebellions, the major objective of Florida's combatants involved not the complete overthrow of slavery or, for many, escape to some other place, but the safeguarding of individual and family freedom and of homes and homelands from white encroachment.[1]

This rebellion meanwhile reflected generations of experience and arose from battle-hardened perspectives on black strength and willingness to fight. Behind the rebels stood memories of previous struggles spanning hundreds of years back to Spain's arrival in La Florida during the sixteenth century. Some participants likely had witnessed or participated personally in more recent landmark events such as the occupation and destruction of the Negro Fort during 1815–16 and Andrew Jackson's subsequent forays into the peninsula that culminated in the First Seminole War of 1817–18 and its highpoint, the Battle of the Suwannee. A will to resist came to the rebels as no recent acquisition.[2]

Further, the events that preceded the Second Seminole War, whether in the short or long term, had touched Florida's white population just as it had helped to prepare so many of its black residents. By 1835, whites would have understood the reality that armed conflict loomed on the horizon or else as an eminent catastrophe. The continued influx of white settlers encroaching on maroon communities in search of cheap land during the 1820s and early 1830s, the lax enforcement of slave codes in northeast Florida, the divided attitudes of East Floridians generally over the institution of slavery, and the immediate support available to blacks from Indian allies all played roles in setting the stage for the race war that was to come.[3]

This rebellion involving Seminoles, Creeks, Mikasukis, free blacks, maroons, and runaways in a struggle to maintain Florida lives and havens additionally reflected the larger movement initiated by the US government during the early 1830s to recapture fugitives and usher Native Americans, as a part of Andrew Jackson's infamous Indian Removal policy, west of the Mississippi River. As the Florida experience illustrated, however, acculturated runaways, maroons, and Indians had come to regard control of land and other property as a human right. Much as when the Founding Fathers took up arms against the oppressor whom they believed had tried to enslave them, so, too, did enslaved blacks and their allies pick up arms to fight the tyranny of slavery in Florida.[4]

Note should be taken at the outset that combined action by the allies in the Second Seminole War did not necessarily represent unity of purpose or cause. While the Indians, maroons, and runaways held some goals in common, marked differences existed as well. With many of them assimilated, the Seminoles did not fear, on the one hand, that they would be enslaved; they simply wanted to retain the land they occupied and be left alone to make lives for themselves and their families. Maroons and fugitives understood, on the other hand, that they lived in a society dominated by powerful and violent whites who also believed they should not only own the land but also own the labor of others. And, the blacks believed, the whites would accomplish those goals by recourse to any means necessary.[5]

No small measure of irony resulted from that fact that many of these white men viewed intransigent blacks as strong, determined, masculine men who would openly fight to defend themselves and their families. And, the fact that autonomous, determined runaways sought to protect their maroon communities evidences the deep and widespread desire for freedom. Beyond those factors and based upon a worldview of black runaways dating back to the Spanish and British eras, white Floridians feared these fugitives more than their Indian counterparts. They were horrified at the possibility of these strong-willed, illegal interlopers increasing in numbers and taking complete control of the peninsula.

Viewing the situation from a nationalistic perspective, white Floridians—much like James Monroe and Andrew Jackson—believed that allowing free-willed, self-determined, enslaved black men and women to establish sanctuaries and remain in the peninsula would thwart their overall expansionist agenda. In swelling the boundaries of the United States, territories such as Florida, Texas, and additional parts of Mexico had to be owned totally and controlled for and by whites only. To this end, ambitious whites would use any means available to accomplish their goals. That backdrop ceded great significance: black escapees had to be stopped from fleeing into Florida. Truly, the whites involved in these dynamics hungered for wealth, honor, prestige, and power; most important, though, the ownership of land and enslaved black labor loomed high indeed as issues to fight about in violent antebellum Florida.[6]

So, in company with Seminoles beginning in 1835, free blacks, maroons, Black Seminoles, and runaways would become a force with which to be reckoned. America's dominance and power would be tested time and again. And the war that ensued would work a major impact on the settlement, character, and course of the territory and state's overall development. This seven-year revolt shook the very foundation of Florida slave society and permanently altered the way in which slaveholders dealt with their bondservants for the next thirty years.[7]

Events Precedent

Unaware of or little appreciating Florida's experience, some historians have suggested that the most significant black uprisings to occur in the antebellum South were the Stono, Denmark Vesey (Telemaque), Gabriel, and Nat Turner rebellions centered in Virginia or the Carolinas. Most recently, one student of the subject interestingly described the Louisiana uprising of 1811 as America's largest slave revolt. To the contrary, historians of Florida's saga have argued that the Second Seminole War in terms of size, scope, and intensity should be considered as the largest sustained slave insurrection to befall the South prior to the Civil War. Actually, this revolt did receive considerable national attention while it flared and in its immediate aftermath, but historians writing thereafter for the most part ignored its meaning and implications.[8]

It was not the first such event, though, to touch the area. Even contemporaries viewed the First Seminole War of 1817–18 as primarily a slave revolt or, at the least, a race war. Writing in 1818, Representative Henry Baldwin of Pennsylvania claimed that Georgia militiamen under Andrew Jackson "were, in fact suppressing an insurrection of slaves, aided by an Indian force, all assembled and armed for purposes hostile to the country."[9]

From the vantage point of the 1850s, Congressman Joshua Giddings agreed that slavery underlay the conflict. Why, Giddings asked, did this fact not appear from the public record "as the cause of this war?" He answered, "There was great delicacy exhibited, and had been for many years previously, in regard to the agitation of any questions touching the institution of Slavery; and the people of the free and slave States appeared to feel that silence on that subject was obligatory upon every citizen who desired a continuance of the Union." Thus, Giddings argued, President James Monroe's administration sold the conflict "as entirely owing to the Indian murders on the frontiers of Georgia, and to the massacre of Lieutenant [Richard W.] Scott and his men" on the Apalachicola River in November 1817. Government officials simply selected words carefully by calling the revolt an Indian war and not a slave rebellion. Much like attempts to minimize the history of the bold actions of rebels and runaways in the Louisiana uprising in 1811, whites at the time, with reference to Florida whites in general and federal government officials in particular, tried to erase from the record the largest and most deadly race war in the nation's history up until that time. This was a pattern seen previously and one their successors would repeat.[10]

Within Florida at the First Seminole War's end lived many men and women, white and black, who recollected even earlier evocations of a will to fight by black Floridians. Some may even have been told that black soldiers had engaged James Oglethorpe's Georgians at Fort Mose near St. Augustine in 1739 and, thanks in part to the leadership of free black captain Francisco Menendez, had recaptured the site from the governor in 1740. Where black militiamen such as Menendez possessed influence in the later years of the first Spanish period, which ended in 1763, black leaders moved during the second Spanish period beginning in 1784 into positions of general authority. Following the 1791 slave revolt in Saint Domingue (Haiti), for instance, authorities drew onetime revolutionary general Jorge (Georges) Biassou to St. Augustine with twenty-five of his followers to direct East Florida's military defense. Southern slaveholders recoiled with trepidation.[11]

After Biassou's death in 1801, the martial tradition among Florida's black population persisted and, if anything, was enhanced. Particularly, a Guinea-born Georgia runaway named Juan Bautista (Prince) Witten, himself a battle-tested veteran, ultimately emerged to replace the general. Notably, during the Patriot War of 1812–14, Witten led Spanish forces including blacks in numerous forays against Patriot rebels backed by President James Madison and leading men of Georgia. Some Georgians spewed and sputtered about Witten and his men but could not defeat them. A turning point in Spain's favor arrived in September 1812 when Witten led a contingent of twenty-five black militiamen, several dozen maroons or Black Seminoles, and what historian Jane Landers described as "a handful of Seminoles" against a detachment of twenty

US Marines and "sixty or seventy Patriots escorting a supply colony through Twelve Mile Swamp" north of St. Augustine. American officialdom naturally misrepresented Witten's victory. "The Patriot accounts (and therefore, most historical treatments based on the English-language sources) reported that the ambush at Twelve Mile Swamp was the work of the Indians," Landers commented, "but [East Florida governor Sebastian] Kindelan wrote that the 'Indians' were actually 'our parties of blacks, whom they [the rebels] think are Indians because they wear the same clothing and go painted.'"[12]

When coupled with Spain's traditional policy of freeing runaways from outside the colony if they met a few conditions, the martial tradition locked in Florida's reputation as a haven for slave fugitives, whether they lived openly in places occupied by Spain or else found refuge in isolated peninsular locations. Little wonder that historian Peter Wood described the origins of South Carolina's 1739 Stono rebellion in these words: "With cries of 'liberty' and the beating of drums, . . . the Rebels raised a standard and headed south to Spanish St. Augustine."[13]

Naturally, particular sites gained a measure of fame as havens for runaways. Fort Mose qualified in that regard until 1763, and the Negro Fort on the Apalachicola also has received mention in these pages. By 1812 at the latest, the place called Angola, which lay at Tampa Bay where the Braden River flows into the Manatee River, harbored blacks seeking refuge from Patriot War fighting. Over the years, its population grew to perhaps seven or eight hundred as survivors of the Negro Fort's destruction and of First Seminole War fighting joined the community. Informed of its existence by aide James Gadsden, Provisional Governor Andrew Jackson appears to have ordered Angola's destruction in the spring of 1821 by his Lower Creek allies. The marauders carried hundreds of individuals back into slavery. The lucky ones made it to Andros Island in the Bahamas. One hundred or more chose to head east into the peninsula toward longtime Indian settlements near the Peace River's headwaters in southern Polk County, close to where Jackson's Upper Creek adversaries had located. A mile or two north of today's Bartow on Lake Hancock's southeastern shore, they took up residence in an existing village that came to be called Minatti. It may have been an alternate spelling of Manatee.[14]

Jackson's allies may have closed Angola as a haven, but until well into the Second Seminole War, other peninsular villages harbored black Floridians. Perhaps the most famous of these was Peliklakaha, located in modern Sumter County not far to the east from a military road constructed during the 1820s to link a new post on Tampa Bay called Fort Brooke (Tampa) with an Indian agency established approximately one hundred miles to the north named Fort King (Ocala). The black leader Abraham presided there from the 1820s until the war commenced and emerged from there as the sense-bearer or principal counselor to the Seminoles and their chief Micanopy. As will be seen, he was to play a crucial role as instigator of the race war and slave rebellion to come.[15]

Armed Conflict Begins

With the Haitian revolutions offering Atlantic world context and Florida's own experiences providing practical training and martial perspectives, free blacks, runaways, and maroons anticipated war as President Andrew Jackson's agents moved treacherously in the early 1830s to inaugurate Indian removal and the capture or recapture of blacks. History in greatest part has remembered the courageous leadership of the Upper Creek war leader Osceola in forging a coalition for resistance, but black leaders such as Abraham played parts of equal significance. Born in 1787 or 1791 at Pensacola, he had spent much of his youth in that town before escaping to join British ranks during the War of 1812. As mentioned, by the mid-1820s he had emerged as an advisor to Chief Micanopy. Thanks in part to his mastery of English, Spanish, and Muscogee, Abraham had become fully acculturated into American and Seminole societies. In fact, he traveled to Washington in 1827 with the chief and other Indian leaders to negotiate with President John Quincy Adams about Indian concerns. Relying on his abilities to read and write, the race leader emerged as powerful and influential.[16]

Abraham used that power and influence to two ends. He plotted slave revolt, and he prodded Seminoles to war. In the former case, he organized maroons and Black Seminoles to visit farms and plantations that ringed the northern and eastern sides of the Indian reservation in the central peninsula. The emissaries forged relationships and prepared the slaves for war. One of the principal historians to investigate the matter found that the task involved no formidable challenges. "Since, for a number of years, the prevalence of peace had encouraged intercourse between Negro slaves and Seminole Indians," concluded Kenneth W. Porter, "it was easy to convince the slaves."[17]

That the slave revolt was organized in this manner and that the effort proved successful appears evident from the record. John Hope Franklin and Loren Schweninger have observed that army commander Thomas Sidney Jesup acknowledged as much in a wartime communiqué. "I have ascertained beyond any doubt," he reported, "not only that a connection exists between a portion of the slave population and the Seminoles, but that there was, before the war commenced, an understanding that a considerable force should join on the first blow being struck." Jesup knew his adversaries well, since white slave owners from Alachua, St. Johns, and Duval Counties had echoed similar thoughts, expressing in one letter that "many slaves were induced or encouraged [to leave their plantations, farms, and industries] by the Indians" before commencement of the Black/Indian Rebellion.[18]

And, leave the plantations, farms, and urban centers they did. J. B. Bird, one student of the subject, identified "at least 385 field slaves [who] defected to the Seminoles." He conceded that true numbers likely were higher. Indeed, the numbers were much higher. Contemporary newspaper accounts published in Florida, Georgia, and South Carolina detailed that over 700 runaways left the Rees, Heriot, Forrester, Depeyster, Humphreys, Hernandez, Bulow, and Dupont plantations and other nearby plantations and farms, many located in the sugar cane country of today's Volusia County. This total did not include numbers of other rebels who absconded from other regions of what quickly became the war zone. On April 1, 1836, one observer acknowledged what virtually all displaced settlers understood by then: the runaways, he insisted, "were quite numerous." Historian Canter Brown Jr. has speculated that the figure ultimately could have reached 750 to 1,000.[19]

Nor were these rebels merely escaping their bonds; instead, many—if not most—of them meant to fight or at least support the fight. Escapees from the plantations and farms of northeast, Central, and South Florida evidenced bold agency rather than an inclination toward marginal participation. When enslaved workers on the Dupont plantation departed, for example, they took all the owner's guns while being encouraged by "Seminoles . . . to kill every white man they saw." These people desired freedom and autonomy as they sought sanctuary among new allies in the remote havens of the peninsula.[20]

While Abraham and his allies plotted and prodded, another black leader partnered with Osceola in instigating resistance through war. That individual was named Harry, and—as a war leader who lived at Minatti—he likely had survived Angola's destruction. It would not have been so unusual for the two men to ally or even to become friends. Minatti lay only fifteen miles north of the Peace River village Talakchopco (modern Fort Meade) where Osceola spent much of his youth after 1819. By late 1835, it appears, Harry had assumed control of all hostiles based at Peace River, whether black or Indian, while Osceola had concentrated his attention more closely on the Indian agency at Fort King. In any event, on New Year's Day 1836, Fort Brooke's commander Francis S. Belton would report, "A negro, [Abraham's] intimate, named *Harry*, controls the Pea creek band of about a hundred warriors, forty miles [east] of us, who have done most of the mischief, and keep this post constantly observed, and communicate with the Mickasukians at Wythlacoochee, by means of powerful bands of Eufollahs and Alafiers, under Little Cloud and the Alligator."[21]

The war had ignited in December 1835, days before Belton's report was issued. The match was struck when Osceola murdered the Indian agent and an army officer at Fort King, and Seminoles and blacks farther south slaughtered troops under the command of Major Francis L. Dade in what amounted at the time to the largest massacre in US Army history. An enslaved black named Louis Fatio Pacheco had led the relief column of over one hundred men from Fort Brooke along the military road to Fort King. Pacheco may have passed word that Major Dade, who was feared and detested for cruelties inflicted almost a decade earlier, commanded the force. One account suggested that, upon receipt of the news of the column's march, "Abraham responded with quite a number of warriors." He, Alligator, and others—it may be supposed that Harry joined them—blocked the road just south of the turnoff to Peliklakaha. At that place, as the year neared its close, Dade and virtually all of his men lost their lives.[22]

Thereafter ensued raids, attacks, and battles throughout the peninsula and northeast Florida, ones that served to cover the rebellion of hundreds of slaves, as already detailed. The forces at work and their purposes came as no surprise to slaveholders and legislators. In fact, as early as September 17, 1835, Jacksonville citizens had talked of a possible slave uprising. About one month later, hysteria about imminent slave rebellion had consumed all of northeast Florida. Conscious of Haiti's proximity to Florida and its ideological influence on bondservants, one newspaper asked, "Shall we wait till the tragic scenes of Hayti are commenced, before we act, and act efficiently?" And within a few weeks of the first attack by Indians and blacks, the territorial council swiftly enacted a measure to tax owners who permitted their slaves to get away. "The present insurrection of the Seminole Nation of Indians," it declared, "has been chiefly excited by diverse mischievous Negroes and mulattoes living with the Indians some claiming to be free . . . and other fugitive slaves, runaways from citizens of Florida." Whites understood that the fight ahead would come down to subduing well-armed blacks in order to restore social order in Florida's ever-growing slave society. They, indeed, had a terrible slave revolt and race war on their hands.[23]

That revolt should not be viewed as a localized form of resistance to slavery of the type that usually occurred. With an Atlantic world perspective, many blacks who joined the war effort apparently viewed the overthrow of slavery not as an individual concern but as a collective, large-scale effort reminiscent of the Haitian precedent. Their goal was to force negotiations with government officials that would lead to freedom and to protection of lands from white encroachment. And, at least at the beginning, it appeared that they would succeed.[24]

Moreover, the struggle differed from typical examples of slave revolt because of a lack of religious purpose or inspiration. True, Baptist and Methodists missionaries slowly were making their way through Florida during the late 1820s and early 1830s. Yet the doctrine of spiritual freedom as preached by revivalist clergy seemingly failed to work an impact on the large majority of slaves who joined the revolt. In fact, no religious or eschatological elements appear to have contributed to sparking this rebellion. Florida's rebel leaders embraced no Gullah Jack, the native-born African "conjurer" and "priest" who helped to stir Christian followers in the Denmark Vesey (Telemaque) conspiracy. Nor did they draw inspirations from biblical sermons about Moses and the children of Israel's quest for freedom from the pharaoh, as in the case of the Nat Turner insurrection. There were no magical or celestial signs (such as an eclipse of the sun) to let leaders and followers know when to strike out for freedom.[25]

The argument can be made that the persistent influence of Roman Catholicism, which historically had sought to reduce rebellious behavior by treating slaves as quasi-human beings and by ameliorating their living and working conditions, may have blunted the appeal of religious fervor to East Florida slaves. Further research may illuminate this point to a greater degree. The fact remains that, however they did so, the Florida leaders succeeded, unlike Nat Turner, in transcending the world of plantation and urban slaves absent the force of a religious dimension to buttress their cause.[26]

Their accomplishment, it should be stressed, additionally was marked by the absence of any messianic figure. Leaders such as Abraham and his associate John Caesar used every opportunity to rally slaves, but no available evidence suggests that they or their peers considered themselves saviors or messiahs. This matched Gabriel's precedent, but where Gabriel focused primarily on urban and skilled bondpeople, the Florida leaders encouraged urban but principally rural residents to join the insurrection. In a sense, freedom with security became the religion of free and enslaved blacks who participated in the Second Seminole War.[27]

Neither was there a single outstanding leader such as a Gabriel or Turner; instead, in a situation similar to that of the Louisiana uprising of 1811, where there were many leaders such as Charles Deslondes, Kook, Quamana, and Harry Kenner, the Black/Indian Rebellion also had many leaders. Abraham may have been the most important strategist and Harry may have stood out as the most active and effective instigator, but many others carried the torch and maintained the cause. The scope of this work does not permit a close examination of all of these men. Scholars including, most recently, Anthony E. Dixon, fortunately have contributed meaningful studies on the subject. Suffice it to say that John Cavallo (John Horse), John Caesar, Cudjoe, King Philip, and Ben Bruno made their marks and left their own legacies of leadership. Many of them spoke English, Spanish, and Muscogee. Some were literate. A few, such as John Horse, boasted mixed parentage of Indian and African backgrounds. Their levels of acculturation permitted them easy contact with urban slaves, while their experience allowed them access to farm and plantation residents. They commanded respect and authority. Incidentally, no women stood within the inner circle. For that matter, few details of any kind come to us regarding women's participation in the insurrection other than for the care of children and the tending of animals and crops.[28]

The Results of Rebellion

Every source makes evident the large-scale successes achieved by blacks and their Indian allies during 1836. Along the way, "maroon communities," protected by the vastness of Florida's interior regions, posed a special problem for the military. The very existence of such communities of armed black warriors separated Florida's experience from that of states to the north. With the exception of the Dismal Swamp region of southeastern Virginia and northeastern North Carolina and a limited number of similar places, communities of runaways were far less evident in the South than in the Caribbean or South America—that is, the South save for Florida.[29]

The strategies employed by maroons to avoid capture and to protect families and loved ones did change over time, however. Where relatively large settlements such as Angola, Mulatto Girl's Town, and Payne's Negro Settlement had existed at times prior to the war, runaways and maroons now developed smaller but interconnected communities where they could more easily uproot and move to safer ground when invaders approached. Military strategy to some extent compelled this approach as army planners targeted the principal existing black settlements as soon as they could. Thus, South Carolina volunteers in early 1835 aimed for Peliklakaha as they traversed the peninsula toward Tampa Bay. Elements of the same army soon ravaged Minatti in the aftermath of its destruction of Talakchopko at Peace River. The tactic adopted by rebels in the wake of the flames frustrated the soldiers and kept them searching, mostly fruitlessly, for the combatants and their dependants during the conflict's first year.[30]

The tactical successes of runaways, free blacks, and Indians during late 1835 and 1836 prolonged the revolution for several years. Maroon leaders directed their cause like a well-oiled military operation in terms of gathering information about their opponents. They benefited particularly from informants among slaves in areas not controlled by them, including in towns. Most of the time, fugitives such as Sampson Forrester, the one-time slave of Indian agent Gad Humphreys, seemingly passed back and forth between white territory and lands controlled by blacks and Indians without much trouble or detection by the authorities. Given that they had wives in the area, even John Caesar and Abraham visited slaves on plantations and farms to the north and east.[31]

By late 1836, the US government had recognized its embarrassing predicament and settled on a change of command to bring new tactics, strategies, and modes of operation into play. Specifically, Secretary of War Lewis Cass assigned General Thomas Sidney Jesup to run the war and combat the blacks and Indians. Cass knew his man. A Virginian born in December 1788, Jesup was the son of a Revolutionary War veteran of solid reputation. Before age twenty, Jesup had accepted a commission in the Seventh Infantry as a second lieutenant and advanced to captain by the outbreak of the War of 1812. Although briefly a prisoner of war, he had distinguished himself to the extent that his "sterling performance" earned him promotion to brevet colonel in 1814. It was in supervising construction of boats for an invasion of Canada, however, that Jesup truly shone. This had brought him designation in 1818 as quartermaster general of the army, a position that he subsequently held for forty-two years. An able and no-nonsense administrator, he had revolutionized the military's supply capabilities.[32]

While Jesup's remarkable ability at managing supplies and equipment impressed Cass, more recent service prompted the appointment to Florida. When violence had flared in the spring of 1836 among Creeks in Alabama, Cass had decided that he needed just such an experienced and practical man to quell the situation and compel removal of the belligerents to the west. "The great object is to remove them immediately," he wrote to the general, "and to this, other considerations must yield." Jesup knew what he was being told. Over the months that followed, in the words of historian Claudio Saunt, "The army's cleanup operation was vicious, and it reflected the contempt that whites felt for native peoples." When a leader was needed in Florida to accomplish the same goal, Jesup already had proven that he was the man for the job. As a son of a Revolutionary War veteran, he obviously knew about the basic ideological tenets of the Declaration of Independence that focused on equality, liberty, and property rights. Yet, he seemingly chose to ignore these principles to leave a legacy of fighting and killing red and black men on behalf of the empire-building efforts of a few white men who desired to build fortunes in frontier Florida.[33]

Florida proved far more of a challenge to Jesup than he had anticipated. These black rebels differed from the foes of Jesup's acquaintance. They had history, demography, and geography on their side, which made possible a large-scale revolt against the general and other whites. As he learned, runaways and maroons would confront the veteran soldier as the most persistent fighters the general would face in his career. At the beginning, though, Jesup felt confident that he had devised a strategy to swiftly end the upheaval, and, to his credit, the plans focused properly on its nature as a race war. Accordingly, the strategy centered more on blacks than on Indians. As he noted, if the war against runaway blacks and Indians was "not speedily put down, the south will feel the effects of it on their slave population before end of next season." Jesup's perception of his black opponents' ability and resolve led him quickly to realize that his struggle probably would be a long one if the runaways could not be subdued swiftly. He initially misjudged, however, the agency of the runaways and maroons and the degree of their determination to keep fighting to maintain their freedom, perhaps because they evidenced willingness to negotiate with military and government officials. In any event, Jesup soon concluded, "Throughout my operations, I found the negroes the most active and determined warriors [that I met]."[34]

One facet of the rebellion actually played in Jesup's favor, though. Few slaves from the Middle Florida region joined the revolt. Geographical, racial, and cultural reasons explained this. The distance between the plantation belt in the panhandle and the heart of the rebellion in the northeast, central, and southern regions of the peninsula amounts to two hundred miles or so. With Middle Florida holding over 50 percent of the slaves in the territory, this worked an impact and a difference. Plus, given the Nat Turner insurrection in 1831 and resulting tendency of whites to solidify based upon their race, the Middle Florida region had come in places to resemble an armed camp. Unlike their northeast Florida counterparts, area slave owners strictly enforced slave codes. Slaves in Middle Florida likely did hear of attacks on the Gamble, Wirt, Johnson, and Gadsden plantations from 1836 to 1839, which left both whites and slaves dead in their wake, but reliable communications otherwise failed them. They possessed no way of knowing whether the Seminoles would accept or kill them. In the circumstances, they mostly opted to stay under the protection of their masters.[35]

The general could not count on this state of facts always remaining the same, of course, and he knew from past experience that he had to strike swiftly in order to get the advantage of the runaways and to end the rebellion "immediately." It appears that he also may have known about the strategy utilized by Gabriel and Charles Deslondes of striking suddenly, forcefully, and sensationally to motivate other slaves to leave their venues in an effort to prolong a major uprising. He appreciated, as well, that black leaders made up the backbone of the rebellion and observed that they "exercised an almost controlling influence over the Indians" and their followers. He initially focused his strategy accordingly on destroying the new maroon communities in Central and South Florida and thereby putting down the revolution. That turned out to be a goal easier stated than accomplished, although the results would carry long-term significance.[36]

For eighteen months, Jesup labored mightily to produce the results he desired. At times they seemed within his grasp, only to be snatched away at the last minute. His frustration level built as time passed, and in April 1838 he asked to be relieved. By then, well over 1,000 officers and 17,000 enlisted men had campaigned to little avail. Starvation rather than military force had proved the general's greatest ally, inducing some Seminoles and blacks to accept payments to depart Florida, labor as free men in the service of the United States, or both. From time to time, groups of runaways surrendered to trusted officers to be returned to owners, but others awaited assurances that they would be allowed to live free. Jesup's greatest prize was Abraham, who turned himself in to the commander personally in January 1838. An officer introduced him at the headquarters as "the terror of the white people, for the last year."[37]

Kenneth W. Porter related what followed. "When Abraham reached the commanding officer's quarters, he saw the general standing inside," the historian began. "He stopped and deliberately thrust his flagstaff into the earth beside the pole bearing Old Glory. . . . He was a chief and would behave as such to the end. Then he crossed his arms as Jesup approached. The officer smiled and extended his hand, which Abraham took."[38]

In May, Jesup left Florida still believing that destroying the maroons and returning runaways to their masters afforded the best approach for putting down the rebellion. He remained adamant, too, in his perception of the nature of conflict. "This . . .," he had insisted, "is a negro, not an Indian war." On the other hand, runaways, free blacks, and Indians maintained their strategic vision as well. They would prolong the upheaval—despite the loss of leaders such as Abraham and, in April 1838, John Cavallo (John Horse)—to obtain certain goals. They would strike plantations, farms, and settlements to obtain food, supplies, and arms; keep the insurrection in the hearts and minds of other slaves; and build support for their cause by exhausting their foes.[39]

The first two years of the conflict had favored runaways and their Indian allies; yet, by Jesup's departure, circumstances had begun to change over time with the goals of the combatants changing with them. The rebellion now took on more of a political dimension for most of Florida's remaining runaways, maroons, and Indians. Instead of merely defending themselves and protecting their homelands, the majority of the rebels and their families sought negotiations with the military and peninsula governmental officials. Jesup, with the assistance of Creek Indian scouts, had learned the landscape of Central and South Florida and, after two years of constantly pursuing the blacks and Indians, had begun to destroy maroon communities along with crops and livestock. As noted, many of the runaways—having barely survived starvation conditions for some time—wanted to negotiate terms that would allow them to remain free, even if it meant the loss of their land and their ultimate removal to the western territory of Arkansas. Finally, the alliance between blacks and Seminoles, largely one of mutual convenience, had begun to show evidence of fissures and stresses. Black rebels now grew concerned that Seminoles might conclude an arrangement with the whites at their expense. They feared particularly that the Seminoles might agree to return them to slavery. Deals thus were struck by many of the remaining black rebels over the next year or two on the best terms that they could get, ones aimed at protecting themselves and their families.[40]

The issue for many ultimately came down to whether the government would agree to send them west or would allow slave catchers access to them. Captain John T. Sprague, writing of events as they appeared early in the 1840s, shared the rationale by which army officials ultimately agreed to frustrate owners and transport survivors away from Florida. "Many of these negroes had escaped, others were captured [by Seminoles], from the citizens of the Territory, and the state of Georgia," he commented. "Years had elapsed, allowing sufficient time for them to have grown from youth to manhood, imbibing the habits of their captors. . . . These habits could not be subdued, nor these ties broken, without a struggle." He continued:

> It was folly to turn the negro, thus imbued, and with such ties, upon his white master. . . . The negroes from the commencement of the Florida war, have, for their numbers, been the most formidable foe, more blood-thirsty, active, and revengeful, than the Indian. To surrender or to be captured, was to them slavery and punishment; while victory gave them plunder, and added confidence to the already excited feelings of their masters. The lives of citizens, and their property, demanded that they should be sent far beyond the country with which they were familiar, and with which were associated many incidents calculated to foster a hostile feeling. . . . It would require blood and money to besiege them, and when forced out, they could remove unseen to other strong-holds, which nature has so abundantly provided.

Sprague concluded, "Ten resolute negroes, with a knowledge of the country, are sufficient to desolate the frontier, from one extent to the other."[41]

Historian Anthony Dixon has explained that not all black combatants departed for the west. "For the remainder of the war, small numbers of Black Seminoles would continue to fight under the remaining Seminole Indian chiefs in Florida," he wrote. "They would no longer play significant roles in battle. . . . Small numbers would remain in Florida for the most part concealed in the dark hammocks and swamps below Lake Okeechobee. . . . They would sporadically be involved in attacks on farms and plantations. These attacks would be instituted primarily as a means to steal supplies. [As late as] 1857, an attack was reported on soldiers at Palm Grove which was led by a Negro . . . in the full costume of a chief."[42]

As Dixon's example makes very clear, Florida's slave owners as late as the eve of the Civil War continued to endure the apparent threat of race war and, in tandem with it, slave revolt. One-time governor Richard Keith Call, who had been defeated by black and Indian warriors early in the Second Seminole War, had declared of the slaves who revolted in 1835 and 1836 his belief that the revolution had been an attack on all whites. The runaways and maroons, he said, "never failed to exercise against the white man, with whom he could expect only slavery and inequity." Those words resonated through the years that followed. Given the history of white violence toward blacks, disruptions of slave families, and overall abuse aimed at enslaved men, women, and children, it might have been a natural response to endeavor to renew revolt and otherwise act as the governor described. But, because of their humanity, Florida's runaways and rebels did not fulfill the dreaded anticipations of widespread, cold-blooded murder articulated by Call. Freedom would come, and a thousand or more black Floridians would fight in the war that brought it. It would be, though, an honorable war for freedom and not murder in the night that eventually brought the Day of Jubilee.[43]

11. The Civil War

> If everything is left with the Negroes . . .
> I know they will not take care of anything.
> —Rabun Scarborough to sister, November 19, 1861

Florida contained nearly 62,000 enslaved persons when it seceded from the Union in January 1861, about 44 percent of its total population. Most bondservants lived in the Middle Florida black belt—the area, it will be remembered, that was framed by the Apalachicola River on the west (but including Jackson County) and by the Suwannee River on the east. Here resided over 50 percent of the state's slave population. Northeast Florida—eastward of the Suwannee and including the peninsula—held the second largest slave concentration, about 20 percent of its population. West Florida (the district in the western panhandle that lay between the Perdido River on the west and the Apalachicola River on the east but excluding Jackson County) had the smallest number of bondservants, who amounted to only 7 percent of total residents. Yet, wherever they lived and worked, enslaved blacks, as scholar W. E. B. Du Bois asserted for the South as a whole, ultimately tipped the Civil War tide in favor of the North by waging a "general strike."[1]

As previously had occurred during the Second Seminole War, many bondservants took the courageous step of fleeing their homes in order to fight in the war effort. These were true rebels, for they knew what the war and its outcome meant to them. "The war was not only a rebellion of southerners against the Union," explained historian Merton Dillon. "It also was a rebellion of slaves against masters or, more exactly, a rebellion of slaves against bondage." They moved outside relatively comfortable and secure environments to participate in a struggle that could very well end their lives but that also would determine their status and place in life. In various enduring ways, these bondservants, as will be seen, expressed agency in their quest for emancipation during the war.[2]

During the Civil War period, bondservants in northeast Florida demonstrated, generally speaking, more agency toward freedom than did their counterparts in other portions of the state. Given the partial or total breakdowns in white authority over enslaved blacks that eventually occurred in much of East Florida and the relative lack of white racial solidarity, slaveholders in the region proved somewhat more complacent when it came to restricting slave movement. Bondpeople in East Florida accordingly emerged as the most vocal in resisting slavery by joining either the US Army or Navy to fight emancipation. Of the over 60,000 slaves of both sexes and all ages listed in the 1860 Florida census, 1,000 or more men, mostly from northeast Florida, served in the military. Many came from Clay, Nassau, and St. Johns Counties and their vicinities, but the largest percentage came from Duval County. These rebels, as it turned out, would contribute to the Union victory in many ways.[3]

The rebels came from diverse backgrounds. Historian Daniel L. Schafer has concluded, based upon a sample of 364 recruits, that "the median age was twenty-four, yet forty-two gave their age at the time of muster as between forty and sixty years." He added, "The majority of the recruits, 65 percent, were engaged in some form of agricultural enterprise." At least 10 to 25 percent were employed as semiskilled and skilled laborers who worked in a variety of occupations, including as carpenters, house servants, tailors, wheelwrights, sawyers, plasterers, shoemakers, and painters. With northeast Florida stretching along the Atlantic coastline, some of the men naturally had worked on and near the water. Among them were boatmen, caulkers, riggers, sailmakers, coopers, mariners, ferrymen, skippers of flats, and pilots.[4]

Masters had leased some of the enlistees to others, while significant numbers were allowed to move about in the process of hiring themselves out. Many lived and worked in port towns such as Fernandina, Jacksonville, and St. Augustine. They might remain out of touch with their owners for months or even years. These prestigious occupations understandably afforded bondservants a sense of worth and dignity, with many becoming well assimilated into society over time. As a result, many became self-assured and self-reliant, able to depend upon their own skills in making a living.[5]

Of all the bondservants who joined the cause for freedom, northeast Florida slaves experienced in maritime trade would prove to be the most helpful, particularly as guides to the US Army and Navy. Their knowledge of the creeks, lakes, streams, rivers, and bays leading to and out of the Atlantic and their familiarity with other waterways abutting the state became essential to the war effort. For example, Israel, an escaped Jacksonville slave, knew the waterways of northeast Florida very well. Among other things, he guided Union troops who had landed along the shore of Pablo Creek near his hometown. According to sources, his presence was welcomed since he was "thoroughly acquainted with all of the country" in East Florida. Maritime slave Isaac Tatwell proved indispensable as well. As a mariner, the fugitive had served as a slave pilot on the steamer *St. Mary* before the conflict. In wartime, he supplied the Union with valuable information about the Confederacy's defenses along the Atlantic coastline.[6]

One Union officer helped to confirm the Atlantic world perspective possessed by some Florida slaves and their resulting usefulness to the Union and to the cause of freedom. "The finest men physically were from Florida," he declared, "and these men, having been pilots and fishermen, had more knowledge of the world than those [slaves] from South Carolina, who had lived chiefly on isolated plantations all their days." Indeed, many Florida runaways who took flight to join the Union army and navy comprehended the outside world in ways that proved quite beneficial.[7]

Owners and persons who were owned, it helps to note, held differing views of the Atlantic. On the one hand, the owners—much like their counterparts through the South—viewed the Atlantic as a large body of water leading to prosperity through the transport of commodities to the Americas, Europe, and Africa. On the other hand, bondservants perceived the Atlantic as a means of travel in search of freedom. For several generations, as has been discussed earlier, they had relied on the Atlantic to bring human beings; other commodities; political, religious, and social ideas; and news and gossip of the world outside. Many in the early 1860s soon came to associate the war with the abolition of slavery. Now, they would rely on the Atlantic and other waterways to deliver them to freedom.[8]

The navy, too, became associated with freedom. With the increasing proximity of Union boats to the various port towns and cities in northeast Florida during 1862, area bondpeople became ever more assertive in seeking to flee farms and plantations. When Federal gunboats began to patrol the St. Johns River region, for example, runaways could hope for freedom if they could reach that stream. As a result, during the war's early stages, northeast Florida slaveholders witnessed significant losses of men, women, and children. For many of northeast Florida's enslaved blacks, as historian Schafer aptly noted, "freedom was as close as the river."[9]

Although the Civil War commenced in 1861, Federal officials initially were reluctant to accept free blacks or escapees into the US military. The Lincoln administration feared border state secession and anti-abolitionist sentiment in the North, plus it did not desire to alienate support of southern Unionists, including those in Florida, by confiscating slave property. As historian Eric Foner correctly noted, Abraham Lincoln remained a complex man throughout his life. His somewhat negative attitude toward blacks would change over time, and, due to a variety of considerations, his administration in the summer and early fall of 1862 altered its position and slowly began allowing blacks to enlist. As in the past, those who chose to do so had to prove, all over again, the ability and resolve of black men to fight. As they succeeded in one theater after another, Lincoln began to admire their abilities. By January 1863, the Emancipation Proclamation offered official endorsement of service by peoples of African descent, and the enlistment of escaped slaves mushroomed. In Florida, as mentioned, more than one thousand eventually stepped forward.[10]

As far as service in the navy was concerned, black seamen followed traditions explored earlier in this volume, as a result of which they were no strangers as sailors or crewmen to boats and ships. This had been true dating back to the Spanish period in Florida. The late eighteenth century, after all, had seen black sailors making up substantial portions of crews, many of them serving in racially integrated units. In Florida during the Civil War era, the Gulf Blockading Squadron utilized black men even before some other naval squadrons of the time. But, much as was true of other black sailors in southern reaches, Florida navy men encountered rampant discrimination and exploitation, particularly after the 1862 reorganization of the Gulf Blockading Squadron into the West Gulf and East Gulf Squadrons. Secretary of the Navy Gideon Wells ordered that blacks "be allowed . . . no higher rating than boys, at a compensation of $10 per month and one ration per day." These wages, like those for black soldiers, averaged far below those of white sailors. But, these wages would increase over time. As with their army comrades, the black mariners would not receive equal pay until January 1, 1864.[11]

One significant naval responsibility involved interdiction of blockade runners. The Federals well understood the importance of the Atlantic economy to the Confederacy, since some foodstuffs, supplies, and munitions came from Havana, the British Bahamas, and other places into Florida and other secessionist coastal states. Federals as a result sought the geographical knowledge of northeast Florida runaways to help them consolidate their blockade. One Union officer, for instance, relied on Corporal Robert Sutton as his guide because of the runaway's experience in navigating area rivers. He had acquired his seafaring knowledge as a slave of Edwin Alberti, who lived along the St. Marys River, Florida's northeastern boundary with Georgia and the waterway that passed into the Atlantic at Fernandina.[12]

The Federals especially aimed at cutting off rebel food supplies as one of the critical steps toward a successful conclusion of the war. The preservation of available food meanwhile became important to the Confederacy's war effort. Preservation processes usually required salt, a commodity most readily available for the Deep South on the coast after boiling seawater. To counter salt harvesting activities, the Union relied in significant part on the memory and knowledge of runaways in locating and destroying coastal salt pans and operations. With their knowledge of the various small and larger beaches up and down the Atlantic and Gulf coastlines, runaways again proved most helpful by aiding naval attempts to destroy the Confederacy's ability to preserve food. At Cedar Keys, for instance, bondpeople who had made salt furnished the Union information used to demolish that operation, at least according to former slave Mary Minus Biddle.[13]

The Nature of Military Service

Runaway contributions to the navy duly acknowledged, the fact remained that 75 percent or more of those who absconded from slavery in Florida became soldiers in the army, and in doing so, they stood among the 180,000 black men who labored and fought for the Union during the war. Sadly and much as occurred to their navy counterparts, Florida's black soldiers faced discrimination. As early as 1862 and the change in administration policy that allowed black men to serve, abolitionists and other Union sympathizers encouraged the Union to take necessary action to recognize black servicemen as full-fledged soldiers, including by providing them with arms and opportunity to fight for the cause. Weapons also allowed them to protect themselves. Discrimination and ill treatment notwithstanding, black soldiers generally conducted themselves with honor and dignity when afforded that chance. On many occasions, they demonstrated a level of heroism equal to that of any white soldiers.[14]

After early 1863, black army service came generally through assignment to a regiment of United States Colored Infantry (USCI), also known as the United States Colored Troops. The regiments to which large numbers of black Floridians were attached included the First, Second, and Third South Carolina Infantry, the Fifty-Fourth Massachusetts Infantry, and the Second, Eighth, Twenty-First, Thirty-First, Thirty-Third, Thirty-Fourth, Thirty-Fifth, Ninety-Ninth, and 102nd USCI. These men, it should be reemphasized, knew what they were fighting for. As respected historians aptly have noted, "Although their owners sought to keep them ignorant of the events that fueled the great conflict, sooner or later slaves came to understand that the war was about them and that their future hinged on its outcome."[15]

A runaway called "long legged Jack" serves as an example of one such man, although many can be cited. Jack had escaped from owner A. M. Reed of Mulberry Grove plantation near Jacksonville to fight the Confederates for his freedom. A year later, he returned to Mulberry Grove with a rifle and bayonet in his possession. According to the owner's daughter Hattie Reed, Jack had come back to settle a score with her father for selling his wife, Etta, into Georgia slavery several years earlier. Jack's superior officer temporarily confined him while in the presence of the Reed family. Bondservant Robert Sutton surprised his owner when he absconded to join the Union army. Once he became a corporal, he too returned with his superior officer. In Sutton's case, the aim was to take possession of his former master's home because the man remained an unrepentant Confederate sympathizer.[16]

Most runaways knew their fate had become inextricably tied to a Union win. They recognized, as well, how difficult that fight would be and that their contributions would make a significant difference in favor of a victory. "If we hadn't become sojers, all might have gone back as it was before; our freedom might have slipped through de two house of Congress and President Linkum's four years might have passed by and notin' been done for us," Private Thomas Long expressed. "But now tings can neber go back, because we have showed our energy and our courage and our naturally manhood." Long and others yearned to make sure that the agency of blacks and their willingness to fight for their own emancipation remained clear. He never wanted his children to hear, "Your fader never fought for he own freedom."[17]

The question of freedom for children and other family members left behind loomed large in the minds of many black servicemen and formed a part of their concept of soldiering. Again, Thomas Long provides an example. Mirroring a situation similar to Long Legged Jack's, Long absconded without his wife and children in late 1862 to join the Union army. But, they remained of utmost importance to the private. So, he went back several months later to get them, rejoining the Thirty-Third USCI in Fernandina with his family intact. Long Legged Jack and Thomas Long reflected the sentiments of thousands of black individuals who put their lives on the line for their families and their own emancipation.[18]

As the war progressed, large numbers of black soldiers participated in engagements throughout the state. The fighting included the two largest of Florida's battles, those of Olustee and Natural Bridge. White officers noted their bravery. For instance, Colonel Thomas Higginson—an ardent abolitionist and one of the Secret Six who had provided financial support for John Brown's 1859 raid on the US Arsenal at Harpers Ferry, Virginia—described the Florida soldiers as bold and brave fighting men. Another Union soldier voiced words of praise for black soldiers who fought at the Battle of Olustee on February 20, 1864. He asserted that the men of the Eighth and Thirty-Fifth USCI and the Fifty-Fourth Massachusetts, including many Florida soldiers, fought "like devils." The Confederates killed over 200 men and wounded more than 1,100 at Olustee. Approximately 300 additional blacks, among them more Floridians, received fatal wounds at the battle of Natural Bridge near Tallahassee in 1865.[19]

Much as was true for other black Union soldiers who fought in theaters of the South, wounded Florida slave recruits sometimes faced savagery and death at Confederates' hands after the fighting had stopped. James A. Seddon, the Confederate secretary of war, set the stage for such atrocities by commanding that captured black soldiers be executed. He ordered, "We ought never to be inconvenienced with such [slave] prisoners . . . summary execution must therefore be inflicted on those taken." At the Battle of Milliken's Bend on the Mississippi River on June 7, 1863, Seddon's orders were enforced by the murder of wounded black soldiers. Some eight months later at the Battle of Olustee, Colonel Abner McCormick of the Second Florida Cavalry acted in accord with Seddon's edict. The colonel directed, "Do not take any negro prisoners in this fight." Confederate officers and soldiers followed his instructions. When a high-ranking officer of the Fourth Georgia Cavalry heard gunshots and asked a Confederate officer what was happening, the man replied, "Shooting niggers sir."[20]

The black soldiers fought and died, even though the war department initially paid them less money than what white soldiers received. Although black enlistees had proven that they would fight, they received, like their black sailor counterparts, ten dollars per month while white privates were allowed thirteen. Most Florida soldiers probably accepted the lesser compensation from necessity in order to provide some assistance to their families, although blacks of the Fifty-Fourth Massachusetts rejected the unequal pay. Money likely persisted as a critical issue for black Floridians who risked their lives in various skirmishes and battles, but the war's outcome remained a bigger one. By the time of the Battle of Olustee, Congress finally had enacted a law that equalized pay between black and white troops.[21]

There were, of course, black supporters of the war effort who did not engage in actual combat. Some men, for instance, worked instead as laborers for the army. However, the majority of runaways who did not fight in battle consisted of women and children. Most of these women were semiskilled, having worked as cooks, seamstresses, domestics, and nannies for their masters prior to absconding. Although none appear to have masqueraded as men to fight on the battlefield as some white women did for both Union and Confederate armies, they nonetheless played a central role in the war's outcome.[22]

These Florida women composed a silent but very effective army of workers who did the day-to-day work of helping to sustain the war effort. In no small way, they formed the backbone of the war endeavor on the home front. These recent bondservants perceived few changes in American slavery yet insisted on persistence unto freedom. For years as the conflict raged, they cooked, washed, and aided the wounded. In one outstanding example, bondservants who had helped to nurture Jacksonville's First Baptist Church (later, Bethel Baptist Institutional Church) utilized the structure as a hospital for the care of Union soldiers. Some slaves such as Lettie and Aunt Eliza prepared food and cared personally for the combatants. Former slave Amanda McCray recalled that she prepared food and washed the uniforms for Federal soldiers and sailors. The services performed by such slaves as Lettie, Aunt Eliza, and McCray mirrored the same types of work accomplished by bondservants throughout the South in support of the Union and freedom.[23]

Even when their roles outside combat nonetheless placed their health and lives at risk, many ex-slaves did not seem to mind working at military installations such as those in the Dry Tortugas and Key West's Fort Taylor. Many died at these facilities from the "yellow jack"—as yellow fever was known—despite the beliefs of some military authorities that the bondservants enjoyed immunity to this disease. Geographic factors, it can be argued, played as well in their willingness to work in such potentially dangerous places. Many of the men and women possessed at least some understanding of the larger world and knew or quickly learned that waterways leading in and out of the Dry Tortugas and Key West also could take them to places such as the British Bahamas, where slavery had been outlawed since the 1830s. If the war did not end in their favor, Nassau at New Providence Island, among other suitable locations, offered options for securing freedom.[24]

West Florida bondpeople, while fewer in number than their East Florida counterparts, also contributed to their freedom by working in various military installations in the region. Most had been concentrated in Escambia and Santa Rosa Counties, which early found themselves under Union influence if not control. In the circumstances, the region's black workers aided the United States in many ways. For one thing, recruits served out their time at Union-controlled Fort Barrancas from 1864 to the war's end. Few actually saw fighting, although Brigadier General Alexander Asboth used a small number of West Florida's black soldiers in his Jackson County raid of September 1864. The majority performed manual labor. They worked, for example, loading and unloading ships, helping to maintain the local railroad system, keeping saltworks running, and assisting in the erection and repair of fortifications and bridges.[25]

A few Florida individuals participated in the war on the side of the Confederacy. Most of these individuals understood that fighting for the South meant the continuation of bondage. Nonetheless, a recognizable number of Florida bondservants could be found voluntarily aiding the Rebel cause. They mainly did so out of loyalty to their masters or else had been hired out by their masters (in which case the service, while it might have been willing, was not voluntary). A case in point involved Aleck, who readily served as a Confederate scout for his Manatee County master, Captain Archibald McNeill. The slave's knowledge of the coastline and waters surrounding the state allowed his master to avoid capture by the Union navy. According to Dr. Etheldred Philips, a black mariner serving as a pilot preferred to lose his life rather than betray his country by leaving his Confederate boat. Benjamin Hopkins rented his skilled cook, Felix, to Captain Winston Stephens as a mess servant for twenty-six dollars per month. In letters to his wife, Stephens would brag about Felix's culinary skills. Generally, though, Florida bondservants had to be forced to serve the Confederacy.[26]

But, unlike the practices adopted by the Union army and navy, the Confederacy sought to impress blacks in Florida into non-combat duties as early as October 1861. This compelled the slaves to do the "dirty and smutty work," as well as the cooking and cleaning, at Fort Steele on the St. Johns River. By February 17, 1864, some three years later, the Confederate Congress officially provided for the impressment of slaves. Whatever may have occurred in Virginia, Tennessee, and, to a lesser degree, North and South Carolina, the Confederacy gave few guns to Florida slaves. They worked, more often than not, in occupations such as cooking, cleaning, caring for livestock, erecting defenses, hauling loads, and similar tasks.[27]

A relatively large number of Florida slaves who served the Confederacy did so as body servants to their masters or, in some cases, to others to whom they were assigned. This especially proved true for individuals from Middle Florida. One of them, Gadsden County's George Washington Witherspoon, attended to his master, Robert Witherspoon. George accompanied the Confederate officer and cared for his every need during the two years he served in the army. Henry Call's experience paralleled that of Witherspoon's. He served his master until the man's demise at the Battle of Clouds near Chattanooga, Tennessee. The bondservant thereafter searched for and secured his master's body from among the dead and returned it to the home place in Jackson County for burial.[28]

The overwhelming majority of enslaved Floridians preferred, though, not to support the Confederate cause, as reflected in Patience Campbell's words. The former bondwoman claimed, "Negroes could [work for] the Southern army if they desired, none of them wished to do so but preferred to join northern forces and fight for the thing they desire most, freedom." Campbell's statement rings true. Few Florida bondservants willingly joined the Confederate cause.[29]

The Quiet Rebellion

Besides voluntarily serving actively in the US military, enslaved Floridians engaged in what the scholar W. E. B. Du Bois called a quiet rebellion, an act of resistance that became more evident as word of Union Civil War victories circulated. The bondmen and bondwomen understood that their labor freed whites to fight for their continued enslavement. Most, as noted, naturally did not want to contribute to the southern cause. In one instance, two East Florida owners concluded that area bondservants intended to help the Union cause by not planting crops for human consumption, efforts that ultimately would impair the Confederacy's ability to feed its troops. They were convinced that the slaves would stop planting crops as early as 1862 when Confederate supplies were in critically short supply in the Upper South.[30]

When owners attempted to force their bondpeople to labor for the South, they faced resistance that intensified over time. William J. Watkins of what is now Bartow hired out his bondservants to aid local Confederate families. His daughter recalled that this did not sit well with one of the slaves. When Watkins lent out this particular person to do laundry for a woman whose husband fought for the Confederacy, the slave would not work for her. The bondwoman communicated to the mistress her position, declaring, "Miss L. she say your father he sending us to wash to help her husband fight to keep us slaves."[31]

It appears that enslaved persons in northeast Florida tended more than those from Middle Florida to vocalize their feelings as the war continued. As early as 1862, Octavia Stephens, the wife of Confederate officer Winston Stephens, found herself dealing with bondservants who refused to be worked hard. They justified their resistance by arguing that the owners did not work, so why should they feel compelled to work hard? The mistress insisted that one slave had the gall to say that his Putnam County slaveholder had worked before getting "married but . . . had not since." The bondservants continued to work poorly and to complain about their assignments. As the resistance built, Stephens urged his wife not to "trust [the] negroes" or to go "in the woods" if the Union army arrived nearby. He also did not want her to let "the negroes know where" she was going. Stephens, like many Floridians, had become convinced that enslaved blacks covertly and overtly were doing what they could to impede the Confederacy's war efforts.[32]

Peninsular residents also forthrightly voiced their thoughts and opinions as signs of the Confederacy's collapse became ever more evident. Tampa's Sarah Brown Bryant reflected the attitude of many. A revealing interview with the former bondwoman by a descendant of her onetime master illustrated her attitude toward her owners and the soldiers fighting for the Confederacy:

> One day during the war, Sarah went into the [John T. Lesley] house and found grandmother rocking Aunt India and both of them crying. She asked them why they were crying, and grandmother replied that her husband and father of her child was away in the war and that he might be killed and they would never see him again, etc. Sarah then asked her if she remembered when she was first brought to Tampa she would cry for her mother and they would spank her. And for her not to cry as it would not do her any good.[33]

Slaves who lived in Middle Florida, where the war's impact reached less directly, and who comprised by far the largest segment of the state's slave population, helped to shake the foundation of slavery in many subtle but effective ways. Given that the Union failed to occupy the region, runaways faced almost two hundred miles of travel to reach Federal lines. Fearing that they easily could be captured moving about in large family groups, most slaves in the region opted to remain in place.[34]

Some Middle Florida whites nonetheless believed through much of the war that a large slave uprising was imminent. Tallahassee's *Florida Sentinel*, on its part, encouraged area residents to arm themselves for rebellion. Some citizens even called for Governor John Milton to declare martial law in the state to protect against the potential of violent slave unrest. As it turned out, no such event occurred.[35]

Although enslaved residents of Middle Florida did not run away to join the Union army or navy in large numbers, they did know about the war. Black wagoner Acie Thomas certainly numbered among them. He, in turn, passed on information about various battles to other blacks during his travels through the region. Enslaved blacks also witnessed the departure of the Confederate army from Florida for more pressing duties in other theaters of battle. Bondservants similarly looked on as masters and overseers left to fight for the southern cause. Former slave Willis Williams saw his master's "eldest son Charlie" volunteer for Confederate service. Louis Napoleon watched as his master's "oldest sons went to war with the Confederate army."[36]

Bondservants—including, among others, Henry Call of Jackson County, George Washington Witherspoon of Gadsden County, and Lewis of Leon County—knew about the war because they had traveled with their masters to the battle front. They, like many other slaves, quietly passed the news on to other bondservants. Former slave Amanda McCray remembered that slaves on her plantation "first heard of the Civil War" from the local slave preacher. "He held whispered prayers for the success of the Union soldiers," she recalled.[37]

As mentioned earlier, W. E. B. Du Bois stressed the significance of the quiet rebellion that took place among the enslaved population throughout the Civil

War South. The phrase "quiet rebellion" well mirrored the Middle Florida situation. Many area whites, from their perspectives, certainly believed this to be the case. The absence of planters and overseers on plantations and farms left many slaves without close supervision. Whites routinely believed that such a lack of close surveillance would encourage assertive behavior aimed at throwing off the shackles of bondage. One fearful Tallahassee editor even called on slaveholders to abandon the fighting and return home. "Many men could serve the Confederacy better out of the military," he insisted, "than in it." The editor went on to add, "The governor should take immediate steps to see that at least one white male adult was left on each plantation."[38]

All the while, many of Middle Florida's enslaved blacks quietly assisted Union efforts to secure their freedom. As historian Peter Kolchin noted, "The actions of slaves themselves helped [to bring down the Confederacy]." In line with this fact, bondservants took every opportunity of weakened authority, in ways large and small, to sabotage the old order through their behavior. As far as some slaves were concerned, slavery had collapsed by war's end thanks to their unwillingness to obey plantation rules. Mrs. M. N. Fletcher, for example, bluntly informed her son that the family's slaves would no longer obey her. She asserted, "In spite of all that I can do they have broke[n] into the sugar house and took my calf skins and nearly a barrel of syrup . . . and I think about two hundred pounds of meat." Mrs. Fletcher went on to note that she had informed the overseer about this disgraceful behavior. He had replied that he "could not help" to stop what the slaves were doing.[39]

Others contributed to the Union cause through their unwillingness to work consistently and productively. At least, Confederate captain Rabun Scarborough thought so. By 1862, the officer was imploring his wife to keep his letters "strictly confidential" since he feared that the laborers on his small Gadsden County plantation might take advantage of their contents. Scarborough asked on one occasion, "Are the negroes more than half done picking cotton[?]" He continued, "Tell Prince [the driver] he must make hands do their best." Being away from home, Scarborough nonetheless grasped that his bondpeople were working poorly for his wife. In a manner seen through much of the South, Florida's bondservants, especially the males, increasingly evidenced only slight or even no respect for or fear of women in control of the farms, plantations, or business enterprises. In a subsequent letter, Scarborough illustrated the point by remarking directly about his bondservants' work ethics. "I have suffered more uneasiness on that point than almost any other," he declared, "for I know if everything is left with the Negroes until the middle of March we will make but a small crop, & I know they will not take care of anything." What the absentee master really meant was that his bondservants would not work as hard for his wife as they might have for him.[40]

In such circumstances, with most white men conspicuously missing during the war from the farms and plantations of Middle Florida, many individuals took advantage of white women who held charge of households. Governor Milton spent most of his time away from his Jackson County home attending to the business of the state during the war. As a result of his chronic absences, his wife and a governess attempted to maintain control of the plantation. The women faced constant challenges from bondservants. Slaves Flora and Jane, for example, grew quite unmanageable, with the former leaving the Miltons' baby unattended while the latter ignored her daily tasks whenever she felt the inclination to do so. When the governess tried to punish the bondservants, the women retaliated.[41]

Some enslaved blacks chose to decrease the amount of work they did while masking any disagreeable attitude toward their masters. Susan Bradford Eppes, daughter of planter Edward Bradford, learned of the true character of one of their "trusted" house servants after the war. Eppes related this story about the house servant who "opened" Eppes's eyes to her true nature:

> [Mrs. Bradford] told her young daughter [Susan] to go to Emeline, the cook, give her the keys to the storeroom and pantry and tell her to provide bountifully for the guests. . . . It seemed an easy thing to deliver the keys and the message to Emeline. Extending the keys, [Susan] said, "Emeline Mother says she wants you to take these keys and have everything just as you know it ought to be. The doctors will bee her [*sic*] to dinner." . . . Imagine the shock and surprise at her answer: "Take dem keys back ter yer Mother an' tell her I don't never 'spects ter cook no more, not while I lives—tell her I's free, bless de Lord!"

Needless to say, young Susan Bradford could not persuade the former bondservant to change her mind. As she learned, the closer freedom came, the more enslaved blacks showed their true selves.[42]

It remains difficult to determine how many slaves actually absconded from Middle Florida during the war years. Many obviously did. Slave owners during this period simply did not advertise their runaways. But if Margrett Nickerson's recollections are reflective of slaves' desires to disappear from Middle Florida farms and plantations, many did so. Nickerson recalled that fellow residents of her former master's plantation ran away but lived in the nearby woods. She claimed that "when de big gun fiahed, de runaway slaves came out of the woods from all directions." Mrs. M. N. Fletcher noted that, on the Oak Grove plantation, Jim and Stephen had disappeared and might "try to get to the yankees."

Joshua Hoyet Frier, a Florida militiaman, recalled tracking Middle Florida fugitives during the war years.[43]

As seen, enslaved blacks in Florida, much like those who resided in other southern states, demonstrated in ways large and small that they wanted their liberty. In West and East Florida, they showed their willingness to effect change in their status by joining the Union military. Some fought in the Union army. Many black soldiers were killed, while most earned a reputation for fighting bravely. Others volunteered for service in the Union navy. Black sailors, especially those from northeast Florida, proved to be very helpful to the Union as guides. Many of these fugitives and their ancestors had plied the numerous creeks, rivers, and bays of East Florida for generations before the Civil War. Because of their knowledge and memory of the East Florida landscape, runaways assisted the Union in cutting off supplies to the Confederacy. Still others in these two regions served as spies, laborers, and informants for the North.

In Middle Florida, enslaved blacks typically did not abscond as often as their West and East Florida counterparts, given demographic and practical restrictions. Yet, they did not simply sit and wait for change to come. Many became unruly by not working consistently and productively, while others took the opportunity to run away or to steal what they could from their owners. Some even quietly resisted during the war years before showing their true character at the war's end. But, as Du Bois noted, a quiet rebellion had started during the war years that would have escalated into more violence had the war not ended as it did.

Afterword

Slave resistance in nineteenth-century Florida, while reflecting many similarities with respect to experiences reported for bondpeople in other southern states, nonetheless differed significantly. But what made Florida bondservants and their experiences unusual? The fact was that Florida's history, geography, and topography combined to set a unique stage for its rebels and runaways. Unlike other southern states, Florida boasted a matchless history as a runaway slave haven, the reality of which changed little over time, at least until the final countdown to the Civil War. Freedom-seeking bondpeople knew about and had sought refuge in its numerous runaway settlements and vast, virtually unpopulated expanses dating back centuries to the opening of the Spanish era. Maroon communities eventually dotted the peninsula, their existence making resistance possible and revolts more likely to succeed. In these settlements, black runaways and their descendants could live free lives while providing for their families as they persisted in a commitment to defend loved ones, if necessary, unto death.

Running counter to Florida's role as a beacon of freedom was the growth of its Middle Florida plantation belt in the decades following cession to the United States in 1821. The desire for cheap land to grow cash crops such as cotton attracted increasing numbers of slaveholders from the Upper and Lower South. While remaining relatively small overall, the territory and state's population nonetheless increased at a pace that made it one of the fastest growing states in the South by the 1840s. As a result, on the eve of the Civil War, almost half of all Floridians were enslaved blacks who lived in proximity to Atlantic world havens, where freedom beckoned under the rule of law or else through the individual and collective initiative of runaways.

Florida slaveholders meanwhile well knew Florida's history and the encouragement given by it to slave resistance and rebellion. With the added influence of the exploitative nature of the peculiar institution, they accordingly faced daily challenges from a rapidly growing dissident army of bondpeople significantly unlike others in the South. So, to accomplish their goal of maximizing profits through the use of enslaved labor, Florida masters—especially those in Middle Florida, where most such laborers lived—ruthlessly sought to control the labor and movement of these dissenters and potential revolters. They would accomplish this objective, by and large, through their control and manipulation of the slave family. Much of the time, their aims were achieved, but at other times, they were not.

For Florida bondservants, as with many of those who lived in other places, the family and family values meant a great deal indeed. In the circumstances, conflict between owners and those who were owned stemmed at times from desires for autonomy in family matters. After 1831, when slavery became a "positive good" in the eyes of many supporters of the institution, the treatment of bondpeople and the slave family by masters ameliorated somewhat. This change over time continued in and after the 1840s as slaveholders grew more keenly aware of how to use the family to control an ever-growing and potentially subversive population. While owners and masters might attempt to direct every aspect of their lives and those of their family members, bondservants comprehended that slave owners often were masquerading as paternalists by pretending to care about slave welfare.[1]

Day-to-day realities, they saw, indicated something far different, just as gut-wrenching, soul-tearing forced separation from loved ones added memories that could not be erased with time. Many bondservants well recalled being separated from family members and uprooted by avaricious owners intent upon dislocation at their slaves' expense in order to better the quality of life for themselves and their white families. The record plainly illustrates that forcible dislocation of thousands of men, women, and children to Florida permanently disrupted countless families. Over time, though, most did manage to rebuild families, despite the challenges. Still, those men and women understood that, as a rule, profit-minded masters cared little for them or their children except as commodities and property to be worked, bought, and sold. Had their paternalism run true, after all, how would masters have explained requiring most bondpeople to work from sunup to sundown, leaving them little time for child-rearing duties or other responsibilities, not to mention pleasures, within their own families?[2]

Resistance naturally resulted. Among other means, persons held in bondage used their labor to bargain with masters for themselves and their families, whether they did so openly or tacitly. Florida bondwomen might challenge, for instance, the long hours they were forced to work in the households of their masters as cooks, servants, and nannies. They knew this unbearable working arrangement left little time for them to rear their own children. Some rebelled openly against work routines involving care of their masters' children. Sometimes through mild and discreet acts of dissidence and at other times through openly aggressive confrontations, women strove to reject the manner in which slaveholders exploited their bodies as well as their labor. By such means of resistance, individuals sought a measure of justice in an unjust society.[3]

Indeed, Florida dissenters and rebels manifested in mighty ways their willingness to fight to protect and provide for their families. They endeavored in the process to maintain the integrity and substance of the slave family, possibly at all costs. There were a variety of measures taken in pursuit of such goals. For one thing, impressive numbers of persons left farms, plantations, and shops in search of family members and did so despite the odds arrayed against them. Runaways such as these reflected practices seen through the South, but there were real differences as well. To cite an example, unlike other eighteenth- and nineteenth-century southern runaways, Florida fugitives tended to take several changes of clothes with them. This hinted at two basic characteristics: resourcefulness coupled with a spirit of independence and creative insight that aimed to confuse owners into giving inaccurate descriptions of what those who fled were wearing at the time they absconded.

Flight might involve long distances, but more typically absconders stayed relatively close to home. Since many were searching for loved ones and family members, it made sense that most would seek havens in nearby counties and communities relatively near to their farm or plantation homes. Loved ones often, though, exerted their pull across regional and state lines, as a consequence of which more than a few persons bravely fled to another slave state farther north while others strove to reach a free state in the North. In the end, some fugitives successfully escaped to other states and managed to reunite with loved ones and family members. Most, unfortunately, did not.

Along gender lines, bondwomen might not have absconded as frequently as did their male counterparts, but they tended to act more quickly and openly than did the men to confront authority figures when they disagreed with them. The hesitancy to flee is easily understandable. Women bore responsibility for children, and they did not desire to leave their children behind. During flight, children slowed absconders down, a fact that reduced the odds on a successful escape.

Florida's runaways differed from their southern counterparts in another and nearly unparalleled manner. Many East and West Florida fugitives possessed an

Atlantic worldview or at least a sense that freedom lay either across the water or through use of the water. Within the territory and state, land blended into water and vice versa, especially in the peninsula. Most regional studies of runaways have concluded that the majority of fugitive slaves who tried to leave the South fled on foot and perhaps utilized the Underground Railroad to lead them to a free state in the North or Midwest. Florida again represented an exception. Interestingly, one in every five Florida fugitives used the various waterways and port towns of the peninsula in making their escapes, the larger Atlantic world having worked an indelible and long-lasting impact on nineteenth-century slave resistance in Florida.[4]

The history and topography of Florida provides the answer why. Dating back to the Spanish era and the 1500s, blacks in Florida had possessed knowledge about and were comfortable using water for travel and commerce, including the international waters of the Atlantic, the Caribbean Sea, and the Gulf of Mexico. Again going back centuries, some had labored as pilots, seamen, and skilled artisans in the maritime industries of East and West Florida, and, to say the least, they knew something about the outside world. Not surprisingly, their nineteenth-century counterparts and those influenced by their nineteenth-century counterparts—as acculturated, self-assured, and knowledgeable individuals—sought freedom over or along the water, even beyond the confines of the United States. The Underground Railroad for these men, women, and children led not farther north but farther south. And, in pursuit of the dream of freedom to the south, many succeeded in obtaining their prize, including those who reached the free British colony of the Bahamas.[5]

Unlike the experience in some other southern locales, abolitionists factored little in the Florida equation. Put another way, Florida fugitives could not rely on the assistance of abolitionists. Absconders who sought to use their feet, the river, the coast, or the high seas to make their escapes did so largely on their own. That is not to argue that slaveholders were not convinced of the diabolical impact that abolitionists were having on their bondservants. White society endured divisions, though, over the enforcement of slave codes and the degree of abolitionist influence. This represented at times a class distinction, but more significantly it was a geographical one. East and, to a lesser extent, West Florida rebels and runaways enjoyed more success in securing freedom and waging revolt than did their Middle Florida counterparts. Different customs and traditions influenced those regions, and the institution of slavery generally rested on other and somewhat weaker foundations.[6]

As opposed to typical West and East Florida bondservants, those who lived in Middle Florida tended to remain on their plantations or farms or in their communities. Few traveled after their relocation to the territory and state; fewer, therefore, held an Atlantic world perspective. This state of affairs served regional slaveholders well in controlling their labor forces. Plus, slave owners strove more or less successfully to combat class divisions within white society by using race and the illusion of "common-man democracy" to manipulate non-slaveholders into working against their personal interests through support of an economic and social system that largely kept the majority of them, literally, dirt poor. The approach worked for the most part at most times. Middle Florida might have possessed a black majority of residents but nonetheless was a white man's country. This fact and, alternatively, the fragility of the system both were evidenced in the manner in which slave patrollers and slave catchers did, or did not, effectively serve their intended purposes.

Florida proved atypical in an additional way. Where word or rumors of revolts circulated generally through the early nineteenth century, open race war erupted in Florida—twice. One conflict became known as the First Seminole War of 1817–18. The other, what this study refers to as the Black/Indian Rebellion, was more commonly called the Second Seminole War of 1835–42. Hundreds, if not thousands, of runaways and rebels fought for freedom by participating in the largest, deadliest, and costliest race war combined with slave rebellion seen in American history. Here again, Florida's uniqueness as a runaway slave haven dotted with maroon communities served the revolt and the rebels well, helping to make the experience for whites and their army and militia protectors at times a living hell. Given their understanding of topography and geography, these insurgents waged a protracted revolt that ended in concessions largely favoring their cause. Unlike other antebellum revolts that ended with the deaths or hangings of surviving rebels, many of these men and women secured freedom for themselves and their families, as well as safe passage to the West. The aftermath, needless to say, stirred an enduring impact on race relations and Florida's development for generations to come.[7]

Generally speaking, most white Floridians and concerned government officials knew full well that a key to increasing the white population and with it the expansion of Florida and western territories centered squarely on controlling slave resistance. Had Florida's enslaved rebels and runaways secured permanent and autonomous settlements in the peninsula, their triumph would have sent a clear and chilling message to whites and offered encouragement and hope to slaves everywhere in the nation. A greater number of enslaved blacks hungry for freedom would have made their way to Florida to join the various maroon and runaway communities as already had occurred in years past. Meanwhile, race-conscious whites, fearing that they would be overrun and possibly killed by vengeful black migrants, would have fled Florida for safer and better-protected territories. Indeed, had the success of the Black/Indian

Rebellion resulted in free and autonomous settlements for Florida's rebels and runaways, the peninsular landscape and, thereby, the history of the nation would have evolved in a significantly different manner than what occurred.

Where the public policy of the United States could have served the cause of freedom in Florida even prior to its cession by Spain, until the Civil War it reinforced and, at times, actively defended the institution of slavery and the interests of slaveholders. Ultimately, the military undertook during the Second Seminole War an all-out effort to completely subordinate blacks in the peninsula, whether slave or free. Not until 1862 was any significant difference seen. Left to their own devices, many enslaved Floridians meanwhile embraced agency in order to ensure their treatment as human beings in an inhumane society. And much as many of them had done during the Black/Indian Rebellion, more than one thousand Florida bondservants demonstrated their continuing courage and resolve when the Civil War came by participating actively with the Union army and navy in furtherance of their freedom and the freedom of their loved ones.

As they put on the uniforms worn in years past by the guarantors of their slavery, men such as Private Thomas Long knew the world was rapidly changing around them. Like other slaves, Long yearned to be a part of—an agent of—that change. He did not want America to develop selective amnesia and write out the contributions of black men and women to the Civil War and the cause of freedom. That is why he, in particular, wanted his words written down by his superior officer so that future generations could read and remember his efforts and those of his comrades in arms. As one historian noted, Long and others fought like "devils" for their freedom. Just as the South wanted to secede from the Union, so too did enslaved blacks want to secede from their masters in the slave South. Florida bondpeople understood, many of them early on, that the Civil War would prove a watershed in their lives. They prayed for the Union to win the war so that they could leave their masters, for most in their struggle for freedom struggled also with bitter memories of their days in bondage.[8]

Given Florida's venerable history as a beacon of freedom and a haven for runaways, its geography and topography, its setting for the largest, deadliest, and costliest race war and slave revolt in American history, and its enslaved inhabitants with an Atlantic world view, Florida's rebels and runaways resisted with mindsets, perceptions, and aims that differed significantly from those of their southern counterparts. Or did they? Without careful examination on the micro level, can we rest easily with general conclusions drawn from the macro standard? Florida's experience provides a test, and that test appears to have found inconsistencies and contradictions. Now, additional studies of nineteenth-century slave resistance are needed to focus on individual southern states and even regional experiences within individual states.

But one thing remains certain. Enslaved Floridians resisted and rebelled. They continued to do so far and wide, when and how they could, until the goal of freedom was achieved. Even when freedom came between 1862 and 1865, the history of the contentious relationship between the former master and the former slave would continue to be played out through race conflicts and violent collisions. That state of affairs, in time, would work an enduring impact on race relations in Florida and, with it, the South and the United States. Indeed, the long and complex saga of Florida's rebels and runaways forms a key element to understanding the history of the nation.

Notes

Introduction

1. John Hope Franklin and Loren Schweninger, *Runaway Slaves: Rebels on the Plantation* (New York: Oxford University Press, 1999), xv. For a similar study completed seven years earlier from a state perspective, see Freddie L. Parker's *Running for Freedom: Slave Runaways in North Carolina 1775–1840* (New York: Routledge, 1993). See also Freddie L. Parker, ed., *Stealing a Little Freedom: Advertisements for Slave Runaways in North Carolina, 1791–1840* (New York: Garland, 1994).

2. Jane Landers, *Black Society in Spanish Florida* (Urbana: University of Illinois Press, 1999), 4.

3. Ibid., 5–6, 45–60.

4. Larry Eugene Rivers, *Slavery in Florida: Territorial Days to Emancipation* (Gainesville: University Press of Florida, 2000).

5. James M. Denham, *"A Rogue's Paradise": Crime and Punishment in Antebellum Florida, 1821–1861* (Tuscaloosa: University of Alabama Press, 1997).

6. *American State Papers: Military Affairs*, 7 vols. (Washington, D.C.: Gales and Seaton, 1832–60), 7:820–21.

7. Walter Johnson, "On Agency," *Journal of Social History* 37 (Fall 2003): 113–24.

Chapter 1. Day-to-Day Resistance

1. See, for example, John P. DuVal, *Compilation of Public Acts of the Legislative Council of the Territory of Florida Passed Prior to 1840* (Tallahassee: Samuel S. Sibley, 1839), 216–28; Leslie Thompson, *A Manual or Digest of the Statute Law of the State of Florida, of a General and Public Character, in Force at the End of the Second Session of the General Assembly of the State, on the Sixth Day of January, 1847* (Boston: C.C. Little and J. Brown, 1847), 537–42; and James M. Denham, *"A Rogue's Paradise": Crime and Punishment in Antebellum Florida, 1821–1861* (Tuscaloosa: University of Alabama Press, 1997), 121.

2. Kenneth M. Stampp, *The Peculiar Institution: Slavery in the Ante-bellum South* (New York: Alfred A. Knopf, 1956; reprinted, New York: Vintage Books, 1964), 34–85, 156. See, for example, John W. Blassingame, *The Slave Community: Plantation Life in the Antebellum South*, 2nd ed. (New York: Oxford University Press, 1979); Al-Tony Gilmore, ed., *Revisiting Blassingame's "The Slave Community": The Scholars Respond* (Westport, Conn.: Greenwood Press, 1978); George P. Rawick, *From Sundown to Sunup: The Making of the Black Community* (Westport, Conn.: Greenwood Press, 1972); George P. Rawick, *The American Slave: A Composite Autobiography*, 41 vols. (Westport, Conn.: Greenwood Press, 1972–79); Donald M. Jacobs, ed., *Index to "The American Slave"* (Westport, Conn.: Greenwood Press, 1981); Eugene D. Genovese, *Roll, Jordan, Roll: The World the Slaves Made* (New York: Pantheon Books, 1974); Eugene D. Genovese, "American Slaves and Their History," in *Red and Black: Marxian Explorations in Southern and Afro-American History*, ed. Eugene D. Genovese (New York: Pantheon Books, 1968), 102–28; Eugene D. Genovese, "Rebelliousness and Docility in the Negro Slave: A Critique of Elkins' Thesis," *Civil War History* 13 (December 1967): 293–314; Eugene D. Genovese, *From Revolution to Rebellion: Afro-American Slave Revolts in the Making of the Modern World* (Baton Rouge: Louisiana State University Press, 1979); John Hope Franklin and Loren Schweninger, *Runaway Slaves: Rebels on the Plantation* (New York: Oxford University Press, 1999); John Hope Franklin and Alfred A. Moss Jr., *From Slavery to Freedom: A History of African Americans* (New York: Alfred A. Knopf, 1947; New York: Alfred A. Knopf, 1994); Donnie D. Bellamy, "Slavery in Microcosm: Onslow County, North Carolina," *Journal of Negro History* 62 (October 1977): 339–50; William Dusinberre, *Them Dark Days: Slavery in the American Rice Swamps* (New York: Oxford University Press, 1996); Paul D. Escott, *Slavery Remembered: A Record of Twentieth-Century Slave Narratives* (Chapel Hill: University of North Carolina Press, 1979); Daniel Flanigan, "The Criminal Law of Slavery and Freedom" (Ph.D. diss., Rice University, 1973); Daniel Flanigan, "Criminal Procedure in Slave Trials in the Antebellum South," *Journal of Southern History* 40 (November 1974): 537–64; Herbert G. Gutman, *The Black Family in Slavery and Freedom, 1750–1925* (New York: Pantheon Books, 1976); Jesse J. Jackson, "Negro and the Law in Florida, 1821–1921" (master's thesis, Florida State University, 1960); Jacqueline Jones, *Labor of Love, Labor of Sorrow: Black Women, Work, and the Family from Slavery to the Present* (New York: Basic Books, 1985); Charles Joyner, *Down by the Riverside: A South Carolina Slave Community* (Urbana: University of Illinois Press, 1984); Charles Joyner, "The World of the Plantation Slaves," in *Before Freedom Came: African American Life in the Antebellum South*, ed. Edward D. C. Campbell Jr. and Kym S. Price (Charlottesville: University of Virginia Press, 1991), 51–100; Wilma King, *Stolen Childhood: Slave Youth in Nineteenth-Century America* (Bloomington: Indiana University Press, 1995); Ann J. Lane, ed., *The Debate over Slavery: Stanley Elkins and His Critics* (Urbana: University of Illinois Press, 1971); Daniel F. Littlefield, *Africans and Seminoles: From Removal to Emancipation* (Westport, Conn.: Greenwood Press, 1977); Daniel C. Littlefield, *Rice and Slaves: Ethnicity and the Slave Trade in Colonial South Carolina* (Baton Rouge: Louisiana State University Press, 1981); Philip D. Morgan, *Slave Counterpoint: Black Culture in the Eighteenth-Century Chesapeake and Lowcountry* (Chapel Hill: University of North Carolina Press, 1998); Ira Berlin, *Many Thousands Gone: The First Two Centuries of Slavery in North America* (Cambridge: Harvard University Press, 1998); Julia Floyd Smith, *Slavery and Plantation Growth in Antebellum Florida, 1821–1860* (Gainesville: University Press of Florida, 1973); E. P.

Southall, "Negroes in Florida Prior to the Civil War," *Journal of Negro History* 19 (January 1934): 77–86; Brenda E. Stevenson, "Distress and Discord in Virginia Slave Families, 1830–1860," in *Joy and in Sorrow: Women, Family, and Marriage in the Victorian South, 1830–1900*, ed. Carol Bleser (New York: Oxford University Press, 1991), 103–24; Brenda E. Stevenson, *Life in Black and White: Family and Community in the Slave South* (New York: Oxford University Press, 1996); Deborah Gray White, *Ar'n't I a Woman? Female Slaves in the Plantation South* (New York: W. W. Norton and Company, 1985); Peter H. Wood, *Black Majority: Negroes in Colonial South Carolina from 1670 through the Stono Rebellion* (New York: Alfred A. Knopf, 1974; New York: W. W. Norton and Company, 1975); Bertram Wyatt-Brown, "Mask of Obedience: Male Slave Psychology in the Old South," *American Historical Review* 93 (1988): 1228–52; Jeffrey Robert Young, *Domesticating Slavery: The Master Class in Georgia and South Carolina, 1670–1837* (Chapel Hill: University of North Carolina Press, 1999); Kenneth M. Stampp, "Rebels and Sambos: The Search for the Negro Personality in Slavery," *Journal of Southern History* 37 (August 1971): 367–92.

3. Dusinberre, *Them Dark Days*, 122–23. See also George M. Fredrickson and Christopher Lasch, "Resistance to Slavery," *Civil War History* 4 (December 1967): 315–29.

4. Gerald W. Mullin, *Flight and Rebellion: Slave Resistance in Eighteenth-Century Virginia* (New York: Oxford University Press, 1972); Blassingame, *Slave Community*; Merton Dillon, *Slavery Attacked: Southern Slaves and Their Allies, 1619–1865* (Baton Rouge: Louisiana State University Press, 1990); Douglas R. Egerton, *Gabriel's Rebellion: The Virginia Slave Conspiracies of 1800 and 1802* (Chapel Hill: University of North Carolina Press, 1993); Douglas R. Egerton, *He Shall Go Out Free: The Lives of Denmark Vesey*, 2nd ed. (Lanham, Md.: Rowan and Littlefield, 2004).

5. Flanigan, "Criminal Law of Slavery and Freedom"; Flanigan, "Criminal Procedure in Slave Trials in the Antebellum South"; Smith, *Slavery and Plantation Growth*, 101–21.

6. Franklin and Schweninger, *Runaway Slaves*, 1–16.

7. See, for example, Canter Brown Jr., *African Americans on the Tampa Bay Frontier* (Tampa: Tampa Bay History Center, 1996); Canter Brown Jr., *Florida's Peace River Frontier* (Orlando: University of Central Florida Press, 1991); Canter Brown Jr. and Barbara Gray Brown, *Family Records of the African-American Pioneers of Tampa and Hillsborough County* (Tampa: University of Tampa Press, 2003); Larry Eugene Rivers, *Slavery in Florida: Territorial Days to Emancipation* (Gainesville: University Press of Florida, 2000).

8. Rawick, *Florida Slave Narratives*, 253–54.

9. Some Florida slaveholders had purchased enslaved blacks from both Atlantic and domestic slave traders; Benjamin Chaires, a large slaveholder who settled in Leon County, was one such person. See Benjamin Chaires to Thomas Fitch, July 1820, folder 11, Thomas Fitch Papers, Florida State Archives, Tallahassee. See also, for example, Edward W. Baptist, *Creating an Old South: Middle Florida's Plantation Frontier before the Civil War* (Chapel Hill: University of North Carolina Press, 2002), 67–72; Stevenson, *Life in Black and White*, 218–25; Herbert G. Gutman, *Slavery and the Numbers Game: A Critique of "Time on the Cross"* (Urbana: University of Illinois Press, 1975); and Walter L. Johnson, *Soul by Soul: Inside the Antebellum Slave Market* (Cambridge: Harvard University Press, 1999), 45–77.

10. Baptist, *Creating an Old South*, 67–72; William Wirt Papers, Maryland Historical Society, Baltimore (hereafter, Wirt Papers); Frances Elizabeth Brown Douglass Memoirs, folder 19, Florida State University Strozier Library Special Collections, Tallahassee; Brown

Memoir, Florida folder 1, Ambler-Brown Papers, Duke University, Durham, N.C.; Joan Cashin, *A Family Venture: Men and Women on the Southern Frontier* (Baltimore: Johns Hopkins University Press, 1991), 57.

11. Laura Randall to Elizabeth Wirt, February 9, July 11, 1828, Ellen McCormick to Laura Randall, October 12, 1842, Wirt Papers; Albert J. Raboteau, *Slave Religion: The "Invisible Institution" in the Antebellum South* (New York: Oxford University Press, 1978); Larry E. Rivers, "Slavery in Microcosm: Leon County, Florida, 1824 to 1860," *Journal of Negro History* 66 (Fall 1981): 235–45; Larry E. Rivers, "Baptist Minister James Page: Alternatives for African American Leadership in Post–Civil War Florida," in *Florida's Heritage of Diversity: Essays in Honor of Samuel Proctor*, ed. Mark I. Greenberg, William Warren Rogers, and Canter Brown Jr. (Tallahassee: Sentry Press, 1997), 43–54.

12. Ulrich Bonnell Phillips and James David Glunt, eds., *Florida Plantation Records from the Papers of George Noble Jones* (St. Louis: Missouri Historical Society, 1927; Gainesville: University Press of Florida, 2006), 131.

13. Ibid., 97–110.

14. Ibid., 112–14.

15. Franklin and Schweninger, *Runaway Slaves,* 182–289; Rivers, *Slavery in Florida.*

16. See Susan Bradford Eppes, *The Negro of the Old South: A Bit of Period History* (Chicago: Joseph Branch, 1925).

17. Joshua Hoyet Frier Journal, pp. 35–36, Florida State Archives, Tallahassee; Eppes, *Negro of the Old South*, 89–90; *St. Augustine Florida Herald*, February 3, 1830.

18. William E. Kilcrease Inventory, May 26, 1860, file 1005, Gadsden County Probate Records, Gadsden County Courthouse, Quincy, Fla.; Alexander S. Webb to Dearest Wife, January 3, 1855, Alexander Stewart Webb Papers, Yale University Library, New Haven, Conn.

19. Phillips and Glunt, *Florida Plantation Records,* 154; Henry Wirt to Elizabeth Wirt, September 13, 1841, Wirt Papers; Amon DeLaughter Journal, entry of March 19, 1857, transcript in collection of Elizabeth H. Sims, Madison County, Fla., xerographic copy in collection of the author.

20. Louis Goldsborough to Elizabeth Wirt Goldsborough, January 2, 1833, August 31, 1835, Louis Goldsborough Papers, Library of Congress, Washington, D.C.

21. Amon DeLaughter Journal, entries of February 16, 1854, and February 19, 1857; John Gamble Diary, Jefferson County Historical Society, Monticello, Fla.

22. Amon DeLaughter Journal, entries of February 16, 1854, and February 19, 1857; William E. Kilcrease Inventory, May 26, 1860; Will of H. Todd, July 15, 1833, file 1806, Miscellaneous Notes, Papers, and Receipts, Gadsden County Probate Records.

23. Eppes, *Negro of the Old South,* 89–90.

24. Jones, *Labor of Love, Labor of Sorrow*, 31.

25. Ellen McCormick to Catharine Wirt, June 14, September 10, 1843, Wirt Papers. See also Randolph B. Campbell, *An Empire for Slavery: The Peculiar Institution in Texas* (Baton Rouge: Louisiana State University Press, 1989), 124.

26. Ellen McCormick to Family, March 18, September 8, 1841, Wirt Papers; Orlando Patterson, *Slavery and Social Death* (Cambridge: Harvard University Press, 1982), 21–17.

27. Ibid., Ellen McCormick to Catharine Wirt, October 1, 1843, Ellen McCormick to Family, March 18, September 8, 1843.

28. Charles Ball, *Fifty Years in Chains; or, The Life of an American Slave* (Indianapolis: Dayton and Asher, 1858), 122–26, 196–200; La Roy Sunderland, *Anti-Slavery Manual Containing A Collection of Facts and Arguments on American Slavery* (New York: S. W. Benedict, 1837), 72.

29. See, for example, Jones, *Labor of Love, Labor of Sorrow*, 11–43.

30. Ibid., 27.

31. Ibid.; Laura Randall to Elizabeth Wirt, February 9, July 11, 1828, Ellen McCormick to Laura Randall, October 12, 1842, Ellen McCormick to Catharine Wirt, October 1, 1843, Wirt Papers.

Chapter 2. Stepping Up the Degrees of Resistance

1. Eugene D. Genovese, *Roll, Jordan, Roll: The World the Slaves Made* (New York: Pantheon Books, 1974), 423; Wilma King, *Stolen Childhood: Slave Youth in Nineteenth-Century America* (Bloomington: Indiana University Press, 1995), 109.

2. See, for example, John David Smith's excellent introduction for information on Evans's sexual relationship with the woman slave named Mariah in Ulrich Bonnell Phillips and James David Glunt, eds., *Florida Plantation Records from the Papers of George Noble Jones* (St. Louis: Missouri Historical Society, 1927; Gainesville: University Press of Florida, 2006), xxvi–xxvii.

3. Ibid., 78, 80, 111–12.

4. Arch Fredric Blakey, Ann Smith Lainhart, and Winston Bryant Stephens Jr., eds., *Rose Cottage Chronicles: Civil War Letters of the Bryant-Stephens Families of North Florida* (Gainesville: University Press of Florida, 1998), 75–77; Phillips and Glunt, *Florida Plantation Records*, 78–80.

5. Petition of Frances C. Blitch, July 17, 1860, Probate Packets, Records of the Probate Court, Marion County, Fla., (available on microfilm at Florida State Archives, Tallahassee).

6. See, for example, John Hope Franklin and Loren Schweninger, *Runaway Slaves: Rebels on the Plantation* (New York: Oxford University Press, 1999), 252–56; and Blakey, Lainhart, and Stephens, *Rose Cottage Chronicles*, 77.

7. Blakey, Lainhart, and Stephens, *Rose Cottage Chronicles*, 281–83.

8. James M. Denham and Keith L. Huneycutt, eds., *Echoes from a Distant Frontier: The Brown Sisters' Correspondence from Antebellum Florida* (Columbia: University of South Carolina Press, 2004), 119–20.

9. Ralph B. Flanders, *Plantation Slavery in Georgia* (Chapel Hill: University of North Carolina Press, 1933; Cos Cob, Conn.: John E. Edwards, 1967), 122; John W. Blassingame, *The Slave Community: Plantation Life in the Antebellum South*, 2nd ed. (New York: Oxford University Press, 1979); Genovese, *Roll, Jordon, Roll*; James Oakes, *The Ruling Race: A History of American Slaveholders* (New York: Alfred A. Knopf, 1998), 22–23; Philip D. Morgan, *Slave Counterpoint: Black Culture in the Eighteenth-Century Chesapeake and Lowcountry* (Chapel Hill: University of North Carolina Press, 1998).

10. On health challenges faced by enslaved women, see, for example, Deborah Gray White, *Ar'n't I a Woman? Female Slaves in the Plantation South* (New York: W. W. Norton and Company, 1985); Brenda E. Stevenson, *Life in Black and White: Family and Community in the Slave South* (New York: Oxford University Press, 1996); King, *Stolen Childhood*; Maria

Jenkins Schwartz, *Born in Bondage: Growing Up Enslaved in the Antebellum South* (Cambridge: Harvard University Press, 2000); Blassingame, *Slave Community*; and Genovese, *Roll, Jordon, Roll.*

11. Deborah Gray White, "Female Slaves in the Plantation South," in *Before Freedom Came: African American Life in the Antebellum South*, ed. Edward D. C. Campbell Jr. and Kym S. Price (Charlottesville: University of Virginia Press, 1991), 110–11.

12. "Diary and Other Papers of William D. Moseley: 1848–1857," 32–35, typescript in Florida Collection, Florida State University, Tallahassee; Linda Brent [pen name of Harriet Jacobs], *Incidents in the Life of a Slave Girl*, ed. L. Maria Child (Boston: Stereotype Foundry, 1861), 34, 39; George P. Rawick, *The American Slave: A Composite Autobiography*, 41 vols. (Westport, Conn.: Greenwood Press, 1972–79), vol. 17, *Florida Slave Narratives*, 166–67. For detailed discussion of consenting and non-consenting relationships between whites and blacks, see, for example, Amon DeLaughter Journal, entry of December 25, 1855, transcript in collection of Elizabeth H. Sims, Madison County, Fla., xerographic copy in collection of the author; Frederick Douglass, *Narrative of the Life of Frederick Douglass* (1836; Upper Saddle River, N.J.: Gregg Press, 1968); Harriet Jacobs, *Incidents in the Life of a Slave Girl* (1861; Cambridge: Harvard University Press, 1987); Brenda E. Stevenson, *Life in Black and White: Family and Community in the Slave South* (New York: Oxford University Press, 1996); Brenda E. Stevenson, "Sally's Choice? Questionable Liaisons and Family Relations," *Journal of African American History* 96 (Summer 2011): 394–405; Winthrop D. Jordon, *White over Black: American Attitudes toward the Negro, 1550–1812* (Chapel Hill: University of North Carolina Press, 1968); Werner Sollors, *Neither Black nor White Yet Both: Thematic Explorations of Interracial Literature* (New York: Oxford University Press, 1997); Elise Lemire, *"Miscegenation": Making Race in America* (Philadelphia: University of Pennsylvania Press, 2002); Annette Gordon-Reed, *Thomas Jefferson and Sally Hemings: An American Controversy* (Charlottesville: University of Virginia Press, 1998); Annette Gordon-Reed, *The Hemingses of Monticello: An American Family* (New York: W. W. Norton, 2008); Larry E. Rivers, *Slavery in Florida: Territorial Days to Emancipation* (Gainesville: University Press of Florida, 2000), 155–61; Canter Brown Jr., *Florida's Peace River Frontier* (Orlando: University of Central Florida Press, 1991), 102–3, 113, 319, 337; Spessard Stone, "Profile of Lloyd Davis," *Sunland Tribune* 17 (November 1991): 25–26; Virginia W. Westergard and Kyle S. Van Landingham, *Parker and Blount in Florida* (Okeechobee, Fla.: private publisher, 1983), 83–89, 160–60; Daina Ramey Berry, *"Swing the Sickle for the Harvest Is Ripe": Gender and Slavery in Antebellum Georgia* (Urbana: University of Illinois Press, 2007), 91.

13. Alexander Randall to Elizabeth Wirt, September 11, 1841, William Wirt Papers, Maryland Historical Society, Baltimore.

14. Phillips and Glunt, *Florida Plantation Records*, 71–72; Alexander Randall to Elizabeth Wirt, September 11, 1841, Wirt Papers.

15. Kathryn T. Abbey, "Documents Relating to El Destino and Chemonie Plantations, Middle Florida, 1828–1868, Part 4," *Florida Historical Quarterly* 8 (October 1929): 80.

16. Charles W. Bannerman Diaries, entries from October 9, 1847, to July 30, 1852, Florida State University Strozier Library Special Collections, Tallahassee.

17. Louis Goldsborough to William Wirt, February 1, 1834, Wirt Papers; John Gamble Diary, Jefferson County Historical Society, Monticello, Fla.

18. Alexander Randall to William Wirt, April 3, October 14, 1842, Thomas Randall to

William Wirt, April 13, October 14, 1828, Elizabeth Wirt to Laura Randall, October 12, 1837, Ellen McCormick to Elizabeth Wirt, July 14, 1844, Ellen Voss to Catharine Wirt, September 4, 1839, Wirt Papers; Abbey, "Documents Relating to El Destino and Chemonie Plantations," 195.

19. See Rivers, *Slavery in Florida*; Orlando Patterson, *Slavery and Social Death* (Cambridge: Harvard University Press, 1982), 21–27; Genovese, *Roll, Jordon, Roll*; Deborah Gray White, "Female Slaves: Sex Roles and Status in the Antebellum Plantation South," *Journal of Family History* 8 (Fall 1983): 248–61.

20. See, for example, Herbert G. Gutman, *The Black Family in Slavery and Freedom, 1750–1925* (New York: Pantheon Books, 1976); Genovese, *Roll, Jordon, Roll*; Charles Joyner, *Down by the Riverside: A South Carolina Slave Community* (Urbana: University of Illinois Press, 1984); Leslie Howard Owens, *This Species of Property: Slave Life and Culture in the Old South* (New York: Oxford University Press, 1976); King, *Stolen Childhood*; Schwartz, *Born in Bondage*; Achille Murat, *The United States of North America* (London: Effingham Wilson, 1833), 92–93.

21. Thomas Randall to William Wirt, December 20, 1828, November 20, 1829, Wirt Papers; Lacy K. Ford, *Deliver Us from Evil: The Slavery Questions in the Old South* (New York: Oxford University Press, 2009), 147–48.

22. Thomas Randall to William Wirt, December 20, 1828, November 20, 1829, Wirt Papers. For excellent studies of free and enslaved settlers moving to Florida from the more established older states to the North, see Edward E. Baptist, "The Migration of Planters to Antebellum Florida: Kinship and Power," *Journal of Southern History* 62 (August 1996): 527–54; William W. Rogers Sr. and Erica R. Clark, *The Croom Family and Goodwood Plantation: Land, Litigation, and Southern Lives* (Athens: University of Georgia Press, 1999).

23. Kingsley G. Gibbs Journal, 1840–43, especially December 25, 1841, p. 24, Florida State University Strozier Library Special Collections, Tallahassee. For an excellent conceptualization of the Atlantic world from 1400 to 1888, see Douglas R. Egerton, Alison Games, Jane G. Landers, Kris Lane, and Donald R. Wright, *The Atlantic World: A History, 1400–1888* (Wheeling: Harlan Davidson, 2007).

24. Gibbs Journal, 1840–43, December 25, 1841, pp. 21–24.

25. Gerald W. Mullin, *Flight and Rebellion: Slave Resistance in Eighteenth-Century Virginia* (New York: Oxford University Press, 1972).

Chapter 3. Away without Leave

1. *St. Augustine East Florida Herald,* February 10, 1830.

2. Ibid., October 16, 1824; *Columbus (Ga.) Enquirer*, August 8, 1834, January 16, October 30, 1835, January 12, 1837.

3. *Tallahassee Floridian*, January 18, 1834.

4. *St. Augustine East Florida Herald,* February 10, 1830.

5. Amon DeLaughter numbered among the many authority figures who seemed more concerned about his slaves—as well as those from neighboring plantations—lurking around on his estate than they did about slaves running away. Amon DeLaughter Journal, February 1854–October 1860, transcript in collection of Elizabeth H. Sims, Madison County, Fla., xerographic copy in collection of the author. See also Ulrich Bonnell Phillips and James

David Glunt, eds., *Florida Plantation Records from the Papers of George Noble Jones* (St. Louis: Missouri Historical Society, 1927; Gainesville: University Press of Florida, 2006), 1–174; Susan Bradford Eppes, *The Negro of the Old South: A Bit of Period History* (Chicago: Joseph Branch, 1925); and Susan Bradford Eppes, *Through Some Eventful Years* (Macon, Ga.: J. W. Burke Company, 1926).

6. Charles W. Bannerman Diaries, October 9, 1847–July 30, 1852, Florida State University Strozier Library Special Collections, Tallahassee; DeLaughter Journal, February 1851–February 1857; Louis Goldsborough Papers, various correspondence, 1930–1834, Library of Congress, Washington, D.C.

7. *St. Augustine Florida Herald,* July 1, 1835; *Tallahassee Floridian and Journal,* July 11, 27, 1857.

8. *Jacksonville Courier,* June 25, 1835; miscellaneous papers and notes of Daniel McLaughlin, 1840–43, file box 1836, Gadsden County Courthouse, Gadsden County, Florida.

9. *Tallahassee Floridian,* October 17, 1835; *Jacksonville Florida Republican,* September 22, 1851, February 21, 1856; *St. Augustine East Florida Herald,* April 17, 1824; *St. Augustine Florida Herald,* February 10, 1830, June 16, 1838; *Tallahassee Star of Florida,* May 21, 1840; *Apalachicola Gazette,* February 2, 1839; *Tallahassee Floridian and Journal,* May 10, 1851; Eugene D. Genovese, *Roll, Jordan, Roll: The World the Slaves Made* (New York: Pantheon Books, 1974), 622.

10. William Kauffman Scarborough, *The Overseer: Plantation Management in the Old South* (Baton Rouge: Louisiana State University Press, 1966), 5.

11. Elizabeth H. Sims remembered descendants of the DeLaughters confirming that Amon, the eldest son, started overseeing in early 1851 but always wanted to quit "bossing" the slaves on the property because they sometimes gave him a "fit" when refusing to work. Several at a time would run away during "cotton picking season" to get some temporary relief, although they usually returned after a couple of days. Sims noted also that Amon's mother, Nancy, required him, as the eldest son, to be the man of the house. Thus, overseeing the slaves and property became a part of his duties. Elizabeth H. Sims, interview with the author, July 16, 1988 (notes in collection of the author); see also Amon DeLaughter Journal, October 31, 1854, March 12, September 14, 1855, April 19, August 20, 25, 1856; and *St. Augustine East Florida Herald*, March 22, 1823. For an in-depth, well-researched study of Edgefield, South Carolina, see Orville Vernon Burton, *In My Father's House Are Many Mansions: Family and Community in Edgefield, South Carolina* (Chapel Hill: University of North Carolina Press, 1987).

12. See, for example, Larry E. Rivers, "Madison County, Florida—1830 to 1860: A Case Study in Land, Labor, and Prosperity," *Journal of Negro History* 78 (Fall 1993): 233–44; Amon DeLaughter Journal, March 8, 9, 1858, November 14, 1860.

13. Amon DeLaughter Journal, September 14, 1855, April 19, 1856; Elizabeth H. Sims interview; Phillips and Glunt, *Florida Plantation Records*, 110.

14. See Jane Landers, *Black Society in Spanish Florida* (Urbana: University of Illinois Press, 1999); and Larry Eugene Rivers, *Slavery in Florida: Territorial Days to Emancipation* (Gainesville: University Press of Florida, 2000).

15. *Tallahassee Floridian and Advocate*, September 7, 21, 1829, September 7, 1830; *Tallahassee Floridian*, July 22, 1837, January 10, 1846; *Pensacola Gazette*, April 18, May 2, 1828, April 28, 1829, June 3, 1837; John Gamble Diary, April 1835–November 12, 1836, Jefferson

County Historical Society, Monticello, Fla.; *Tallahassee Florida Sentinel*, December 2, 1845, June 3, 1855. See also Jerrell H. Shofner, *Jefferson County, Florida: A History* (Tallahassee: Sentry Press, 1976), 137–39.

16. Gamble Diary, April 10, 1835–November 12, 1836; *Tallahassee Florida Sentinel*, June 3, 1855. See also Shofner, *Jefferson County*, 137–39.

17. *Pensacola Gazette*, January 16, 1830, February 1, 1840; *Apalachicola Gazette*, November 2, December 21, 1839; *Tallahassee Floridian*, May 4, 1839; *Tallahassee Floridian and Journal*, May 20, 1854.

18. Philip D. Morgan, *Slave Counterpoint: Black Culture in the Eighteenth-Century Chesapeake and Lowcountry* (Chapel Hill: University of North Carolina Press, 1998), 329.

19. Phillips and Glunt, *Florida Plantation Records*, 156–57; will of William Harris, December 20, 1827, Case Style No. 1, Leon County probate records, Leon County Courthouse, Tallahassee, Fla.

20. George P. Rawick, *The American Slave: A Composite Autobiography*, 41 vols. (Westport, Conn: Greenwood Press, 1972–79), vol. 17, *Florida Slave Narratives*, 243–46, 259, 337.

21. Ibid., 17, 35; Jacqueline Jones, *Labor of Love, Labor of Sorrow: Black Women, Work, and the Family from Slavery to the Present* (New York: Basic Books, 1985), 27.

22. John W. Malone File, miscellaneous papers and notes of Jonathan Thomas, case no. 1804-05, and miscellaneous papers and inventory, 1845–49, Gadsden County probate records, Gadsden County Courthouse, Quincy, Fla.; *Tallahassee Florida Watchman*, May 5, 1838; *Tallahassee Floridian and Journal*, September 7, 1850.

23. *Apalachicola Gazette*, April 20, 1839.

24. *Pensacola Gazette*, May 18, 1829, May 1, 1830, July 25, 1840; *Tallahassee Floridian*, August 16, September 2, 1837, July 7, November 3, 1838, September 1840; *Apalachicola Commercial Advertiser*, January 1, March 11, October 19, 1844; *Jacksonville News*, October 13, 1858; Ernest F. Dibble, "Slave Rentals to the Military: Pensacola and the Gulf Coast," *Civil War History* 23 (June 1977): 101–13; Ernest F. Dibble, *Antebellum Pensacola and the Military Presence*, 3 vols. (Pensacola: Pensacola News-Journal, 1974), 1:66; *St. Augustine Florida Gazette*, December 10, 1821.

25. *Quincy Sentinel*, September 18, 1840.

26. *Apalachicola Commercial Advertiser*, March 11, 1844.

27. Landers, *Black Society in Spanish Florida*, 1–6; W. Jeffrey Bolster, *Black Jacks: African American Seamen in the Age of Sail* (Cambridge: Harvard University Press, 1997), 4, 17, 20, 27, 37. For further information on blacks as seafaring men in the Atlantic world, see Roger Morris, *Atlantic Seafaring: Ten Centuries of Exploration and Trade in the North Atlantic* (New York: International Marine Publications, 1992); Gary B. Nash, *Red, White, and Black: The Peoples of Early North America* (Upper Saddle River, N.J.: Prentice Hall, 2000); and Douglas R. Egerton, Alison Games, Jane G. Landers, Kris Lane, and Donald R. Wright, *The Atlantic World: A History, 1400–1888* (Wheeling, W.V.: Harlan Davidson, 2007), 1–38.

28. Landers, Black Society in Spanish Florida, 7–28.

29. *Pensacola Gazette*, May 27, 1837.

30. Landers, *Black Society in Spanish Florida*, 7–28.

31. *Tallahassee Weekly Floridian*, September 2, 1848; *Tallahassee Star of Florida*, September 1, 1843; *Jacksonville Courier*, February 4, 1835; *Tallahassee Floridian and Advocate*, July 12, 1844.

32. Philip M. Hamer, "Great Britain, the United States, and the Negro Seamen Acts, 1822–1848," *Journal of Southern History* 1 (February 1935): 3–28; Philip M. Hamer, "British Consuls and the Negro Seamen Acts, 1850–1860," *Journal of Southern History* 1 (May 1935): 138–68; *Acts of the Legislative Council of the Territory of Florida: Passed at the Tenth Session, Commencing January 2d. and Ending February 12 1832* (Tallahassee: William Wilson, Territorial Printer, 1832), 143–45; *Acts and Resolutions of the Legislative Council of the Territory of Florida Passed at Its Twentieth Session, Which Commenced on the third day of January, and ended on the fifth day of March, 1842* (Tallahassee: C. S. Bartlett, Printer, 1842), 36. See an earlier unsuccessful attempt to pass a law restricting free blacks and seamen from coming into the Territory of Florida in *Pensacola Gazette and West Florida Advertiser*, February 9, 1827.

33. *Tallahassee Floridian*, January 30, 1836; *Tallahassee Floridian and Journal*, December 28, 1850; Amon DeLaughter Journal, January 16, 1860.

34. *St. Augustine Florida Gazette*, September 15, 1821; *St. Augustine Florida Herald and Southern Democrat*, May 8, 18, 1840; *Jacksonville Florida News*, July 16, 1847, May 19, 1855; *Tallahassee Floridian and Journal*, July 7, 1849; *Tallahassee Floridian*, November 11, 1845.

Chapter 4. A Yearning for Freedom

1. Larry Eugene Rivers, *Slavery in Florida: Territorial Days to Emancipation* (Gainesville: University Press of Florida, 2000), 226–27; Edward E. Baptist, "The Slave Labor Camps of Antebellum Florida and the Pushing System," in *Florida's Working-Class Past: Current Perspectives on Labor, Race, and Gender from Spanish Florida to the New Immigration*, ed. Robert Cassanello and Melanie Shell-Weiss (Gainesville: University Press of Florida, 2009), 31.

2. George P. Rawick, *The American Slave: A Composite Autobiography*, 41 vols. (Westport, Conn: Greenwood Press 1972–79), vol. 17, *Florida Slave Narratives*, 253–54.

3. Freddie L. Parker, *Running for Freedom: Slave Runaways in North Carolina 1775–1840* (New York: Routledge, 1993), 93–94; John Hope Franklin and Loren Schweninger, *Runaway Slaves: Rebels on the Plantation* (New York: Oxford University Press, 1999), 218–19.

4. Rivers, *Slavery in Florida*, 18; Edward W. Baptist, *Creating an Old South: Middle Florida's Plantation Frontier before the Civil War* (Chapel Hill: University of North Carolina Press, 2002), 43, 165–74, 232, 235, 262; *Fifth Census; or Enumeration of the Inhabitants of the United States, 1830* (Washington, D.C.: Duff Green, 1832), 156–57; *Sixth Census of the United States, 1840* (Washington, D.C.: Rives and Blair, 1841), 454–55; *Seventh Census of the United States, 1850* (Washington, D.C.: Government Printing Office, 1853–55), 391–401; *Population of the United States in 1860, Compiled from the Original Returns of the Eighth Census* (Washington, D.C.: Government Printing Office, 1864), 50–54; *Statistics of the United States (Including Mortality, Property, etc.) in 1860; Compiled from the Original Returns and Being the Final Exhibit of the Eighth Census* (Washington, D.C.: Government Printing Office, 1864), 340–41.

5. See, for example, Ernest F. Dibble, "Slave Rentals to the Military: Pensacola and the Gulf Coast," *Civil War History* 23 (June 1977): 101–13; Ernest F. Dibble, *Antebellum Pensacola and the Military Presence*, 3 vols. (Pensacola: Pensacola News-Journal, 1974), 1:66; *St.*

Augustine Florida Gazette, December 10, 1821; Ellen McCormick to Catherine Wirt, June 14, September 10, 1843, William Wirt Papers, Maryland Historical Society, Baltimore.

6. Alexander S. Webb to Dearest Wife, January 3, 1855, Alexander Stewart Webb Papers, Yale University Library, New Haven, Conn.

7. *St. Augustine News*, April 3, 1839, September 17, 1842, March 18, June 3, 1843; *Tallahassee Star of Florida*, September 9, 1843; *Tallahassee Floridian and Journal*, January 22, 29, 1851, December 22, 29, 1853.

8. *Tallahassee Floridian and Journal*, April 12, June 12, July 31, 1852; *St. Augustine Ancient City*, March 13, 1852; *Jacksonville Florida News*, January 1, 1853.

9. *Tallahassee Weekly Floridian*, April 20, 1839; *Tallahassee Floridian*, May 1, July 3, 1841.

10. *St. Augustine East Florida Herald*, March 1823; *Pensacola Gazette*, January 18, 1828, July 17, 1830, April 15, May 6, 1837; *Tallahassee Floridian*, February 9, 1839, July 3, 1841; *Tallahassee Floridian and Journal*, November 6, 1850, May 6, 1852; *Jacksonville St. Johns News*, April 13, 1840.

11. *Jacksonville Courier*, December 10, 1835.

12. David Walker, *Walker's Appeal, in Four Articles; Together with a Preamble, to the Coloured Citizens of the World, but in Particular, and Very Expressly, to Those of the United States of America* (Boston, 1829); Merton L. Dillon, *Slavery Attacked: Southern States and Their Allies, 1619–1865* (Baton Rouge: Louisiana State University Press, 1990), 137–77.

13. Donorena Harris, "Abolitionist Sentiment in Florida, 1821–1860" (master's thesis, Florida State University, 1989), 14; *Apalachicola Commercial Advertiser*, September 30, 1844; *Tallahassee Floridian*, August 8, 1835; *St. Joseph Times*, April 7, 1840; Ray Granade, "Slave Unrest in Florida," *Florida Historical Quarterly* 55 (July 1976): 18–36; Charlton W. Tebeau, *A History of Florida* (Miami, Fla.: University of Miami Press, 1971), 181. For a telling and dramatic story of the Underground Railroad, see Scott Christianson, *Freeing Charles: The Struggle to Free a Slave on the Eve of the Civil War* (Urbana: University of Illinois Press, 2010).

14. See Sally E. Hadden, *Slave Patrols: Law and Violence in Virginia and the Carolinas* (Cambridge: Harvard University Press, 2001); Rivers, *Slavery in Florida*.

15. *Tallahassee Floridian*, April 4, 1840; *Jacksonville News*, August 8, 1851; *Jacksonville Courier*, October 8, 1835; *Tallahassee Weekly Floridian*, September 5, 1835; *Fernandina Florida News*, June 23, 1858. On a few occasions, Middle Florida whites expressed concern over the influence of abolitionists in the region. See Ulrich Bonnell Phillips and James David Glunt, eds., *Florida Plantation Records from the Papers of George Noble Jones* (St. Louis: Missouri Historical Society, 1927; Gainesville: University Press of Florida, 2006), 113–14.

16. Peter S. Smith to Gerrit Smith, September 13, 1842, Peter Skenandoah Smith to Gerrit Smith, November 22, 1852, Gerrit Smith Papers, Family Correspondence, Peter Skenandoah Smith, 1813–58, George Brent Library, Syracuse University, Syracuse, N.Y.; *St. Augustine Florida Herald and Southern Democrat*, June 21, 1835, January 26, 1837, July 5, August 11, November 8, 1858; *Tallahassee Floridian*, May 9, 1840.

17. Peter S. Smith to Gerrit Smith, November 22, 1852, Gerrit Smith Papers; *St. Augustine Herald and Southern Democrat*, June 21, 1835, January 26, 1837, December 17, 1844, July 5, August 11, November 8, 1858; *Pensacola Gazette*, June 29, 1844, February 8, 1845; *Jacksonville Courier*, August 3, October 8, 1835.

18. *St. Augustine Herald and Southern Democrat*, December 17, 1844; Jonathan Walker,

Trial and Imprisonment of Jonathan Walker (Boston: Anti-Slavery Office, 1845; Gainesville: University Press of Florida, 1974), 8–14, 32–45, 72–73, 108–10; *Pensacola Gazette*, June 29, 1844, February 8, 1845; *St. Augustine News*, July 26–29, 1844; *Boston Liberator*, December 6, 1844; *Jacksonville Courier*, August 3, October 8, 1835; James M. Denham, *"A Rogue's Paradise": Crime and Punishment in Antebellum Florida, 1821–1861* (Tuscaloosa: University of Alabama Press 1997), 97.

19. J. Walker, *Trial and Imprisonment*, 82–85; *Cincinnati Philanthropist*, cited in the *Boston Liberator*, March 28, 1845, p. 50; *Jacksonville Courier*, September 17, October 8, December 10, 1835; *Pensacola Gazette*, February 8, 1845.

20. *Tallahassee Floridian and Journal*, November 20, 1858; Christian Boyd to his son, Key West, Fla., September 23, 1862, State and Local History Collection, Monroe County May Hill Russell Public Library, Key West, Fla. (also quoted in Wiley L. Housewright, *A History of Music and Dance in Florida, 1856–1865* [Tuscaloosa: University of Alabama Press, 1991], 237–38).

21. Rawick, *Florida Slave Narratives*, 337.

22. *Pensacola Gazette*, May 20, 1837; *St. Augustine Florida Herald*, March 17, 1846, August 5, 1859; *Tallahassee Florida Sentinel*, May 5, 1839; *Tallahassee Florida Herald*, October 28, 1829, October 15, 28, 1858; *Jacksonville Florida Republican*, July 4, November 14, 1850.

23. *Tallahassee Floridian*, December 20, 1840, November 13, 1847; *Jacksonville News*, January 23, 1846. For an excellent discussion on the kidnapping of free blacks and enslaved people in the North and South, see Carol Wilson, *Freedom at Risk: The Kidnapping of Free Blacks in America, 1780–1865* (Lexington: University Press of Kentucky, 1994), 9–39.

24. *Jacksonville Florida Republican*, April 16, November 26, December 3, 1856; Brian R. Rucker, "Blackwater and Yellow Pine: The Development of Santa Rosa County, 1821–1865," 2 vols. (Ph.D. diss., Florida State University, 1990), 2:592.

25. Petition dated 1843 to the US government by the St. Augustine city council to protect northeast Florida from "slave smuggling and pirate activities," St. Augustine Historical Society Library, St. Augustine, Fla.

26. Minute Book 4, December 23, 1844, Leon County court records, Leon County Courthouse; Order Book A, November 1844, Jefferson County circuit court records (available on microfilm at Florida State Archives, Tallahassee).

27. J. Walker, *Trial and Imprisonment*, 16–100; *Tallahassee Florida Sentinel*, November 11, 1845; Rucker, "Blackwater and Yellow Pine," 2:592; Order Book A, case files, October 23, 1850, *State vs. Redding Evans*, 215, Jefferson County circuit court records; Rawick, *Florida Slave Narratives*, 337; *Jacksonville Courier*, August 3, 20, September 2, 13, 1835; Harris, "Abolitionist Sentiment in Florida," 1–16; Denham, *"Rogue's Paradise,"* 97.

28. *St. Augustine Florida Herald*, June 16, 1832, June 23, July 7, 14, 1838.

29. *Tallahassee Floridian*, July 5, 1834; *Pensacola Gazette*, September 22, 1838; *Tallahassee Floridian and Journal*, August 20, 1853, November 4, 1854; *Jacksonville Florida News*, October 14, 28, November 4, 1854; *Jacksonville Standard*, May 31, 1860; *Tampa Florida Peninsular*, October 6, 1860.

30. *Jacksonville Florida News*, October 12, 14, 28, November 4, 1854.

31. *Pensacola Floridian*, March 23, 1822; *Tallahassee Floridian*, May 11, 1833, June 1, 1839; *Jacksonville Courier*, January 14, 1836; *Key West Gazette*, April 8, 1840; *Tallahassee Star of Florida*, May 21, 1840; *Tampa Herald*, October 25, 1854.

32. *Pensacola Gazette*, August 12, 1837; *Tallahassee Floridian and Journal*, October 27, 1849, May 10, 1851; *St. Augustine Florida Herald*, June 16, 1832; *Gainesville Cotton States*, February 9, 1861.

33. See W. Jeffrey Bolster, *Black Jacks: African American Seamen in the Age of Sail* (Cambridge: Harvard University Press, 1997); Marcus Rediker, *Between the Devil and the Deep Blue Sea: Merchant Seamen, Pirates, and the Anglo-American Maritime World* (Cambridge: Cambridge University Press, 1987); Huge Thomas, *The Slave Trade: The Story of the Atlantic Slave Trade, 1440 -1870* (New York: Simon and Schuster, 1997); Philip D. Curtin, *The Atlantic Slave Trade: A Census* (Madison: University of Wisconsin Press, 1969); and David Eltis, *The Rise of African Slavery in the Americas* (Cambridge: Harvard University Press, 2000).

34. *Apalachicola Commercial Advertiser*, January 4, 25, 1849; *Tallahassee Floridian and Journal*, July 7, 1849. On Apalachicola as a cotton port and its slave-related actions and activities, see Lynn Willoughby, *Fair to Middlin: The Antebellum Cotton Trade of the Apalachicola/Chattahoochee River Valley* (Tuscaloosa: University of Alabama Press, 1993); and William W. Rogers, *Outposts on the Gulf: St. George Island and Apalachicola from Early Exploration to World War II* (Pensacola: University of West Florida Press, 1986).

35. *Pensacola Gazette*, August 11, 1829; *Key West Enquirer*, January 25, February 7, April 11, 1835; *Tallahassee Floridian and Advocate*, July 12, 1834; *Apalachicola Apalachicolan*, December 26, 1840; *Pensacola Gazette*, August 17, 1822.

36. *Apalachicola Gazette*, June 3, August 19, September 9, 1837; *St. Augustine Floridian Herald and Southern Democrat*, July 9, 16, 30, August 6, 13, 20, September 2, 10, 1834, October 13, 1855; *Jacksonville Weekly Republican*, March 18, 1855.

37. Clarence E. Carter, ed., *Territorial Papers of the United States*, 28 vols. (Washington, 1856), 22:745, 764; Harris, "Abolitionist Sentiment in Florida," 39; Canter Brown Jr., "Sarrazota, or Runaway Negro Plantations: Tampa Bay's First Black Community, 1812–21," *Tampa Bay History* 12 (Fall/Winter 1990), 14–16; Canter Brown Jr., "Tales of Angola: Free Blacks, Red Stick Creeks, and International Intrigue in Spanish Southwest Florida, 1812–1821," in *Go Sound the Trumpet! Selections in Florida's African American History*, ed. David H. Jackson Jr. and Canter Brown Jr. (Tampa: University of Tampa Press, 2005), 5–21. See also Rosalyn Howard, *Black Seminoles in the Bahamas* (Gainesville: University Press of Florida, 2002).

Chapter 5. Destinations of Runaways

1. John Hope Franklin and Loren Schweninger, *Runaway Slaves: Rebels on the Plantation* (New York: Oxford University Press, 1999), 97–123. See also David J. Weber, *The Spanish Frontier in North America* (New Haven: Yale University Press, 1994); Paul E. Hoffman, *Florida's Frontiers* (Bloomington: Indiana University Press, 2002); Michael V. Gannon, *The Cross in the Sand* (Gainesville: University Press of Florida, 1965); Rosalyn Howard, *Black Seminoles in the Bahamas* (Gainesville: University Press of Florida, 2002); and Canter Brown Jr., "Tales of Angola: Free Blacks, Red Stick Creeks, and International Intrigue in Spanish Southwest Florida, 1812–1821," in *Go Sound the Trumpet! Selections in Florida's African American History*, ed. David H. Jackson Jr. and Canter Brown Jr. (Tampa: University of Tampa Press, 2005), 5–21.

2. Jane Landers, *Black Society in Spanish Florida* (Urbana: University of Illinois Press, 1999), 7–28; Jane Landers, ed., *Colonial Plantations and Economy in Florida* (Gainesville: University Press of Florida, 2000); Larry Eugene Rivers, *Slavery in Florida: Territorial Days to Emancipation* (Gainesville: University Press of Florida, 2000), 210–28; William S. Coker and Thomas D. Watson, *Indian Traders of the Southeastern Spanish Borderlands: Panton, Leslie & Company and John Forbes & Company, 1783–1847* (Pensacola: University of West Florida Press, 1986). See also Whittington B. Johnson, *Post-Emancipation Race Relations in the Bahamas* (Gainesville: University Press of Florida, 2006).

3. Landers, *Black Society in Spanish Florida,* 7–28; Rivers, *Slavery in Florida,* 210–28. See also Sidney Walter Martin, *Florida during the Territorial Days* (Athens: University of Georgia Press, 1944); Joshua R. Giddings, *The Exiles of Florida; or, The Crimes Committed by Our Government against the Maroons, Who Fled from South Carolina and Other Slave States, Seeking Protections under Spanish Laws* (Columbus: Follett, Foster, 1858; Gainesville: University Press of Florida, 1964); and Canter Brown Jr., *Florida's Peace River Frontier* (Orlando: University of Central Florida Press, 1991).

4. Landers, *Black Society in Spanish Florida*, 7–28; Rivers, *Slavery in Florida*, 210–28. See also Gerald W. Mullin, *Flight and Rebellion: Slave Resistance in Eighteenth-Century Virginia* (New York: Oxford University Press, 1972), 36–112. See also other whites who described enslaved blacks who ran away but returned shortly after cooling off in Ulrich Bonnell Phillips and James David Glunt, eds., *Florida Plantation Records from the Papers of George Noble Jones* (St. Louis: Missouri Historical Society, 1927; Gainesville: University Press of Florida, 2006); Susan Bradford Eppes, *The Negro of the Old South: A Bit of Period History* (Chicago: Joseph G. Branch Publishing, 1925); and Susan Bradford Eppes, *Through Some Eventful Years* (Macon: J. W. Burke Company, 1926).

5. See Mullin, *Flight and Rebellion*, 94–95; Freddie L. Parker, *Running for Freedom: Slave Runaways in North Carolina 1775–1840* (New York: Routledge, 1993), 142–43; Lathan A. Windley, "A Profile of Runaway Slaves in Virginia and South Carolina from 1730 through 1787" (Ph.D. diss., University of Iowa, 1974), 137; Lathan A. Windley, *A Profile of Runaway Slaves in Virginia and South Carolina from 1730 through 1787* (New York: Routledge, 1995), 84; and Franklin and Schweninger, *Runaway Slaves*, 230. For an excellent study of African identities and the acculturation process from African to African American, see Michael Gomez, *Exchanging Our Country Marks* (Chapel Hill: University of North Carolina Press, 1998).

6. *St. Augustine Florida Herald*, July 1, 1835.

7. *Jacksonville News*, March 4, 1848.

8. Franklin and Schweninger, *Runaway Slaves*, 99–103.

9. *Quincy Sentinel*, July 7, 1840.

10. Ibid., January 1, 1841.

11. *Tallahassee Floridian and Journal*, October 27, 1849, May 10, November 22, 1851.

12. *St. Augustine Florida Herald*, June 18, 1832; *Fernandina Weekly East Floridian*, August 30, 1860.

13. *St. Augustine Florida Herald*, June 16, 1838; *Milledgeville (Ga.) Southern Recorder*, July 16, 1850.

14. *St. Augustine Florida Herald*, June 16, 1832, September 10, 1835.

15. *Fernandina Weekly East Floridian*, August 30, 1860.

16. *Tallahassee Weekly Floridian*, March 6, 1847; Charlyn Rainville, "The Story of a Son of a Slave" (master's thesis, Florida State University, 1976), 19–26; *Tallahassee Sentinel*, May 23, 1842.

17. *Tallahassee Florida Sentinel*, October 15, December 18, 1841, January 1, February 18, 1842; *Magnolia Advertiser*, February 23, March 2, 1830; *Tallahassee Florida Watchman*, February 17, 1838.

18. *Tallahassee Floridian*, August 22, 1835; *Monticello Family Friend*, March 15, 1859; *Marianna Florida Whig*, December 16, 1848; *Marianna Star of Florida*, June 6, 1844; *Tallahassee Star of Florida*, May 9, 1843; *Tallahassee Floridian*, December 17, 1831, March 13, 1832; *Apalachicola Gazette*, August 28, 1839, September 4, 19, October 31, 1840; Eppes, *Negro of the Old South*, 92–102.

19. *Jacksonville St. Johns Mirror*, May 7, 1861; *Jacksonville Standard*, May 31, 1860; *Fernandina East Floridian*, May 1, 1860; *Jacksonville News*, January 9, 1836; *Fernandina Florida News*, May 19, 1858, March 22, 1860; *Jacksonville Florida Republican*, June 6, 1850; *Tampa Florida Peninsular*, February 2, 1856, March 30, 1861; *St. Augustine Ancient City*, June 14, 1851, March 9, 1859; *Tallahassee Florida Sentinel*, April 20, 1852, June 15, 1853; *Jacksonville Standard*, May 22, 1834; *Jacksonville Florida News*, May 25, 1852.

20. See Rivers, *Slavery in Florida.*

21. *Fernandina Weekly East Floridian*, August 30, 1860.

22. *Quincy Sentinel*, May 16, 1840; *Cedar Keys Telegraph*, February 15, 1860; Estate of Cyrus Dearborn, miscellaneous notes and paper, 1830 and 1831, Gadsden County Courthouse, Quincy, Fla.

23. See Amon DeLaughter Journal, December 7 and 9, 1855, p. 30, transcript in collection of Elizabeth H. Sims, Madison County, Fla., xerographic copy in collection of the author.

24. George P. Rawick, *The American Slave: A Composite Autobiography*, 41 vols. (Westport, Conn.: Greenwood Press, 1972–79), vol. 17, *Florida Slave Narratives*, 97, 166–67, 336.

25. Eppes, *Negro of the Old South*, 98–102; *St. Augustine Florida Herald*, February 10, 1830; Ernest F. Dibble, *Antebellum Pensacola and the Military Presence*, 3 vols. (Pensacola: *Pensacola News-Journal*, 1974), 2:66.

26. *St. Augustine East Florida Herald*, March 1, 1823.

27. *Pensacola Gazette*, December 19, 1829.

28. See Canter Brown, Jr., "The Florida Crisis of 1826–27 and the Second Seminole War," *Florida Historical Quarterly* 73 (April 1995): 419–42; Canter Brown Jr., "Race Relations in Territorial Florida, 1821–1845," *Florida Historical Quarterly* 73 (January 1995): 287–307; *Pensacola Floridian*, September 22, 1821. See also Rivers, *Slavery in Florida.*

29. Landers, *Black Society in Spanish Florida*, 14–15; Giddings, *Exiles of Florida*, v.

30. James W. Covington, "The Negro Fort," *Gulf Coast Historical Review* 5 (Spring 1990): 79–91; James W. Covington, *The Seminoles of Florida* (Gainesville: University Press of Florida, 1993).

31. See Kenneth W. Porter, *The Black Seminoles: History of a Freedom-Seeking People*, rev. and ed. Alcione M. Amos and Thomas P. Senter (Gainesville: University Press of Florida, 1996); Kevin Mulroy, *Freedom on the Border: The Seminole Maroons in Florida, the Indian Territory, Coahuila, and Texas* (Lubbock: Texas Tech University Press, 1993); and Kevin Mulroy, *The Seminole Freedmen: A History* (Norman: University of Oklahoma Press, 2007).

32. Brown, *Florida's Peace River Frontier*, 8–9; Canter Brown Jr., *Tampa before the Civil*

War (Tampa: University of Tampa Press, 1999), 3–10; "Defences of the Floridas: A Report of Captain James Gadsden, Aide-de-Camp to General Andrew Jackson," *Florida Historical Quarterly* 15 (April 1937): 242–48.

33. Brown, "Tales of Angola," 5–21. See also Canter Brown Jr., *African Americans on the Tampa Bay Frontier* (Tampa: Tampa Bay History Center, 1997); Brown, "The Florida Crisis of 1826–27 and the Second Seminole War"; Brown, *Florida's Peace River Frontier*; Brown, "Race Relations in Territorial Florida, 1821–1845"; and Larry Rivers and Canter Brown Jr., "'The Indispensable Man': John Horse and Florida's Second Seminole War," *Journal of the Georgia Association of Historians* 18 (1997): 1–23.

34. *St. Augustine East Florida Herald*, October 16, 1824; *Jacksonville Courier*, December 10, 24, 1835, January 7, 14, February 11, December 17, 1836; *Tallahassee Floridian*, February 15, 1837.

35. *Ocala Argus*, March 16, 1848; *Ocala Florida Home Companion*, December 23, 1857, February 2, 23, 1858; *St. Augustine Ancient City*, March 16, 1850; *Tampa Tribune*, November 3, 1957. See also, Porter, *Black Seminoles*; and Brown, *Florida's Peace River Frontier*. On Peliklakaha, see "Interview with Terrance Weik" at http://lookingforangola.org.

36. *St. Augustine Ancient City*, March 16, 1850; *Ocala Florida Home and Companion*, February 2, May 5, 11, 1858; *Tampa Tribune*, November 3, 1957; William H. French to Captain J. C. Casey, November 19, 1853, John C. Casey Papers, Thomas Gilcrease Institute, Tulsa, Okla.

Chapter 6. Flight Away from Florida

1. See, for example, Jane Landers, *Black Society in Spanish Florida* (Urbana: University of Illinois Press, 1999); Larry Eugene Rivers, *Slavery in Florida: Territorial Days to Emancipation* (Gainesville: University Press of Florida, 2000).

2. A helpful introduction to Spanish colonial history in Florida can be found in Michael Gannon, ed., *The New History of Florida* (Gainesville: University Press of Florida, 1996), 40–166. On St. Augustine, see also Jean Parker Waterbury, ed., *The Oldest City: St. Augustine, Saga of Survival* (St. Augustine: St. Augustine Historical Society, 1983). On Pensacola, see also John J. Clune and Margo S. Stringfield, *Historic Pensacola* (Gainesville: University Press of Florida, 2009).

3. See, for example, Sidney Walter Martin, *Florida during the Territorial Days* (Athens: University of Georgia Press, 1944); and Gannon, *New History of Florida*, 207–32.

4. See, for example, correspondence between City Council of St. Augustine and Secretary of the Treasury, August 14, 1843, H. G. Wright to Colonel F. G. Totten, July 21, 1847, St. Augustine Historical Society Library, St. Augustine; *St. Augustine News*, August 12, October 7, November 4, 11, 25, 1843, January 20, 1844; *Fernandina Florida News*, February 17, 1857, March 17, September 1, November 8, December 16, 1858, January 27, 1859; *Tallahassee Floridian*, July 5, September 6, 1834, November 1, 1837, March 30, April 20, 1839, November 1, 4, 1845, September 2, 1848, February 20, 1858; *Tallahassee Floridian and Journal*, July 7, 1849; *Tallahassee Sentinel*, April 14, 1841, January 18, February 18, 1842; *Newnansville Florida Dispatch*, May 11, 1860; *St. Augustine Gazette*, September 15, 1821; *St. Augustine East Floridian*, August 14, 1843; *St. Augustine Florida Herald*, June 7, August 9, 1832, May 22, 1834, September 10, 1835, April 20, 1839, May 15, 1840, June 3, 1846, February 9, 1847;

St. Augustine Florida Herald and Southern Democrat, August 7, 1843; *Tallahassee Weekly Floridian*, November 4, 1845, January 10, 1846, September 2, 1848; *Tallahassee Floridian and Advocate*, November 11, 1830, July 18, 1834; *Jacksonville News*, July 16, 1847, May 19, October 13, 1855, October 10, 1857, October 13, 1858; *Apalachicola Gazette*, February 2, March 30, April 20, August 28, 1839; *Pensacola Gazette*, July 7, 1829, May 6, 27, 1837, June 9, 30, 1838, August 29, 1840; *Marianna Star of Florida*, June 28, 1844; *Jacksonville East Florida Advocate*, June 16, 1840; *Key West Enquirer*, January 24, February 7, April 11, 1835, January 17, 1836; *St. Augustine Ancient City*, June 14, 1851; *Apalachicola Commercial Advertiser*, January 4, 25, 1849; *St. Augustine East Florida Herald*, March 1, 1823; *Tallahassee Star of Florida*, July 18, September 6, 1844; *Tallahassee Florida Intelligencer*, October 6, 1826; *Jacksonville Republican*, November 5, 1856; *Cedar Keys Telegraph*, February 15, 1860; *St. Augustine Herald and Southern Democrat*, May 8, 1840; *Quincy Sentinel*, January 1, 1841.

5. *Tallahassee Weekly Floridian*, May 22, 1877; *Jacksonville Republican*, June 5, 1851. For a sound analysis of traditional African religious practices employed by many enslaved Africans and persons of African descent in the antebellum South, especially in South Carolina, Georgia, and North Florida, see Sterling Stuckey, *Slave Culture: Nationalist Theory and the Foundation of Black America* (New York: Oxford University Press, 1987); Michael Gomez, *Exchanging Our Country Marks* (Chapel Hill: University of North Carolina Press, 1998); and Jason Young, *Rituals of Resistance: African Atlantic Religion in Kongo and the Lowcountry South in the Era of Slavery* (Baton Rouge: Louisiana State University Press, 2002).

6. See Sitiki, *The Odyssey of an African Slave*, ed. Patricia C. Griffin (Gainesville: University Press of Florida, 2009).

7. For the period prior to 1821, see Landers, *Black Society in Spanish Florida*, 29–106. See also *St. Augustine Florida Herald*, August 5, 1829, September 10, 1835; An Ordinance Prohibiting Slaves Occupying Separate Houses and in reference to houses of free persons of color, passed November 22, 1856, the 1860 Petition of Sundry Citizens of the City of St. Augustine asking the action of the Council in removing Charles, a slave of O. M. Dorman, from the City, the 1838 Ordinance for the Better Regulation of Negro Slaves and Free Persons of Color, and the letter of Mayor F. L. Dancey of St. Augustine, 1841, establishing the use of Patrols, St. Augustine Historical Society Library, Fla.; *St. Augustine Florida Herald and Southern Democrat*, May 8, 1840; *Tallahassee Florida Intelligencer*, October 6, 1826.

8. *St. Augustine News*, August 12, 14, October 7, November 4, 11, 25, 1843.

9. *Jacksonville Republican*, October 3, 1850; *Jacksonville Florida News*, October 13, 1858. On Jacksonville's early development, see Thomas Frederick Davis, *A History of Jacksonville Florida and Vicinity, 1513 to 1924* (Jacksonville: Florida Historical Society, 1925; Jacksonville: San Marco Bookstore, 1990).

10. *Tallahassee Floridian*, February 20, 1858. On Key West, see also Maureen Ogle, *Key West: History of an Island of Dreams* (Gainesville: University Press of Florida, 2003).

11. *Pensacola Floridian*, April 27, 1822; *Pensacola Gazette*, August 17, 1822, August 3, 1835.

12. *Pensacola Gazette*, March 13, 18, April 17, June 26, September 4, 1824, April 2, October 8, 1825, April 15, May 6, August 4, 1826, April 20, 1827, January 18, February 1, May 2, July 1, November 7, 1828, May 19, August 11, November 14, 1829, January 16, February 6, March 13, August 21, 1830, January 2, March 14, 1833, January 9, May 14, June 4, July 9, 16, September 10, October 22, November 26, 1836, May 6, 13, 20, July 8, 22, August 19, September

23, October 7, 10, 1837, February 24, May 5, June 9, 30, July 7, September 22, November 3, 1838, April 6, 1839, February 22, July 4, 1840, April 15, 1843.

13. *Pensacola Floridian*, April 27, 1822; *Pensacola Gazette*, August 29, 1840.

14. *Tallahassee Floridian*, October 13, 17, 1835; *Quincy Sentinel*, January 1, 1841; *Magnolia Advertiser*, February 9, 1830.

15. *Tallahassee Floridian and Journal*, January 4, 1838; *Apalachicola Commercial Advertiser*, January 22, 1844, June 6, 1846, January 4, 1849.

16. *Tallahassee Floridian*, June 1, 1833; *Quincy Sentinel*, January 1, 1841; *Tallahassee Weekly Floridian*, January 1, 1836; George W. Honk to Thomas Brown, January 10, 1853, Governor's Correspondence, Record Group 101, series 557, box 3, Florida State Archives, Tallahassee. On the Fugitive Slave Act of 1850, see, for example, Stanley W. Campbell, *The Slave Catchers: Enforcement of the Fugitive Slave Law, 1850–1860* (Chapel Hill: University of North Carolina Press, 1970); and "Edinbur Randall, interviewed, 1854," in *Slave Testimony: Two Centuries of Letters, Speeches, Interviews, and Autobiographies*, ed. John W. Blassingame (Baton Rouge: Louisiana State University Press, 1977), 320–25.

17. Freddie L. Parker, *Running for Freedom: Slave Runaways in North Carolina 1775–1840* (New York: Routledge, 1993), 181–84; Lathan A. Windley, *A Profile of Runaway Slaves in Virginia and South Carolina from 1730 through 1787* (New York: Routledge, 1995), 133, 180–81; John Hope Franklin and Loren Schweninger, *Runaway Slaves: Rebels on the Plantation* (New York: Oxford University Press, 1999), 115.

18. *St. Augustine News*, April 13, 1839, September 17, 1842, March 18, June 3, 1843; *Tallahassee Star of Florida*, September 1, 1843; *Jacksonville Republican*, September 9, 1851.

19. *Magnolia Advertiser*, March 13, 1829.

20. *Tallahassee Floridian*, May 19, 1838.

21. *Tallahassee Floridian*, May 19, 1838; *Tallahassee Weekly Floridian*, March 6, 1847; *Columbus (Ga.) Enquirer*, May 11, 1833; *Milledgeville (Ga.) Southern Recorder*, May 8, 1833.

22. *Tallahassee Floridian*, January 10, 1846.

23. *Pensacola Gazette and Florida Advertiser*, January 16, 1830.

24. Ibid., May 2, 1828.

25. Amon DeLaughter Journal, October 31, 1854, transcript in collection of Elizabeth H. Sims, Madison County, Fla., xerographic copy in collection of the author; *Tallahassee Florida Watchman*, April 28, 1838.

26. *Tallahassee Floridian Watchman*, April 21, 1838.

27. *Tallahassee Floridian and Advocate*, September 7, 21, 1829, September 7, 1830; *Tallahassee Star of Florida*, May 1, 1840, August 9, 1844; *Key West Key of the Gulf*, April 10, 1845; *Tallahassee Floridian*, April 11, 1840; *Tallahassee Floridian and Journal*, June 16, 1855, May 22, 1858.

28. *Pensacola Gazette*, May 18, June 8, October 26, 1827, April 18, 1828; *Tallahassee Floridian and Advocate*, November 1, 1828, October 6, 13, 22, November 3, 10, 17, December 1, 15, 22, 1829; *Magnolia Advertiser*, January 12, 19, 26, 1830; *Tallahassee Floridian*, June 1, 1833, July 5, 1834, January 2, August 28, 1841; *Tallahassee Florida Sentinel*, April 4, 1846.

29. *Pensacola Gazette and West Florida Advertiser*, December 7, 1827; *Pensacola Gazette*, June 30, 1838, January 18, 1849; *Jacksonville Standard*, May 31, 1860; *Tallahassee Floridian*, September 2, 1848.

30. *Tallahassee Weekly Floridian*, January 10, 1846; *Tallahassee Florida Sentinel*, November 4, 1845; *Newnansville Florida Dispatch*, May 11, 1860.

31. *Tallahassee Floridian and Journal*, January 29, 1853, May 20, 1854; *Tallahassee Florida Sentinel*, November 4, 1845; *Tallahassee Weekly Floridian*, January 10, 1846; *Jacksonville Florida News*, October 13, 1855.

32. See, for example, Larry E. Rivers, "A Troublesome Property: Master-Slave Relations in Florida, 1821–1865," in *The African American Heritage of Florida*, ed. David R. Colburn and Jane L. Landers (Gainesville: University Press of Florida, 1995), 104–27; and Larry E. Rivers, "Baptist Minister James Page: Alternatives for African American Leadership in Post–Civil War Florida," in *Florida's Heritage of Diversity: Essays in Honor of Samuel Proctor*, ed. Mark I. Greenberg, William Warren Rogers, and Canter Brown Jr. (Tallahassee: Sentry Press, 1997), 43–54.

33. Canter Brown Jr., "'Where are now the hopes I cherished?' The Life and Times of Robert Meacham," *Florida Historical Quarterly* 69 (June 1990): 2–3.

34. *St. Augustine Florida Herald*, June 7, 1832; April 17, 1834; *Pensacola Floridian*, March 23, 1822; *Tallahassee Floridian*, June 1, 1833, November 19, 1842; *Jacksonville Florida News*, December 12, 1855, October 10, 1857; *Pensacola Florida Democrat*, January 18, 1849; *Key West Enquirer*, January 24, 1835; *Apalachicola Gazette*, June 3, August 19, September 19, October 11, 1837, November 16, 1839, August 29, 1840; *Tallahassee Star of Florida*, May 1, 1840, May 1, 1846; *Tallahassee Floridian and Journal*, December 20, 1851.

Chapter 7. In Search of Kinfolk and Loved Ones

1. Herbert G. Gutman, *Slavery and the Numbers Game: A Critique of "Time on the Cross"* (Urbana: University of Illinois Press, 1975), 106–7; Herbert G. Gutman, *The Black Family in Slavery and Freedom, 1750–1925* (New York: Pantheon Books, 1976), 144–84; Frederic Bancroft, *Slave Trading in the Old South* (New York: Frederick Ungar Publishing Company, 1931), 15–46; Ann Patton Malone, *Sweet Chariot: Slave Family and Household Structure in Nineteenth-Century Louisiana* (Chapel Hill: University of North Carolina Press, 1992), 10–39; Eugene D. Genovese, *Roll, Jordan, Roll: The World the Slaves Made* (New York: Pantheon Books, 1974), 419, 453; Leslie Howard Owens, *This Species of Property: Slave Life and Culture in the Old South* (New York: Oxford University Press, 1976), 174–91; John W. Blassingame, *The Slave Community: Plantation Life in the Antebellum South*, 2nd ed. (New York: Oxford University Press, 1979), 173–77; Walter L. Johnson, *Soul by Soul: Life Inside the Antebellum Slave Market* (Cambridge: Harvard University Press, 1999), 5, 24–25, 178–79; Marie Jenkins Schwartz, *Born In Bondage: Growing Up Enslaved in the Antebellum South* (Cambridge: Harvard University Press, 2000), 17–18; Edward E. Baptist, *Creating an Old South: Middle Florida's Plantation Frontier before the Civil War* (Chapel Hill: University of North Carolina Press, 2002), 191–218. See also Larry E. Rivers, "Dignity and Importance: Slavery in Jefferson County, Florida—1827 to 1860," *Florida Historical Quarterly* 61 (April 1983): 404–30; Larry E. Rivers, "Madison County, Florida—1830–1860: A Case Study in Land, Labor, and Prosperity," *Journal of Negro History* 78 (Fall 1993): 233–44.

2. Ira Berlin, *Many Thousands Gone: The First Two Centuries of Slavery in North America* (Cambridge: Harvard University Press, 1998), 359; Ira Berlin, "The Slaves' Changing

World," in *The History Of The American People: The History, Traditions and Culture of African Americans*, ed. James Oliver Horton and Louise E. Horton (Detroit: Wayne State University Press, 1997), 44–45; Edward E. Baptist, "The Migration of Planters to Antebellum Florida: Kinship and Power," *Journal of Southern History* 62 (August 1996): 527–54.

3. Baptist, *Creating an Old South*, 61–87.

4. *1830 United States Decennial Census, Leon and Jackson Counties, Florida* (population schedules), National Archives, Washington, D.C. (available on microfilm at the Florida State Archives, Tallahassee; Harriet Randolph to Lucy Beverly Randolph, September 8, 1829, Randolph Family Papers, Virginia Historical Society, Richmond; Steven F. Miller, "Plantation Labor Organization and Slave Life on the Cotton Frontier: The Alabama-Mississippi Black Belt, 1815–1845," in *Cultivation and Culture: Labor and the Shaping of Slave Life in the Americas*, ed. Ira Berlin and Phillip D. Morgan (Charlottesville: University of Virginia Press, 1989), 156–57; Baptist, *Creating an Old South*, 68–69.

5. *Tallahassee Floridian and Advocate*, September 7, 1830; Achille Murat, *The United States of North America: With a Note on Negro Slavery* (London: Effingham Wilson, 1833), 64; Achille Murat to John G. Gamble, October 1, 1834, Murat to Thomas Botts, October 4, 1835, Lipona Letter Book, 1830–35, 46, 459–61, Murat Papers, Bibliotheque Nationale, Paris (available on microfilm at Florida State University Strozier Library).

6. Daniel Campbell will, June 18, 1832, John Branch, testamentary, February 16, 1863, Richard Witaker will, August 15, 1854, Book A, 52–53, 383–88, Gadsden County probate records, Gadsden County Courthouse, Quincy, Fla.

7. Daniel Campbell will; John Branch testamentary.

8. John Hope Franklin and Loren Schweninger, *Runaway Slaves: Rebels on the Plantation* (New York: Oxford University Press, 1999), 51; Thomas Randall to William Wirt, December 20, 1828, November 20, 1829, William Wirt Papers, Maryland Historical Society, Baltimore.

9. Rivers, "Dignity and Importance," 404–30; Rivers, "Madison County, Florida," 233–55; Larry E. Rivers, "Slavery in Microcosm: Leon County, Florida, 1824 to 1860," *Journal of Negro History* 66 (Fall 1981): 235–45.

10. See, for example, the probate records of slaveholders of Florida, 1821 to 1865, deposited by the author in the Florida A&M University Black Archives, Research Center, and Museum, Tallahassee.

11. *Quincy Sentinel*, December 11, 1840; *Tallahassee Florida Sentinel*, April 15, 1842; *Tallahassee Florida Advertiser*, July 11, 1829; *Tallahassee Floridian and Advocate*, January 5, 1830; *Jacksonville Standard*, April 5, 1860.

12. "Diary and Other Papers of William D. Moseley: 1848–1857," 45–46, typescript in Florida Collection, Florida State University, Tallahassee; see also George Rawick, *The American Slave: A Composite Autobiography*, 41 vols. (Westport, Conn.: Greenwood Press, 1972–79), vol. 17, *Florida Slave Narratives*, 166–67. See also the interesting interview of former bondservant Mary Gomez, *St. Augustine Record*, October 21, 1934.

13. *Tallahassee Florida Advertiser*, July 11, 1839; *Tallahassee Floridian and Advocate*, January 5, 1830. See also Larry Eugene Rivers, *Slavery in Florida: Territorial Days to Emancipation* (Gainesville: University Press of Florida, 2000); Emily West, *Chains of Love: Slave Couples in Antebellum South Carolina* (Urbana: University of Illinois Press, 2004); and Wilma King, *Stolen Childhood: Slave Youth in Nineteenth-Century America* (Bloomington: Indiana University Press, 1995).

14. Franklin and Schweninger, *Runaway Slaves*, 51; William Kilcrease estate, probate file no. 1005, Gadsden County probate records; Rawick, *Florida Slave Narratives*, 95, 167.

15. Rivers, *Slavery in Florida*, 210–28; King, *Stolen Childhood*, 102–3; Schwartz, *Born in Bondage*, 88–91.

16. *Jacksonville Republican*, September 25, 1851.

17. *Jacksonville Courier*, January 4, 1851; *St. Augustine Ancient City*, March 13, 1852; *Jacksonville Florida News*, May 25, October 30, 1852, January 1, 1853; *Tallahassee Floridian and Journal*, April 12, 1851, June 12, July 31, 1852; *Tallahassee Florida Sentinel*, June 15, 1852; *Jacksonville Republican*, October 9, 1851; "Diary and Other Papers of William D. Moseley."

18. Schwartz, *Born in Bondage*, 88–91; Charles Ball, *Fifty Years in Chains; or, The Life of An American Slave* (Indianapolis: Dayton and Asher, 1858), 122.

19. *Tallahassee Floridian*, February 2, 1839.

20. *Pensacola Gazette*, August 17, 1822; *Tallahassee Florida Intelligencer*, October 6, 1826; *St. Augustine Florida Herald*, July 3, 1838.

21. William W. Rogers and Erica R. Clark, *The Croom Family and Goodwood Plantation: Land, Litigation, and Southern Lives* (Athens: University of Georgia Press, 1999), 140.

22. *Tallahassee Floridian and Advocate*, November 1, 1828, October 6, 1829, September 7, 1830; *Tallahassee Floridian*, February 9, 1839; *Tallahassee Florida News*, February 17, 1837; *Jacksonville Republican*, February 21, 1856; *Columbus (Ga.) Enquirer*, May 11, 1833; *Milledgeville Georgia Journal*, February 15, 1825.

23. *Tallahassee Floridian*, May 26, 1838; *St. Augustine News*, June 19, 1840; *Tallahassee Floridian and Advocate*, November 1, 1828; *St. Augustine Florida Herald*, July 3, 1838.

24. *Pensacola Gazette*, April 18, 1828; *St. Augustine Florida Herald*, April 21, May 13, 1830; *Milledgeville (Ga.) Southern Recorder*, May 8, 1833; *Tallahassee Floridian*, March 2, 1839; *Jacksonville News*, June 10, 19, 1848; *Jacksonville Courier*, August 6, 1835; *Fernandina Florida News*, February 2, 1858.

25. *Tallahassee Florida Sentinel*, May 5, 1839, April 4, 1842; *St. Joseph Mirror*, May 7, 1861; *Jacksonville Standard*, May 31, 1860; *Apalachicola Gazette*, September 4, 1839; *Jacksonville Courier*, May 17, 1835.

26. *Tampa Florida Peninsular*, April 20, 1858.

27. *Tallahassee Florida Sentinel*, March 4, 1842; *Tallahassee Star of Florida*, May 21, 1840; *Tallahassee Floridian and Journal*, November 30, 1850.

28. Edward E. Baptist, "The Slave Labor Camps of Antebellum Florida and the Pushing System," in *Florida's Working-Class Past: Current Perspectives on Labor, Race, and Gender from Spanish Florida to the New Immigration*, ed. Robert Cassanello and Melanie Shell-Weiss (Gainesville: University Press of Florida, 2009), 45; Franklin and Schweninger, *Runaway Slaves*, 212.

29. *St. Augustine East Florida Herald*, October 16, 1824; *Jacksonville News*, March 4, 1848; Deborah Gray White, "Female Slaves in the Plantation South," in *Before Freedom Came: African-American Life in the Antebellum South*, ed. Edward D. C. Campbell (Charlottesville: University of Virginia Press, 1991), 101, 119, 121; Deborah Gray White, "Female Slaves: Sex Roles and Status in the Antebellum Plantation South," *Journal of Family History* 8 (Fall 1983): 248–61; Deborah Gray White, *Ar'n't I a Woman? Female Slaves in the Plantation South* (New York: W. W. Norton and Company, 1985).

30. *St. Augustine East Florida Advocate*, October 12, 1839; *Jacksonville Courier*, April 16, 1835; *Tallahassee Floridian and Journal*, May 22, 1858; *Pensacola Floridian*, March 23, 1822; *Tallahassee Floridian*, November 11, 1845; *St. Augustine Florida Herald*, March 25, 1829, May 11, 1833, April 6, 1839; *Magnolia Advertiser*, January 13, 19, 26, 1830; *Tallahassee Florida Sentinel*, April 4, 1842; *Tallahassee Floridian and Advocate*, October 6, 13, 20, November 10, 17, December 1, 15, 22, 1829.

31. *Tallahassee Floridian*, December 12, 1840.

32. *Pensacola Floridian*, March 23, 1822.

33. *Tallahassee Floridian*, June 15, 1839; *Tallahassee Weekly Floridian*, September 2, 1848.

34. *Tallahassee Weekly Floridian*, September 2, 1848; *Tallahassee Floridian*, January 10, 1846, February 20, 1858; *Jacksonville Republican*, October 3, 1850.

35. *Jacksonville News*, July 16, 1847; *Tallahassee Floridian and Journal*, October 3, 1857.

36. Jane Murray-Sheldon Reminiscences, 1884, 3–4, Beaches Historical Society, Key West, Fla.

37. *Jacksonville Florida Times-Union*, July 20, 1891.

38. See, for example, Canter Brown Jr., "Sarrazota, or Runaway Negro Plantations: Tampa Bay's First Black Community, 1812–21," *Tampa Bay History* 12 (Fall/Winter 1990): 14–17; Canter Brown Jr., "Tales of Angola: Free Blacks, Red Stick Creeks, and International Intrigue in Spanish Southwest Florida, 1812–1821," in *Go Sound the Trumpet! Selections in Florida's African American History*, ed. David H. Jackson Jr. and Canter Brown Jr. (Tampa, Fla., 2005), 17–18; *Nassau Royal Gazette and Literary Register*, March 20, 1822; *Tallahassee Floridian and Journal*, February 20, 1858; Julia Floyd Smith, *Slavery and Plantation Growth in Antebellum Florida, 1821–1860* (Gainesville: University of Florida Press, 1973), 105–6. For more information on early black flight from Florida to various Atlantic world communities in the Caribbean, see Rosalyn Howard, *Black Seminoles in the Bahamas* (Gainesville: University Press of Florida, 2002); David E. Wood, comp., *Guide to Selected Sources for the History of the Seminole Settlements at Red Bays, Andros, 1817–1980* (Nassau: Department of Archives, 1980); Kenneth W. Porter, "Notes on the Seminole Negroes in the Bahamas," *Florida Historical Quarterly* 24 (July 1945): 56–60; John M. Goggin, "The Seminole Negroes of Andros Island," *Florida Historical Quarterly* 24 (January 1946): 201–6; Harry A. Kersey Jr., "The Seminole Negroes of Andros Island Revisited: Some New Pieces to an Old Puzzle," *Florida Anthropologist* 34 (December 1981): 169–76; and R. J. M. Blackett, *Building an Anti-slavery Wall: Black Americans in the Atlantic Abolitionist Movement, 1830–1860* (Baton Rouge: Louisiana State University Press, 1983), 137.

39. H. G. Wright to F. G. Totten, July 21, 1847, Monroe County May Hill Russell Public Library Florida Collection, Key West; *St. Augustine Florida Herald*, March 1, 1823; *Tallahassee Floridian*, February 20, 1858.

40. Franklin and Schweninger, *Runaway Slaves*, 55; Bertram H. Groene, *Ante-Bellum Tallahassee* (Tallahassee: Florida Heritage Foundation, 1971), 111–13.

41. *Tallahassee Florida Watchman*, April 2, 1838; *Tallahassee Floridian*, June 8, August 2, 1839, January 15, September 12, 1840; *Tallahassee Floridian and Advocate*, October 6, 1829.

42. *Tallahassee Florida Sentinel*, June 3, 1855; *St. Augustine East Florida Advocate*, September 1, 1840.

43. *Jacksonville Republican*, October 1, 1851; *Tallahassee Floridian*, February 9, 1834,

August 22, October 17, 1835; *Tallahassee Floridian and Advocate*, September 7, 1830; Laura Randall to Mother, December 14, 1827, Wirt Papers.

44. Ulrich Bonnell Phillips and James David Glunt, eds., *Florida Plantation Records from the Papers of George Noble Jones* (St. Louis: Missouri Historical Society, 1927; Gainesville: University Press of Florida, 2006), 107–8, 111, 152–53.

45. See, for example, Rivers, "Dignity and Importance," 404–30; Rivers, "Madison County," 233–44; Larry E. Rivers, "Slavery and the Political Economy of Gadsden County, Florida: 1823–1861," *Florida Historical Quarterly* 70 (July 1991): 1–19; Rivers, "Slavery in Microcosm," 235–45; Larry E. Rivers, "A Troublesome Property: Master-Slave Relations in Florida, 1821–1865," in *The African American Heritage of Florida*, ed. David R. Colburn and Jane L. Landers (Gainesville: University Press of Florida, 1995), 104–27. Among newspapers that carried descriptions of Florida runaways in search of spouses from 1821 to 1865 were the *Apalachicola Commercial Advertiser*, *Apalachicola Gazette*, *Jacksonville Courier*, *Jacksonville East Florida Advocate*, *Jacksonville Florida News*, *Jacksonville Florida Union*, *Jacksonville News*, *Magnolia Advertiser*, *Pensacola Gazette*, *St. Augustine East Florida Herald*, *St. Augustine Florida Gazette*, *St. Augustine Florida Herald and Southern Democrat*, *Tallahassee Florida Advocate*, *Tallahassee Florida Intelligencer*, *Tallahassee Florida Sentinel*, *Tallahassee Florida Watchman*, *Tallahassee Floridian*, *Tallahassee Floridian and Journal*, *Tallahassee Star of Florida*, *Tallahassee Weekly Floridian*, and *Tampa Florida Peninsular*.

Chapter 8. Catch the Runaway

1. On the subject of slave patrols generally, see, for instance, Sally E. Hadden, *Slave Patrols: Law and Violence in Virginia and the Carolinas* (Cambridge: Harvard University Press, 2001); Stanley W. Campbell, *The Slave Catchers: Enforcement of the Fugitive Slave Law, 1850–1860* (Chapel Hill: University of North Carolina Press, 1970).

2. *Acts of the Legislative Council of the Territory of Florida, Passed at Their Third Session, 1824, Together with the former Acts, and parts of Acts now in force, the Laws of Congress organizing the government of the Territory of Florida, and Constitution of the United States* (Tallahassee: Office of the *Tallahassee Florida Intelligencer,* 1825), 290.

3. *Jacksonville Courier*, September 2, 17, October 8, December 10, 1835; *Acts of the Legislative Council of the Territory of Florida, Passed at Their First Session, 1822, Together With The Treaty of Cession—Governor Jackson's Ordinances—The Act of Congress Organizing the Territorial Government Constitution of the United States—Spanish Regulations for the allotment of Lands, &c., &c., &c.* (Pensacola: Floridian Press, 1823), 181–85; *Acts of the Legislative Council of the Territory of Florida: Passed at Their Second Session 1823* (Pensacola: John Fitzgerald and Co., 1823, 2–5; *Acts of the Legislative Council of the Territory of Florida, Passed at Their Third Session, 1824*, 289–92; *Acts of the Legislative Council of the Territory of Florida, Passed at Their 5th Session, 1826–7* (Tallahassee: A. S. Thruston, 1827), 141–50; *Acts of the Legislative Council of the Territory of Florida, Passed at Their 7th Session, 1828* (Tallahassee: William Wilson, 1829), 97–110; *Acts of the Governor and Legislative Council, of the Territory of Florida: Passed at the Fourteenth Session, Begun and Held at the City of Tallahassee, on Monday, January 4th, and Ended Sunday, February 14th, 1836* (Tallahassee: William Wilson Printer, 1836), 13–15; *Acts and Resolutions of the Legislative Council of the*

Territory of Florida, Passed at Its Eighteenth Session, Which commenced on the sixth day of January, and ended on the second day of March, 1840 (Tallahassee: B. F. Whitner, Printer, 1840), 13; *Acts and Resolutions of the General Assembly of the State of Florida: Passed at Its Fifth Session, Begun and Held at the Capitol, in the City of Tallahassee, on Monday, November 25, 1850, and Ended January 24, 1851* (*Tallahassee Floridian and Journal*, 1851), 390; *St. Augustine East Florida Herald*, June 7, 1823.

4. John Hope Franklin and Loren Schweninger, *Runaway Slaves: Rebels on the Plantation* (New York: Oxford University Press, 1999), 156–57; *Acts of the Legislative Council of the Territory of Florida, Passed at Their Third Session, 1824*, 291; *Pensacola Gazette*, June 15, 1839.

5. *Acts of the Legislative Council of the Territory of Florida, Passed at the Eleventh Session, Commencing January the Seventh and Ending February the Seventeenth, 1833* (Tallahassee: William Wilson, Territorial Printer, 1833), 26–27; *Laws of the Legislative Council of the Territory of Florida, Passed at the Twelfth Session, Commencing January Sixth, and Ending February Sixteenth, One Thousand Eight Hundred and Thirty-Three [Thirty-Four]* (Tallahassee: William Wilson, Printer, 1834), 31.

6. *Acts of the Legislative Council of the Territory of Florida, Passed at the Eleventh Session* (1833), 27; Franklin and Schweninger, *Runaway Slaves*, 152.

7. *Acts of the Legislative Council of the Territory of Florida, Passed at the Eleventh Session* (1833), 93.

8. George P. Rawick, *The American Slave: A Composite Autobiography*, 41 vols. (Westport, Conn.: Greenwood Press, 1972–79), vol. 17, *Florida Slave Narratives*, 338.

9. Ibid., 97.

10. Ibid., 37, 244; *Key West Key of the Gulf*, November 4, 1882.

11. *St. Augustine News*, August 12, October 7, November 4, 1843.

12. *Quincy Sentinel*, September 18, 1840; *Ocala Argus*, March 26, 1848; *Jacksonville Courier*, December 12, 24, 1835, January 7, February 11, 1836, December 17, 1837; *St. Joseph Times*, September 26, 1840.

13. *Jacksonville Courier*, September 2, 3, 1835.

14. See, for example, Amon DeLaughter Journal, April 28, May 7, 1859, October 1, 30, November 5, 1859, transcript in collection of Elizabeth H. Sims, Madison County, Fla., xerographic copy in collection of the author.

15. *St. Augustine East Florida Herald*, March 1, 1823; *St. Augustine Ancient City*, March 16, 1850. Most studies suggest that the majority of slaves were caught by slave catchers or other civilians. See, for example, Franklin and Schweninger, *Runaway Slaves*, 149–81; Randolph B. Campbell, *An Empire for Slavery: The Peculiar Institution in Texas* (Baton Rouge: Louisiana State University Press, 1989), 180–84; and Gerald W. Mullin, *Flight and Rebellion: Slave Resistance in Eighteenth-Century Virginia* (New York: Oxford University Press, 1972), 39–47.

16. *St. Augustine East Florida Herald*, March 15, 1860; *Fernandina Weekly East Floridian*, August 30, 1860; *Cedar Keys Telegraph*, February 15, 1860.

17. *Pensacola Gazette*, April 28, 1837; John Missall and Mary Lou Missall, *The Seminole Wars: America's Longest Indian Conflict* (Gainesville: University Press of Florida, 2004), 169–73.

18. Franklin and Schweninger, *Runaway Slaves*, 161.

19. Amon DeLaughter Journal, December 7, 9, 1855, March 19, 1857, March 29, 1858, May 26, 1860.

20. *Tallahassee Floridian*, June 12, 1841.

21. Amon DeLaughter Journal, May 18, 1857; "Diary and Other Papers of William D. Moseley: 1848–1857," 5, 23, typescript in Florida Collection, Florida State University, Tallahassee.

22. William H. French to Captain J. C. Casey, November 19, 1853, John C. Casey Papers, Thomas Gilcrease Institute, Tulsa, Okla.

23. French to Casey, November 19, 1853, William J. Sloan to Dear Captain, June 16, 1853, ibid.

24. French to Casey, November 19, 1853.

25. Franklin and Schweninger, *Runaway Slaves*, 170; Mullin, *Flight and Rebellion*, 39–41.

26. *Tallahassee Florida Sentinel*, February 18, 1842, February 2, September 21, 1847, April 16, November 26, 1850, October 12, 1852; *St. Augustine Ancient City*, March 16, 1850; *Apalachicola Gazette*, November 23, 1856; *Magnolia Advertiser*, March 13, 1829; *Tallahassee Floridian and Journal*, February 20, 1858, November 17, 1860; *Pensacola Gazette*, August 29, 1840; *Tallahassee Weekly Floridian*, April 20, 1839; *Tallahassee Floridian and Advocate*, October 6, 1828; *Tallahassee Floridian*, September 6, 1834, April 7, May 19, November 3, 1838, April 20, May 4, 1839.

27. *Tallahassee Floridian*, May 31, June 15, 1839, March 21, 1840.

28. *Tallahassee Floridian and Journal*, April 27, 1850, November 20, 1858; *Tallahassee Star of Florida*, September 1, 1843.

29. *Tallahassee Floridian and Journal*, January 29, 1853; *Tallahassee Floridian*, June 15, 1839, April 18, 1846; *Jacksonville News*, July 16, 1847, July 7, December 22, 1855, October 10, 1857; *Pensacola Florida Democrat*, January 18, 1849.

30. *Quincy Sentinel*, January 1, 1841; *Apalachicola Commercial Advertiser*, January 25, 1845; *Tallahassee Star of Florida*, August 9, 1844; *Tallahassee Floridian*, March 30, 1839, June 19, 1841; *Apalachicola Gazette*, April 20, 1839; *Jacksonville Courier*, January 4, 1851.

31. *Tallahassee Florida Sentinel*, October 13, 1841, February 2, 1847; *Jacksonville News*, October 12, 14, 28, November 4, 1854; *Tallahassee Floridian and Journal*, August 20, 1853; *Pensacola Gazette*, October 11, 1837, February 1, 1840; *Tallahassee Floridian and Advocate*, July 13, 1830; *Tallahassee Floridian*, December 26, 1840, November 13, December 25, 1847.

32. *Tallahassee Florida Sentinel*, November 26, 1850, November 25, 1851, October 12, 1852.

33. *Key West Gazette*, April 8, 1840; *Tallahassee Floridian*, August 15, 1846; Carol Wilson, *Freedom at Risk: The Kidnapping of Free Blacks in America, 1780–1865* (Lexington: University Press of Kentucky, 1994), 9–39.

34. *Tampa Florida Peninsular*, October 3, 1857; *Tallahassee Floridian*, October 17, 1835, April 20, 1839, January 10, April 18, 1846; *Pensacola Gazette*, October 7, 1837, December 12, 1840.

35. *Pensacola Gazette*, September 23, 1828; *Quincy Sentinel*, August 14, 1840; *Tallahassee Floridian*, August 22, October 3, 1835, February 3, 1838, September 12, 1840; *Tallahassee Floridian and Advocate*, September 1, 1829, November 9, 1830; *Tallahassee Floridian and Journal*, May 10, 1851.

36. *Tallahassee Floridian*, February 14, 1835, January 22, December 30, 1851, January

22, 29, 1853; *Tallahassee Star of Florida*, September 1, 8, 1843; *Tallahassee Floridian and Journal*, December 20, 1851.

37. *Tallahassee Floridian*, August 9, 1834.

38. Ibid., June 12, 1841.

39. Amon DeLaughter Journal, May 4, 1860, 113; *Acts of the Legislative Council of the Territory of Florida, Passed at Their Third Session, 1824*, 289–92; *Tampa Florida Peninsular*, March 17, 24, May 5, 26, 1860.

Chapter 9. Slave Violence

1. See John Hope Franklin and Loren Schweninger, *Runaway Slaves: Rebels on the Plantation* (New York: Oxford University Press, 1999), 77–88, 149–50, 169, 211; Gerald W. Mullin, *Flight and Rebellion: Slave Resistance in Eighteenth-Century Virginia* (New York: Oxford University Press, 1972), 58–61, 177; Herbert Aptheker, *American Negro Slave Revolts* (New York: Columbia University Press), 207, 176, 346; Ray Granade, "Slave Unrest in Florida," *Florida Historical Quarterly* 55 (July 1976): 18–36; Darlene Clark Hine, William C. Hine, and Stanley Harrold, *The African-American Odyssey* (Upper Saddle River, N.J.: Prentice Hall, 2000), 60–90; Julia Floyd Smith, *Slavery and Plantation Growth in Antebellum Florida, 1821–1860* (Gainesville: University Press of Florida, 1973), 102–8; John W. Blassingame, *The Slave Community: Plantation Life in the Antebellum South*, 2nd ed. (New York: Oxford University Press, 1979), 120, 179–212; Randolph B. Campbell, *An Empire for Slavery: The Peculiar Institution in Texas* (Baton Rouge: Louisiana State University Press, 1989), 184–85; Peter Kolchin, *American Slavery: 1619–1877* (New York: Hill and Wang 1993), 159–60; Larry E. Rivers, "A Troublesome Property: Master-Slave Relations in Florida, 1821–1865," in *The African American Heritage of Florida*, ed. David R. Colburn and Jane L. Landers (Gainesville: University Press of Florida, 1995), 104–27; Donorena Harris, "Abolitionist Sentiment in Florida, 1821–1860" (master's thesis, Florida State University, 1989), 71–96; James M. Denham, *"A Rogue's Paradise": Crime and Punishment in Antebellum Florida, 1821–1861* (Tuscaloosa: University of Alabama Press, 1997), 120–40.

2. Jane Landers, *Black Society in Spanish Florida* (Urbana: University of Illinois Press, 1999), 29–60; Jane Landers, "Gracia Real de Santa Teresa de Mose: A Free Black Town in Spanish Colonial Florida," *American Historical Review* 95 (February 1990): 9–30; Jane Landers, "Slave Resistance on the Southeastern Frontier: Fugitives, Maroons, and Banditti in the Age of Revolutions," *El Escribano* 32 (1995): 12–24; Jane Landers, "Spanish Sanctuary: Fugitives in Florida, 1687–1790," *Florida Historical Quarterly* (January 1984): 296–313; Jane Landers, "Free and Slave," in *The New History of Florida*, ed. Michael Gannon (Gainesville: University Press of Florida, 1996), 167–82; Jane Landers, "Traditions of African American Freedom and Community in Spanish Colonial Florida," in *African American Heritage of Florida*, ed. David R. Colburn and Jane L. Landers (Gainesville: University Press of Florida, 1995), 17–41; Ira Berlin, *Many Thousands Gone: The First Two Centuries of Slavery in North America* (Cambridge: Belknap Press of Harvard University Press, 1998), 73–76; Philip D. Morgan, *Slave Counterpoint: Black Culture in the Eighteenth-Century Chesapeake and Lowcountry* (Chapel Hill: University of North Carolina Press 1998), 450.

3. Edward W. Baptist, *Creating an Old South: Middle Florida's Plantation Frontier before the Civil War* (Chapel Hill: University of North Carolina Press, 2002), 191–218. On the

concept of "southern honor," see, particularly, Bertram Wyatt-Brown, *Honor and Violence in the Old South* (New York: Oxford University Press, 1986); and Bertram Wyatt-Brown, *Southern Honor: Ethics and Behavior in the Old South, Twenty-fifth Anniversary Edition* (New York: Oxford University Press, 1983).

4. *Acts of the Legislative Council of the Territory of Florida, Passed at Their Third Session, 1824, Together with the former Acts, and parts of Acts now in force, the Laws of Congress organizing the government of the Territory of Florida, and Constitution of the United States* (Tallahassee: Office of the *Florida Intelligencer,* 1825), 289–92.

5. *Acts of the Legislative Council of the Territory of Florida, Passed at Their 5th Session, 1826–7* (Tallahassee: A. S. Thruston 1827), 141–44; Smith, *Slavery and Plantation Growth*, 101–3.

6. Peter Alba to William P. DuVal, March 10, 1831, Office of the Governor, Correspondence of the Territorial Governor, box 1825–36, Florida State Archives, Tallahassee; Drew Gilpin Faust, "Slavery in the American Experience," in *Before Freedom Came: African American Life in the Antebellum South*, ed. Edward D. C. Campbell Jr. and Kym S. Price (Charlottesville: University of Virginia Press, 1991), 1–19.

7. Jerrell H. Shofner, *Jefferson County, Florida: A History* (Tallahassee: Sentry Press, 1976), 144; Denham, *"Rogue's Paradise,"* 120–40; *Tallahassee Floridian and Journal*, December 12, 20, 1851; *Tallahassee Florida Advocate*, March 19, 1829.

8. J. L. Taylor to Sue, October 2, 1859, Pine Hill Plantation Papers, Special Collections, Robert M. Strozier Library, Florida State University, Tallahassee; Ulrich Bonnell Phillips and James David Glunt, eds., *Florida Plantation Records from the Papers of George Noble Jones* (St. Louis: Missouri Historical Society, 1927; Gainesville: University Press of Florida, 2006), 114.

9. Linda Brent [pen name of Harriet Jacobs], *Incidents in the Life of a Slave Girl*, ed. L. Maria Child (Boston: Stereotype Foundry, 1861), 26; Charles Ball, *Fifty Years in Chains; or, The Life of An American Slave* (Indianapolis: Dayton and Asher, 1858), 39; Phillips and Glunt, *Florida Plantation Records*; Kenneth M. Stampp, *Peculiar Institution: Slavery in the Ante-Bellum South* (New York: Vintage Books, 1989), 86–140; *Tallahassee Floridian and Journal*, April 7, 1849.

10. *Tampa Florida Peninsular*, May 26, 1860; Amon DeLaughter Journal, entries of April 16–May 4, 1860, pg. 113, transcript in collection of Elizabeth H. Sims, Madison County, Fla., xerographic copy in collection of the author; Denham, *"Rogue's Paradise,"* 120–40.

11. *Fernandina East Floridian*, March 29, 1860; *Jacksonville Florida Republican*, April 16, 1856.

12. *Tampa Florida Peninsular*, October 20, November 3, 1860.

13. Deborah Gray White, *Ar'n't I a Woman? Female Slaves in the Plantation South* (New York: W. W. Norton and Company, 1985), 79; *Pensacola Gazette*, May 12, 1829.

14. Laura Randall to Father, June 30, 1832, William Wirt Papers, Maryland Historical Society, Baltimore; Shofner, *Jefferson County*, 136; Deborah Gray White, "Female Slaves in the Plantation South," in *Before Freedom Came: African American Life in the Antebellum South*, ed. Edward D. C. Campbell Jr. and Kym S. Price (Charlottesville: University of Virginia Press, 1991), 110–11.

15. Charles Joyner, "The World of the Plantation Slaves," in *Before Freedom Came: African American Life in the Antebellum South*, ed. Edward D. C. Campbell Jr. and Kym S. Price

(Charlottesville: University of Virginia Press, 1991), 91; George P. Rawick, *The American Slave: A Composite Autobiography*, 41 vols. (Westport, Conn.: Greenwood Press, 1972–79), vol. 17, *Florida Slave Narratives*, 94–95; *Jacksonville Republican*, November 5, 1856.

16. Daniel Flanigan, "Criminal Procedure in Slave Trials in the Antebellum South," *Journal of Southern History* 40 (November 1974): 537–64; Daniel Flanigan, "The Criminal Law of Slavery and Freedom, 1800–1868" (Ph.D. diss., Rice University, 1973), 47–48. See also, for example, Minor Walker to Samuel H. Duval, in *Territory vs. Dick, a Negro Slave*, 1840, Territorial Court of Appeals Case Files, Record Group 970, series 73, box 12, folder 376, Florida State Archives, Tallahassee; Pardon of Isaac by Governor Richard K. Call, December 8, 1841, *Territory v. Isaac, a Slave*, 1841, and Bill of Indictment of Stepney, and Charge of the Court, in *State v. Stepney, a Slave*, 1849, Escambia County Case Files, Minutes of the Circuit Court, Book A, 1849, n.p., Book B, 65, Book 4, 155, 181, Escambia County Courthouse, Pensacola; *State v. Charles, a Slave*, in folder 1, *Florida Reports*, 298–300; *State v. Charles, a Slave*, 1847, in Comptroller's Vouchers, Criminal Prosecutions, Record Group 350, series 565, box 3, folder 2 (Hamilton County), Florida State Archives; *Magnolia Advertiser*, October 2, 1829; Alachua, Columbia, and Hillsborough Counties Minutes of the Superior Court, 1828–35, pp. 22, 24–25, P. K. Yonge Library of Florida History, University of Florida, Gainesville; Jacob Holbrook to Charles Downing, December 29, 1830, in *Territory of Florida vs. Monday*, December Term 1829, Alachua County, Territorial Auditor, Vouchers, Record Group 352, series 584, box 1, folder 3, Florida State Archives; *State vs. Cato*, 1860, Jackson County, Case Files, Jackson County Courthouse, Marianna; *Cato, a Slave, Plaintiff in Error, v. the State*, 1860, in folder 1, *Florida Reports*, 162–87; Bill of Indictment of Cato, a Slave for Rape, Spring Term 1859, U. S. District Court, Northern District, Civil Cases, box 17, bundle entitled Miscellaneous Court Papers, Unidentified Criminal Records, Record Group 21, Records of the US District Court for the Northern District of Florida, National Archives, Atlanta, Georgia; *State vs. Cato*, 1860, Comptroller's Vouchers, Criminal Prosecutions, box 2, folder 6 (Franklin County); *Pensacola Gazette*, November 27, December 18, 1841; *Territory v. Isaac, a Slave*, in Territorial Auditor, Vouchers, Record Group 352, series 584, box 3, folder 1, Florida State Archives.

17. *Pensacola Gazette and West Florida Advertiser*, October 27, 1827; indictment of Ben, October 2, 1827, Superior Court Minute Book, I, 37–76, Leon County Courthouse; Clifton Paisley, *Red Hills of Florida: 1528–1865* (Tuscaloosa: University of Alabama Press, 1989), 91.

18. Phillips and Glunt, *Florida Plantation Records*, 110–11.

19. *Tampa Florida Peninsular*, September 9, 17, November 5, 1859, January 21, 1860; Canter Brown Jr., "Politics, Greed, Regulator Violence, and Race in Tampa, 1858–1859," *Sunland Tribune* 20 (November 1994): 25–29; Canter Brown Jr., *Ossian Bingley Hart, Florida's Loyalist Reconstruction Governor* (Baton Rouge: Louisiana State University Press, 1997), 105–7, 158–59.

20. Granade, "Slave Unrest in Florida," 18–36; *Tampa Florida Peninsular*, December 15, 1856; *Pensacola West Florida Times*, February 17, 1857.

21. *Jacksonville Courier*, September 3, 1835.

22. *Tampa Florida Peninsular*, September 18, 1858.

23. Ibid., February 25, 1860; E. Ashby Hammond, *The Medical Profession in 19th Century Florida: A Biographical Register* (Gainesville: University Press of Florida, 1996), 329–30.

24. *Jacksonville News*, December 10, 1847.

25. *St. Augustine Ancient City*, December 27, 1851.

26. *Territory vs. Simon, a Slave*, 1848, Jefferson County Case Files; Jefferson County, Minutes of the Circuit Court, Book A, 214, 217, 223, 226; see also Denham, *"Rogue's Paradise,"* 135.

27. Rawick, *Florida Slave Narratives*, 97, 254, 336–37; see also Orlando Patterson, *Slavery and Social Death* (Cambridge: Harvard University Press, 1982), 21–27.

28. *Tallahassee Florida Intelligencer*, October 6, 1826; *Tampa Florida Peninsular*, May 5, 12, 1860; *Jacksonville St. Johns Mirror*, May 7, 1861; Amon DeLaughter Journal, April 16–May 4, 1860, 113.

29. *Fernandina Weekly East Floridian*, August 30, 1860; Landers, *Black Society in Spanish Florida*, 166–68; Landers, "Free and Slave," 180–81.

Chapter 10. The Second Seminole War

1. See Gerald W. Mullin, *Flight and Rebellion: Slave Resistance in Eighteenth-Century Virginia* (New York: Oxford University Press, 1972), 140–63. See also Herbert Aptheker, *American Negro Slave Revolts* (New York: Columbia University Press, 1943); Herbert Aptheker, *Nat Turner's Slave Rebellion: Including the 1831 "Confession"* (New York: Dover, 2006); Douglas R. Egerton, *He Shall Go Out Free: The Lives of Denmark Vesey*, 2nd ed. (Lanham, Md.: Rowman and Littlefield, 2004); Edward A. Pearson, *Designs Against Charleston: The Trial Record of the Denmark Vesey Slave Conspiracy of 1822* (Chapel Hill: University of North Carolina Press, 1999); Douglas R. Egerton, *Gabriel's Rebellion: The Virginia Slave Conspiracies of 1800 and 1802* (Chapel Hill: University of North Carolina Press, 1993); Eric Foner, *Nat Turner* (Englewood Cliffs, N.J.: Prentice Hall Trade, 1971); Roy F. Johnson, *The Nat Turner Story: History of the South's Most Important Slave Revolt, with New Material Provided by Black Tradition and White Tradition* (Chicago: Johnson Publishing Company, 1966); Robert S. Starobin, *Denmark Vesey: The Slave Conspiracy of 1822* (Englewood Cliffs, N.J.: Prentice Hall., 1971); Daniel Rasmussen, *American Uprising: The Untold Story of America's Largest Slave Revolt* (New York: Harper, 2011); Michael P. Johnson, "Denmark Vesey and His Co-conspirators," *William and Mary Quarterly* 58 (Spring 2001): 915–76; Robert L. Paquett, "The Great Louisiana Slave Revolt of 1811 Reconsidered," *Historical Reflections* 35 (Spring 2009): 72–96.

2. The principal source on black military experiences and traditions during Florida's Spanish colonial era is Jane Landers, *Black Society in Spanish Florida* (Urbana: University of Illinois Press, 1999).

3. On Florida's development in the 1820s and early 1830s, see Sidney Walter Martin, *Florida during the Territorial Days* (Athens: University of Georgia Press, 1944); Julia Floyd Smith, *Slavery and Plantation Growth in Antebellum Florida, 1821–1860* (Gainesville: University Press of Florida, 1973); Larry Eugene Rivers, *Slavery in Florida: Territorial Days to Emancipation* (Gainesville: University Press of Florida, 2000); Edward W. Baptist, *Creating an Old South: Middle Florida's Plantation Frontier before the Civil War* (Chapel Hill: University of North Carolina Press, 2002); Canter Brown Jr., *Florida's Peace River Frontier* (Orlando: University of Central Florida Press, 1991), 3–59; and Paul E. Hoffman, *Florida's Frontiers* (Bloomington: Indiana University Press, 2002), 282–316.

4. George Klos, "Blacks and the Seminole Removal Debate, 1821 to 1835," in *The African American Heritage of Florida*, ed. David R. Colburn and Jane L. Landers (Gainesville: University Press of Florida, 1995), 128–56; Rembert W. Patrick, *Florida Fiasco: Rampant Rebels on the Georgia-Florida Frontier* (Athens: University of Georgia Press, 1954), 35–47; John D. Milligan, "Slave Rebelliousness and the Florida Maroon," *Prologue* 6 (Spring 1974): 4–18; Smith, *Slavery and Plantation Growth*, 18; Mark F. Boyd, "Horatio Dexter and Events Leading to the Treaty of Moultrie Creek with the Seminole Indians," *Florida Anthropologist* 6 (September 1958): 81–92; Kenneth W. Porter, *The Negro on the American Frontier* (New York: Arno Press, 1971), 204–41. For more on Andrew Jackson's Indian Removal policy, see Sean Michael O'Brien, *In Bitterness and in Tears: Andrew Jackson's Destruction of the Creeks and Seminoles* (Westport, Conn.: Greenwood Press, 2003); Robert V. Remini, *Andrew Jackson and His Indian Wars* (New York: Viking Press, 2001); Anthony F. C. Wallace and Eric Foner, eds., *The Long, Bitter Trail: Andrew Jackson and the Indians* (New York: Farrar, Straus and Giroux, 1993); and Alfred A. Cave, "Abuse of Power: Andrew Jackson and the Indian Removal Act of 1830," *Historian* 65 (Winter 2003): 1330–53.

5. See Kenneth W. Porter, *The Black Seminoles: History of a Freedom-Seeking People*, rev. and ed. Alcione M. Amos and Thomas P. Senter (Gainesville: University Press of Florida, 1996); Kevin Mulroy, *The Seminole Freedmen: A History* (Norman: University of Oklahoma Press, 2007); James W. Covington, *The Seminoles of Florida* (Gainesville: University Press of Florida, 1993).

6. See Daniel L. Schafer, *Thunder on the River: The Civil War in Northeast Florida* (Gainesville: University Press of Florida, 2010), 136–38; and Larry E. Rivers, "A Troublesome Property: Master-Slave Relations in Florida, 1821–1865," in *The African American Heritage of Florida*, ed. David R. Colburn and Jane L. Landers (Gainesville: University Press of Florida, 1995), 104–27. See also Canter Brown Jr., "The Florida Crisis of 1826–27 and the Second Seminole War," *Florida Historical Quarterly* 73 (April 1995): 419–42; and Ulrich B. Phillips, "The Central Theme of Southern History," *American Historical Review* 34 (October 1928): 30–43.

7. Daniel L. Schafer, "A Class of People Neither Freemen nor Slaves: From Spanish to American Race Relations in Florida, 1821–1861," *Journal of Social History* 26 (Spring 1993): 587–610; Rivers, *Slavery in Florida*, 148–49, 189–209.

8. Annals of Congress, 15th Cong., 2nd Sess., 1040, 16th Cong. 1st Sess., 1194; Merton Dillon, *Slavery Attacked: Southern Slaves and Their Allies, 1619–1865* (Baton Rouge: Louisiana State University Press, 1990), 84–86; *Jacksonville Courier*, October 8, 1835, January 14, December 17, 1836; *American State Papers: Military Affairs*, 7 vols. (Washington D.C.: Gales and Seaton, 1832–60), 7:821 (hereafter cited as *ASPMA*); Mullin, *Flight and Rebellion*, 140; John Hope Franklin and Loren Schweninger, *Runaway Slaves: Rebels on the Plantation* (New York: Oxford University Press, 1999), 12, 291; Aptheker, *American Negro Slave Revolts*, 35–37; Richard Keith Call Journal, Florida State Archives, Tallahassee; *Tallahassee Floridian*, November 11, 1837, June 8, 1839; Clarence E. Carter, ed., *Territorial Papers of the United States*, 28 vols. (Washington, D.C.: Government Printing Office, 1956–62), 22:763. See also Mary Kemp Davis, *Nat Turner before the Bar of Judgment: Fictional Treatments of the Southampton Slave Insurrection* (Baton Rouge: Louisiana State University Press, 1999); Peter H. Wood, *Black Majority: Negroes in Colonial South Carolina from 1670 through the Stono Rebellion* (New York: Alfred A. Knopf, 1974); and Eugene D. Genovese, *From Rebellion*

to Revolution: Afro-American Slave Revolts in the Making of the Modern World (Baton Rouge: Louisiana State University Press, 1979). The following works by historians perceive the Second Seminole War in terms of a slave uprising: Joshua R. Giddings, *The Exiles of Florida; or, The Crimes Committed by Our Government against the Maroons, Who Fled from South Carolina and Other Slave States, Seeking Protections under Spanish Laws* (Columbus: Follett, Foster, 1858; Gainesville: University Press of Florida, 1964); Rivers, *Slavery in Florida*, 189–209; Larry E. Rivers and Canter Brown Jr., "'The Indispensable Man': John Horse and Florida's Second Seminole War," *Journal of the Georgia Association of Historians* 18 (1997): 1–23; Canter Brown Jr., "Persifor F. Smith, the Louisiana Volunteers, and Florida's Second Seminole War," *Louisiana History* 34 (Fall 1993): 407–10; Brown, *Florida's Peace River Frontier*, 41–59; Brown, "Florida Crisis," 419–41; Porter, *Black Seminoles*, 33–68; Kenneth W. Porter, "Farewell to John Horse: An Episode of Seminole Negro Folk History," *Phylon* 8 (1947): 265–73; Kenneth W. Porter, "Florida Slaves and Free Negroes in the Seminole War, 1835–1842," *Journal of Negro History* 28 (April 1943): 390; Kenneth W. Porter, "The Negro Abraham," *Florida Historical Quarterly* 25 (July 1946): 1–42; Kenneth W. Porter, "Negro Guides and Interpreters in the Early Stages of the Seminole War, Dec. 28, 1835–March 6, 1837," *Journal of Negro History* 35 (April 1950): 174–82; and J. B. Bird, "Part 1: The Largest Slave Rebellion in US History" and "Tally of Plantation Slaves in the Black Seminole Slave Rebellion, with Sources" at www.johnhorse.com. Besides the Stono, Gabriel, Turner, and Prosser rebellions, the New York City conspiracy of 1712 and the Louisiana revolt of 1811 may be cited among the major slave revolts prior to 1865. James Dormon, "The Persistent Specter: Slave Rebellion in Territorial Louisiana," *Louisiana History* 18 (1977): 389–40; Robert L. Paquette, "The Great Louisiana Slave Revolt of 1811 Reconsidered," *Historical Reflections* 35 (Spring 2009): 30–43; Rasmussen, *American Uprising*, 1. For the most recent general study of archaeology and slave resistance, see Terrence M. Weik, *The Archaeology of Antislavery Resistance* (Gainesville: University Press of Florida, 2011).

9. Annals of Congress, 15th Cong., 2nd Sess., 1040, 16th Cong. 1st Sess., 1194. On the First Seminole War, see Virginia Bergman Peters, *The Florida Wars* (Hamden, Conn.: Archon Books, 1979), 17–62; John Missall and Mary Lou Missall, *The Seminole Wars: America's Longest Indian Conflict* (Gainesville: University Press of Florida, 2004), 39–64; John K. Mahon, *History of the Second Seminole War* (Gainesville: University Press of Florida, 1967), 18–28; and Joe Knetsch, *Florida's Seminole Wars, 1817–1858* (Charleston: Arcadia Publishing, 2003), 23–41.

10. Giddings, *Exiles of Florida*, 50; Rasmussen, *American Uprising*, 2.

11. Landers, *Black Society in Spanish Florida*, 35–39, 81.

12. Ibid., 220–27. For interesting interpretations of the Patriot War, see Frank Lawrence Owsley Jr. and Gene A. Smith, *Filibusters and Expansionists: Jeffersonian Manifest Destiny, 1800–1821* (Tuscaloosa: University of Alabama Press, 1997); James G. Cusick, *The Other War of 1812: The Patriot War and the American Invasion of Spanish East Florida* (Athens: University of Georgia Press, 2007); Joseph Burkholder Smith, *James Madison's Phony War* (New York: Arbor House, 1983); and Rembert W. Patrick, *Florida Fiasco: Rampant Rebels on the Georgia-Florida Border, 1810–1815* (Athens: University of Georgia Press, 1954).

13. Colin A. Palmer, ed., *Encyclopedia of African-American Culture and History: The Black Experience in the Americas*, 2nd ed., 6 vols. (Detroit: Macmillan, 2006), 5:5–10; Wood quote found in Jack Salzman, David L. Smith, and Cornel West, eds., *The Encyclopedia*

of African American Culture and History, vol. 1 (New York: Macmillan Library Service, 1996), 2580.

14. John Goggin, "The Seminole Negroes of Andros Island, Bahamas," *Florida Historical Quarterly* 24 (January 1946): 201–6; Harry A. Kersey Jr., "The Seminole Negroes of Andros Island Revisited: Some New Pieces to an Old Puzzle," *Florida Anthropologist* 34 (December 1981): 169–76; Janet Snyder Matthews, *Edge of Wilderness: A Settlement History of Manatee River and Sarasota Bay, 1529–1885* (Tulsa: Caprine Press, 1983), 71; Jane Landers, "Gracia Real de Santa Teresa de Mose: A Free Black Town in Spanish Colonial Florida," *American Historical Review* 95 (February 1990): 9–30; James W. Covington, "The Negro Fort," *Gulf Coast Historical Review* 5 (Spring 1990): 79–91; Brown, *Florida's Peace River Frontier*, 17–25; Canter Brown Jr., "Sarrazota, or Runaway Negro Plantations: Tampa Bay's First Black Community, 1812–21," *Tampa Bay History* 12 (Fall/Winter 1990): 5–19; Canter Brown Jr., "Tales of Angola: Free Blacks, Red Stick Creeks, and International Intrigue in Spanish Southwest Florida, 1812–1821," in *Go Sound the Trumpet! Selections in Florida's African American History*, ed. David H. Jackson Jr. and Canter Brown Jr. (Tampa: University of Tampa Press, 2005), 5–21; Rosalyn Howard, *Black Seminoles in the Bahamas* (Gainesville: University Press of Florida, 2002).

15. Porter, "Negro Abraham"; Brown, "Florida Crisis," 428–33, 441; Terrance M. Weik, "African Enemies and Kin in the African-Seminole Communities of Florida: Archaeology at Pilaklikaha," in *Archaeology of Atlantic Africa and the African Diaspora*, ed. Akinwumi Ogundiran and Toyin Falola (Bloomington: Indiana University Press, 2007), 311–31.

16. Porter, "Negro Abraham," 2–11; Brown, "Florida Crisis," 418–32; George A. McCall, *Letters from the Frontiers* (Philadelphia: J. B. Lippincott, 1868), 160. See also Klos, "Blacks and the Seminole Removal Debate, 1821–1835," 128–56; Alfred N. Hunt, *Haiti's Influence on Antebellum America: Slumbering Volcano in the Caribbean* (Baton Rouge: Louisiana State University Press, 1988); and C. L. R. James, *The Black Jacobins: Toussaint L'Ouverture and the San Domingo Revolution*, 2nd ed. (New York: Vintage Books, 1989).

17. Porter, "Negro Abraham," 17–18.

18. Canter Brown Jr., "Race Relations in Territorial Florida, 1821–1845," *Florida Historical Quarterly* 73 (January 1995): 304; Kenneth W. Porter, *Negro on the American Frontier* (New York: Arno Press, 1971), 266–75; Franklin and Schweninger, *Runaway Slaves*, 87–88.

19. Contemporary and near-contemporary accounts, including those of eyewitnesses, gave varying and fragmented estimates of the number of runaways from northeast, Central, and South Florida who left plantations, farms, and industries during the Black/Indian Rebellion. For example, John T. Sprague, adjutant to Colonel William Jenkins Worth, noted on December 20, 1836, the capture and return of "upwards of three hundred" enslaved runaways to their masters. Thomas Hart Benton, then a congressman from Missouri and certainly no abolitionist, cited "five hundred runaway negroes mixed up with them [the Seminoles]." Joshua R. Giddings estimated about 1,200 Indians and maroons, along with another 200 enslaved runaways from the various farms and plantations. Yet, seemingly reliable contemporary reports reflect that many hundreds of runaways left the northeast region alone to join the rebellion. For example, at the height of the first explosion of the insurrection on January 29, 1836, approximately 400 enslaved runaways left the Bulow, Forrester, and Hernandez plantations. Some 15 rebels left the farms of John Mizell (7), J. Hunter (4), Woodruff (3), and Maxey Dell (1). Another 162 escapees burned and left O. S. Rees's

Spring Garden plantation. Between the plantations of Heriot and Depeyster (148), as well as Humphreys (47), 195 enslaved blacks rose up in rebellion, spreading havoc, burning and destroying everything in their paths as they journeyed to join other runaways in the remote maroon settlements of the peninsula. Other owners in the region such as Philip Solano, Ann Bryck, Mrs. Murphy, Mary Hamny, and Hugh Love lost an untold number from their places. It thus can be documented generally that over 750 enslaved rebels rose up during the Black/Indian Rebellion. *Negroes, &c., Captured from Indians in Florida, &c.* (Washington, D.C.: War Department, 1839), 11, 89, 95–96; *Macon Georgia Telegraph*, January 21, February 4, 11, 25, 1836; *Columbus (Ga.) Enquirer*, January 29, February 5, 12, March 18, 1836; *Niles' Weekly Register*, February 6, 27, 1836; *Savannah (Ga.) Republican*, December 23, 28, 1835, January 4, 12, February 22, March 9, 11, 1836; *St. Augustine Florida Herald*, January 6, 13, April 1, May 12, 1836, January 21, 1837; *Jacksonville Courier*, September 17, 1835; *New York Star*, April 16, 1836; John T. Sprague, *The Origin, Progress, and Conclusion of the Florida War* (New York, 1848; Tampa: University of Tampa Press, 2000), 216; *The Extra Globe: Containing Political Discussions, Documentary Proofs, &c for 1838* (Washington, D.C.: Globe Printing Office, 1838), 203–7; Giddings, *Exiles of Florida*, 97; Matthew Clavin, "It Is a Negro, Not an Indian War," in *America's Hundred Years' War: US Expansion to the Gulf Coast and the Fate of the Seminole, 1763–1858*, ed. William S. Belko (Gainesville: University Press of Florida, 2011), 181–208; Brown, "Race Relations," 304; Bird, "Part 1: The Largest Slave Rebellion in US History" and "Tally of Plantation Slaves in the Black Seminole Slave Rebellion, with Sources."

20. *Macon Georgia Telegraph*, February 4, 11, 25, 1836; *Columbus (Ga.) Enquirer*, February 5, 12, March 18, 1836; *Savannah (Ga.) Republican*, February 22, March 9, 11, 1836. The runaways and maroons thus had use of many more guns and rifles when compared to the clubs, sticks, and sword blades utilized by the participants of the New York conspiracy of 1712, Stono rebellion, Gabriel's conspiracy, Louisiana revolt of 1811, Denmark Vesey plot, and Turner rebellion.

21. Brown, *Florida's Peace River Frontier*, 36–42; Canter Brown Jr., *Tampa before the Civil War* (Tampa: University of Tampa Press, 1999), 45–51; *Niles' Weekly Register*, January 30, 1836, 367.

22. Sprague, *Florida War*, 89–91; Brown, "Florida Crisis," 439–42; *Jacksonville Florida Times-Union*, February 16, 1895. The most complete history of the Dade massacre can be found in Frank Laumer, *Dade's Last Command* (Gainesville, Fla., 1995).

23. *Acts of the Governor and Legislative Council, of the Territory of Florida: Passed at the Fourteenth Session, Begun and Held at the City of Tallahassee, on Monday, January 4th, and Ended Sunday, February 14th, 1836* (Tallahassee: William Wilson Printer, 1836), 13–15; Richard Keith Call Journal, 365; *ASPMA*, 7:827–31; James Oakes, *The Ruling Race: A History of American Slaveholders* (New York: Alfred A. Knopf, 1987), 235–42. Runaways received some assistance from free blacks when it came to securing guns, powder, and shot. Two free blacks particularly were charged with "furnishing ammunition . . . to the hostile Indians and negroes." *St. Augustine Florida Herald*, January 26, 1837; *Jacksonville Courier*, September 17, October 8, December 24, 1835, January 1, 1836.

24. Dillon, *Slavery Attacked*, 45–62; Mullin, *Flight and Rebellion*, 140–63.

25. Gerald Mullin, "Religion, Acculturation, and American Negro Slave Rebellions: Gabriel's Insurrection," in *American Slavery: The Question of Resistance*, ed. John H. Bracey

Jr., August Meier, and Elliott Rudwick (Belmont, Calif.: Wadsworth, 1971), 140–64; Dillon, *Slavery Attacked*, 97–103; Margaret Washington, *"A Peculiar People": Slave Religion and Community-Culture among the Gullahs* (New York: New York University Press, 1988); Albert J. Raboteau, *Slave Religion: The "Invisible Institution" in the Antebellum South* (New York: Oxford University Press, 1978); Sylvia R. Frey and Betty Wood, *Come Shouting to Zion: African American Protestantism in the American South and British Caribbean to 1830* (Chapel Hill: University of North Carolina Press, 1998); Allan Gallay, *The Formation of the Planter Elite: Jonathan Bryan and the Southern Colonial Frontier* (Athens: University of Georgia Press, 1978).

26. Mullin, "Religion, Acculturation, and American Negro Slave Rebellions," 160–61; Dillon, *Slavery Attacked*, 97–103.

27. See Egerton, *Gabriel's Rebellion*, 50–53, 179–81; Egerton, *He Shall Go Out Free*, 97–121; Mullin, "Religion, Acculturation, and American Negro Slave Rebellions," 160–61; Dillon, *Slavery Attacked*, 97–103.

28. Porter, *Black Seminoles*, 33; Mahon, *History of the Second Seminole War*, 129; Rivers and Brown, "'Indispensable Man,'" 3–15; Brown, *Florida's Peace River Frontier*, 39–43; Brown, "Florida Crisis," 428–32; Kenneth W. Porter, "John Caesar, Seminole Negro Partisan," *Journal of Negro History* 31 (April 1946): 362–84; Egerton, *He Shall Go Out Free*, 128–47; Egerton, *Gabriel's Rebellion*, 3–69; Porter, *Black Seminoles*, 37–92; Porter, "Negro Abraham," 2–11; Dillon, *Slavery Attacked*, 97–103, 201–23; Starobin, *Denmark Vesey*; Eric Foner, ed., *Nat Turner: Great Lives Observed* (Englewood Cliffs, N.J.: Prentice Hall, 1971); Stephen B. Oates, *The Fires of Jubilee: Nat Turner's Fierce Rebellion* (New York: Harper Perennial, 1990); Junius P. Rodriquez, ed., *Encyclopedia of Slave Resistance and Rebellion* (Westport, Conn.: Greenwood Press, 2007); Rasmussen, *American Uprising*, 97–111. On the subject of black leadership, see especially Anthony E. Dixon, "Black Seminole Involvement and Leadership during the Second Seminole War, 1835–1842" (Ph.D. diss., Indiana University, 2007).

29. *St. Augustine Florida Herald*, April 1, 1825, April 1, 1833; Peter J. Parish, *Slavery: History and Historians* (New York: Westview Press, 1989), 72; Franklin and Schweninger, *Runaway Slaves*, 114–15. See also Richard Price, ed., *Maroon Societies: Rebel Slave Communities in the Americas*, 3rd ed. (Baltimore: Johns Hopkins University Press, 1996); Hugo Prosper Learning, *Hidden Americans: Maroons of Virginia and the Carolinas* (New York: Routledge, 1995); Alvin O. Thompson, *Flight to Freedom: African Runaways and Maroons in the Americas* (Kingston, Jamaica: University of the West Indies Press, 2006); and Timothy James Lockley, ed., *Maroon Communities in South Carolina: A Documentary Record* (Columbia: University of South Carolina Press, 2009), 128.

30. Myer M. Cohen, *Notices of East Florida and The Campaigns* (Charleston: General Books LLC, 1836), 173–74; Brown, *Florida's Peace River Frontier*, 43–45; Rivers and Brown, "'Indispensable Man,'" 3–15; Porter, *Black Seminoles*, 54–65. A fascinating look at the activities, ambitions, and ultimate frustration of the South Carolina volunteers in Florida may be found in James M. Denham and Canter Brown Jr., "South Carolina Volunteers in the Second Seminole War: A Nullifier Debacle as Prelude to the Palmetto State Gubernatorial Election of 1836," in *America's Hundred Years' War: US Expansion to the Gulf Coast and the Fate of the Seminole, 1763–1858*, ed. William S. Belko (Gainesville: University Press of Florida, 2011), 209–36.

31. *Savannah Daily Georgian*, November 8, 1841; Canter Brown Jr. and Barbara Gray Brown, *Family Records of the African American Pioneers of Tampa and Hillsborough County* (Tampa: University of Tampa Press, 2003), 86–88; Porter, *Black Seminoles*, 66–107; Porter, "Negro Abraham," 1–43; Porter, "John Caesar," 362–84; *St. Augustine Florida Herald*, January 6, 1836.

32. John C. Fredrikson, *American Military Leaders: From Colonial Times to the Present* (Santa Barbara, Calif.: ABC-CLIO, 1999), 2:372–73; Keith E. Bonn, *Army Officer's Guide*, 50th ed. (Mechanicsburg, Pa.: Stackpole Books, 2005), 165; Claudio Saunt, *Black, White, and Indian: Race and the Unmaking of an American Family* (New York: Oxford University Press, 2006); Chester L. Kieffer, *Maligned General: The Biography of Thomas Sidney Jesup* (San Rafael, Calif.: Presidio Press, 1979).

33. Fredrikson, *American Military Leaders*, 2:372–73; Bonn, *Army Officer's Guide*, 165; Saunt, *Black, White, and Indian*, 50–51.

34. Thomas Jesup to J. R. Poinsett, June 7, 1837, Jesup to J. R. Poinsett, June 6, 1838, Office of Indian Affairs, Letters Received, M-234, roll 290, National Archives, Washington, D.C.; Jesup to William L. Marcy, April 3, July 1, 1838, Office of Indians Affairs, Special Files, M-574, roll 13, National Archives, Washington, D.C.; Porter, "Florida Slaves and Free Negroes in the Seminole War," 390–421; Kenneth Wiggins Porter, "Negroes and the Seminole War: 1835–1842," *Journal of Southern History* 30 (November 1964): 427–50; Mahon, *History of the Second Seminole War*, 235–36; Rivers and Brown, "'Indispensable Man,'" 13; Covington, *Seminoles of Florida*, 79–95; Edwin C. McReynolds, *The Seminoles* (Norman: University of Oklahoma Press, 1957; Norman: University of Oklahoma Press, 1975), 240; Kevin Mulroy, *Freedom on the Border: The Seminole Maroons in Florida, the Indian Territory, Coahuila, and Texas* (Lubbock: Texas Tech University Press, 1993), 32; Rivers, *Slavery in Florida*, 201–6.

35. Smith, *Slavery and Plantation Growth*, 11, 129–30; Larry E. Rivers, "Slavery in Microcosm: Leon County, Florida, 1824 to 1860," *Journal of Negro History* 66 (Fall 1981): 235–45; Larry E. Rivers, "Dignity and Importance: Slavery in Jefferson County, Florida—1827 to 1860," *Florida Historical Quarterly* 61 (April 1983): 404–18; Larry E. Rivers, "Slavery and the Political Economy of Gadsden County, Florida: 1824–1861," *Florida Historical Quarterly* 70 (July 1991): 1–19; Larry E. Rivers, "Madison County, Florida—1830–1860: A Case Study in Land, Labor, and Prosperity," *Journal of Negro History* 78 (Fall 1993): 233–44; Brown, "Troublesome Property," 113–13; Carter, *Territorial Papers*, 25:283; Legislative Council to Governor William P. DuVal [1823], Florida Legislative Council Records (Unicameral), Record Group 6, series 5, folder 6, box 1, Florida State Archives, Tallahassee; *Tallahassee Floridian*, June 8, 1839. On attacks upon the Randall, Wirt, and Gadsden families from the 1820s to the late 1830s, see Thomas Randall to William Wirt, December 3, 1827, William Wirt Papers, Maryland Historical Society, Baltimore; Louis Goldsborough to Mr. William Wirt, February 1834, Louis Goldsborough to Elizabeth W. Goldsborough, August 28, 1836, Louis Goldsborough Papers, Library of Congress, Washington, D.C.; Brown, *Tampa before the Civil War*, 55–56; and William McKee Evans, *Open Wound: The Long View of Race in America* (Urbana: University of Illinois Press, 2009), 1–38.

36. *ASPMA*, 7:827–32.

37. Mahon, *History of the Second Seminole War*, 239–42; Sprague, *Florida War*, 219; Porter, *Black Seminoles*, 66–73.

38. Porter, *Black Seminoles*, 72.

39. *ASPMA*, 7:827–32; Jesup to J. M. Hernandez, January 21, 1837, box 14, Thomas Jesup Papers, Library of Congress, Washington, D.C.; Covington, *Seminoles of Florida*, 72–95; Mahon, *History of the Second Seminole War*, 200–204; Peters, *Florida Wars*, 142–43; Rivers and Brown, "'Indispensable Man,'" 8–13; Giddings, *Exiles of Florida*, 157; Brown, "Persifor F. Smith," 407; Brown, *Florida's Peace River Frontier*, 43–46; Porter, "Negroes and the Seminole War," 436.

40. Jesup to J. R. Poinsett, June 6, 1838, box 14, Thomas Jesup Papers; Mahon, *History of the Second Seminole War*, 235–36; Jesup to William L. Marcy, April 3, July 1, 1838, Office of Indian Affairs, Special Files, M-574, roll 13; Rivers and Brown, "'Indispensable Man,'" 13; Covington, *Seminoles of Florida*, 79–95; McReynolds, *Seminoles*, 447; Mulroy, *Freedom on the Border*, 32; Rivers, *Slavery in Florida*, 201–6; Carter, *Territorial Papers*, 25:385–86.

41. Sprague, *Florida War*, 309; *Tallahassee Floridian*, September 16, 1837. Besides settling in the west, some self-determined runaways and rebels with an Atlantic worldview persisted in efforts to secure freedom in the Bahamas and, possibly, Cuba. Unlike other New World slave revolts, in Florida, rebels and runaways were more successful in reaching terms more favorable to them due to the overall leniency received from slave owners and Florida society in general at the rebellion's conclusion. No heads or body parts were severed and placed on pikes or poles for all to see. Reportedly, none were executed when the Black/Indian Rebellion ended. See also Rasmussen, *American Uprising*, 147–63.

42. Dixon, "Black Seminole Involvement and Leadership," 110.

43. *Laws of Territorial Florida* (1836), 13–15; Richard Keith Call Journal, 365; *ASPMA*, 7:827–32.

Chapter 11. The Civil War

1. *Seventh Census of the United States, 1850* (Washington, D.C.: Government Printing Office, 1853–55), 399–400. See also John E. Johns, *Florida during the Civil War* (Gainesville: University Press of Florida, 1963), 285; W. E. B. Du Bois, *Black Reconstruction in America: An Essay toward a History of the Part Which Black Folk Played in the Attempt to Reconstruct Democracy in America, 1860–1880* (New York: Harcourt and Brace, 1992), 31–34.

2. Merton Dillon, *Slavery Attacked: Southern Slaves and Their Allies, 1619–1865* (Baton Rouge: Louisiana State University Press, 1990), 243.

3. Daniel L. Schafer, *Thunder on the River: The Civil War in Northeast Florida* (Gainesville: University Press of Florida, 2010), 137.

4. Ibid., 137–38; Julius S. Scott, "Afro-American Sailors and the International Communication Network: The Case of Newport Bowers," in *Jack Tar in History: Essays in the History of Maritime Life and Labour*, ed. Colin Howell and Richard Twomey (Fredericton, New Brunswick: Acadiensis Press, 1991), 41; W. Jeffrey Bolster, *Black Jacks: African American Seamen in the Age of Sail* (Cambridge: Harvard University Press, 1997), 4, 20, 27, 37. See also W. Jeffrey Bolster, "To Feel Like a Man: Black Seamen in Northern States, 1800–1860," *Journal of American History* 76 (1990): 1173–99.

5. Larry Eugene Rivers, *Slavery in Florida: Territorial Days to Emancipation* (Gainesville: University Press of Florida, 2000), 30–32, 44–45, 80–83, 235, 241, 254. For examples of those skilled and self-assured workers in the maritime industry, see Frederick Douglass,

Narrative of the Life of Frederick Douglass, An American Slave, Written by Himself, ed. David W. Blight (Boston: Bedford/St. Martin's Press, 2002), 91–93; and Paul Gilroy, *The Black Atlantic: Modernity and Double Consciousness* (Cambridge: Harvard University Press, 1987), 1–15.

6. Valentine Chamberlain to (unidentified), October 10, 1862, P. K. Yonge Library of Florida History, University of Florida, Gainesville; Daniel L. Schafer, "Freedom Was as Close as the River: African Americans and the Civil War in Northeast Florida," in *The African American Heritage of Florida*, ed. David R. Colburn and Jane L. Landers (Gainesville: University Press of Florida, 1995), 158; *War of the Rebellion: A Compilation of the Official Records of the Union and Confederate Armies*, 128 vols. (Washington, D.C., 1880–1901), ser. 1, vol. 25, pt. 2, 53 (hereafter, *ORA*); Brian R. Rucker, "Blackwater and Yellow Pine: The Development of Santa Rosa County, 1821–1865," 2 vols. (Ph.D. diss., Florida State University, 1990), 2:700.

7. See Thomas Wentworth Higginson, *Army Life in a Black Regiment* (Boston: Fields, Osgood and Company, 1870; Boston: Beacon Press, 1962), 528; Schafer, *Thunder on the River*, 137; Jane Landers, *Black Society in Spanish Florida* (Urbana: University of Illinois Press, 1999), 1–60.

8. Dillon, *Slavery Attacked*, 243–66.

9. Schafer, "Freedom Was as Close as the River," 158.

10. David J. Coles, "Unpretending Service: The James L. Davis, the Tahoma, and the East Gulf Blockading Squadron," *Florida Historical Quarterly* 71 (July 1992): 41–62; George E. Buker, *Blockaders, Refugees, and Contrabands: Civil War on Florida's Gulf Coast, 1861–1865* (Tuscaloosa: University of Alabama Press, 1993), 42–58. For a recent and well-balanced account of Abraham Lincoln within the general construct of the antislavery establishment, see Eric Foner, *The Fiery Trial: Abraham Lincoln and American Slavery* (New York: W. W. Norton, 2010), xv–xxi, 117–31. Over the past decade, a multiplicity of scholarly works have reached publication that address Lincoln's evolving attitudes toward blacks, the Civil War, and social, political, and economic issues. See, for instance, Michael Burlingame, *Abraham Lincoln: A Life* (Baltimore: Johns Hopkins University Press, 2009); James M. McPherson, *Tried by War: Abraham Lincoln as Commander in Chief* (New York: Penguin Press, 2008); Drew Gilpin Faust, *This Republic of Suffering: Death and the American Civil War* (New York: Alfred A. Knopf, 2008); Craig L. Symonds, *Lincoln and His Admirals: Abraham Lincoln, the US Navy, and the Civil War* (New York: Oxford University Press, 2008); James Oakes, *The Radical and the Republican: Frederick Douglass, Abraham Lincoln, and the Triumph of Antislavery Politics* (New York: Oxford University Press, 2007); Douglas L. Wilson, *Lincoln's Sword: The Presidency and the Power of Words* (New York: Vintage Books, 2006); Doris Kearns Goodwin, *Team of Rivals: The Political Genius of Abraham Lincoln* (New York: Simon and Schuster, 2005); Allen C. Guelzo, *Lincoln's Emancipation Proclamation: The End of Slavery in America* (New York: Simon and Schuster, 2004); Allen C. Guelzo, *Abraham Lincoln: Redeemer President* (New York: William B. Eerdmans, 1999); Richard J. Carwardine, *Lincoln* (New York: Longman, 2003); David W. Blight, *Race and Reunion: The Civil War in American Memory* (Cambridge: Harvard University Press, 2001); Russell F. Weigley, *A Great Civil War: A Military and Political History, 1861–1865* (Bloomington: Indiana University Press, 2000); and Orville Vernon Burton, *The Age of Lincoln* (New York: Hill and Wang, 2007).

11. *Official Records of the Union and Confederate Navies in the War of the Rebellion*, 30 vols. (Washington, D.C.: Government Printing Office, 1894–1922), ser. 1, vol. 16, 689, vol. 17, 737–39, 744 (hereafter, *ORN*); Darlene Clark Hine, William C. Hine, and Stanley Harrold, *The African-American Odyssey* (Upper Saddle River, N.J.: Prentice Hall, 2000), 246–47; Benjamin Quarles, *Negro in the Civil War* (Boston: Little and Brown, 1953), 200–202.

12. Schafer, *Thunder on the River*, 138.

13. George P. Rawick, *The American Slave: A Composite Autobiography*, 41 vols. (Westport, Conn.: Greenwood Press, 1972–79), vol. 17, *Florida Slave Narratives*, 35; Sarah Brown Bryant interview, box 7, folder 3, pg. 4, Florida Negro Papers, University of South Florida Library Special Collections, Tampa; Buker, *Blockaders, Refugees, and Contrabands*, 46; *Dade City Banner*, April 4, 1924; Canter Brown Jr., *African Americans on the Tampa Bay Frontier* (Tampa: Tampa Bay History Center, 1997), 40; Robert A. Taylor, *Rebel Storehouse: Florida in the Confederate Economy* (Tuscaloosa: University of Alabama Press, 1995), 3–5.

14. Higginson, *Army Life*, 12–14; *New York Times*, March 25, 1863; Thomas Wentworth Higginson, *Complete Civil War Journal and Selected Letters of Thomas Wentworth Higginson*, ed. Christopher Looby (Chicago: University of Chicago Press, 2000), 110.

15. Ira Berlin, Marc Favreau, and Steven F. Miller, eds., *Remembering Slavery* (New York: New Press, 1998), 209.

16. Higginson, *Complete Civil War Journal*, 94–95; Thomas Wentworth Higginson, "Up the St. Mary's," *Atlantic Monthly*, April 1865, 432.

17. Higginson, *Army Life*, 19–20; Schafer, "Freedom Was as Close as the River," 157–71; Charles Sumner Long, *History of the A.M.E. Church in Florida* (Philadelphia: AME Book Concern, 1939), 75; Canter Brown Jr., *Florida's Black Public Officials, 1867–1924* (Tuscaloosa: University of Alabama Press, 1998), 105–6.

18. Long, *History of the A.M.E. Church in Florida*, 75.

19. David J. Coles, "'They Fought Like Devils': Black Troops in Florida during the Civil War," in *Florida's Heritage of Diversity: Essays in Honor of Samuel Proctor* (Tallahassee: Sentry Press, 1997), 37; David J. Coles, "'Far from Fields of Glory': Military Operations in Florida during the Civil War, 1864–1865" (Ph.D. diss., Florida State University, 1996), 155–85; Brown, *African Americans on the Tampa Bay Frontier*, 39; Canter Brown Jr., *Florida's Peace River Frontier* (Orlando: University of Central Florida Press, 1991), 181; Brown, *Florida's Black Public Officials*, 5–6, 72–73, 75–78, 88–89, 105–6, 135, 142; Canter Brown Jr., "Civil War in Florida," in *The New History of Florida*, ed. Michael Gannon (Gainesville: University Press of Florida, 1996), 241; Johns, *Florida during the Civil War*, 190; Richard A. Martin and Daniel L. Schafer, *Jacksonville's Ordeal by Fire: A Civil War History* (Jacksonville: Florida Publishing Company, 1984), 141; Thomas Frederick Davis, *History of Jacksonville Florida and Vicinity, 1513 to 1924* (Jacksonville: Florida Historical Society, 1925; Jacksonville: San Marco Bookstore, 1990), 134; Joseph T. Wilson, *Black Phalanx: A History of the Negro Soldiers of the United States in the Wars of 1775–1812, 1861–65* (Hartford, Conn.: American Publishing, 1980), 269; Faust, *This Republic of Suffering*, 44–55.

20. Lawrence Jackson, "As I Saw" (transcript), Lawrence Jackson Papers, P. K. Yonge Library of Florida History, University of Florida, Gainesville; William Penniman Reminiscences, Southern Historical Collection, University of North Carolina, Chapel Hill; "Letters from Confederate Solders, 1861–1865" (typescript), 481, Georgia Department of Archives and History, Atlanta; *A Voice from Rebel Prisons: Giving an Account of Some of the Horrors of*

Stockades at Andersonville, Milan, and Other Prisons, by a Returned Prisoner of War (Boston: George C. Rand and Avery, 1865), 4; *Jacksonville Florida Union*, March 11, 1865; Frankie H. Fennell, "Blacks in Jacksonville, 1840–1865" (master's thesis, Florida State University, 1978), 77–100; Coles, "'They Fought Like Devils,'" 38–39; John David Smith, ed., *Black Soldiers in Blue: African American Troops in the Civil War Era* (Chapel Hill: University of North Carolina Press, 2002), 18–39.

21. Hine, Hine, and Harrold, *African-American Odyssey*, 241–56; Leon Litwack, *Been in the Storm So Long: The Aftermath of Slavery* (New York: Vintage Books, 1979), 10–51; Quarles, *Negro in the Civil War*, 10–42. See also Dudley Taylor Cornish, *The Sable Arm: Negro Troops in the Union Army, 1861–1865* (New York: Longman, Green, and Company, 1956); and George Washington Williams, *History of the Negro Troops in the War of the Rebellion* (New York: Harper and Brothers, 1988).

22. Quarles, *Negro in the Civil War*, 1–104; Tracy J. Revels, *Grander in Her Daughters: Florida's Women during the Civil War* (Columbia: University of South Carolina Press, 2004), 92–109; Rivers, *Slavery in Florida*, 229–50.

23. Wilson W. Rice, "Negro Religion, Bethel Baptist Institutional Church" (typescript, Jacksonville, Fla., 1936); Rawick, *Florida Slave Narratives*, 178–80; *Fernandina Peninsula*, August 13, 1863; Tracy J. Revels, "Grander in Her Daughters: Florida's Women during the Civil War," *Florida Historical Quarterly* 77 (Winter 1999): 261–82; Revels, *Grander in Her Daughters*, 92–109.

24. *ORN*, ser. 1, vol. 26, 689, vol. 27, 737–39; Quarles, *Negro in the Civil War*, 200–202; quarantine regulations, March 15, 1864, in Letters Received, Department and District of Key West, 1861–65, Record Group 393, series 3, National Archives, Washington, D.C.; Charles Smart, *Medical and Surgical History of the War of the Rebellion* (Washington, D.C.: Government Printing Office, 1888), 675–83; *Philadelphia Inquirer*, September 26, 1872; William H. Foster, "'This Place is Safe': Engineer Operations at Fort Zachary Taylor, Florida, 1845–1864" (master's thesis, Florida State University, 1974), 181; Higginson, *Army Life*, 237; John Wilder to Richard Wilder, July 25, 1864, Wilder-Loomis Family Papers, Yale University Library, New Haven, Conn.; Frederick H. Dyer, *Compendium of the War of the Rebellion*, 3 vols. (New York: Thomas Yoseloff, 1959), 3:1723. See also Mark A. Smith, *Engineering Security: The Corps of Engineers and the Third System Defense Policy, 1815–1861* (Tuscaloosa: University of Alabama Press, 2009).

25. Mark F. Boyd, "Battle of Marianna," *Florida Historical Quarterly* 30 (April 1951): 225–42; Charlotte C. Farley, "Florida's Alamo: The Battle of Marianna 'Twas Said to Me'" (n.p., n.d.), no pagination; Coles, "'They Fought Like Devils,'" 40; Rucker, "Blackwater and Yellow Pine," 2:700. The Third, Seventh, and Thirty-Fifth United States Colored Troops (USCT) took part also in the June 1864 capture of Camp Milton. The Thirty-Fourth, Thirty-Fifth, and 102nd USCT were involved in the Florida Railroad raid of August 1864. *ORA*, ser. 1, vol. 25, pt. 1, 393–98, 400–404, 427–40, 443–45.

26. Buker, *Blockaders, Refugees, and Contrabands*, 44–50; Lillie B. McDuffee, *The Lures of Manatee: A True Story of South Florida's Glamorous Past* (Nashville: Marshall and Bruce, 1933), 150–52; Arch Fredric Blakey, Ann Smith Lainhart, and Winston Bryant Stephens Jr., eds., *Rose Cottage Chronicles: Civil War Letters of the Bryant-Stephens Families of North Florida* (Gainesville: University Press of Florida, 1998), 73–76, 97, 135; DeAnn Blanton and Lauren M. Cook, *Conflicting Worlds: New Dimensions of the American Civil War* (Baton

Rouge: Louisiana State University Press, 2002), 36–69; Etheldred Philips to James J. Philips, December 24, 1862, James J. Philips Papers, Southern Historical Collection, University of North Carolina, Chapel Hill.

27. Rawick, *Florida Slave Narratives*, 60; William Bryant to Davis Bryant, October 30, 1861, Bryant-Stephens Family Papers, P. K. Yonge Library of Florida History, University of Florida, Gainesville.

28. Canter Brown Jr., "George Washington Witherspoon: Florida Second Generation of Black Political Leadership," *A.M.E. Church Review* 119 (January-March 2003), 66; Long, *History of the A.M.E. Church in Florida*, 56–57.

29. Rawick, *Florida Slave Narratives*, 60.

30. Du Bois, *Black Reconstruction*, 55–83; Blakey, Lainhart, and Stephens, *Rose Cottage Chronicles*, 130; S. Fairbanks to G. Fairbanks, August 27, 1862, George R. Fairbanks Papers, Florida State University Library Special Collections, Tallahassee.

31. Margaret Watkins Gibbs Memory Diary, St. Augustine Historical Society Research Library, St. Augustine, Fla.; Rodney E. Dillon, "Civil War in South Florida" (master's thesis, University of Florida, 1980), 243–329.

32. Blakey, Lainhart, and Stephens, *Rose Cottage Chronicles*, 99–100, 106.

33. Sarah Brown Bryant interview, box 7 folder 3, Florida Negro Papers, Special Collections, University of South Florida Library, Tampa; Leland Hawes, "One-Time Slave Sheds Light on Life in Tampa," *Tampa Sunday Tribune*, June 5, 1988; Brown, *African Americans on the Tampa Bay Frontier*, 40; Canter Brown Jr., *Tampa in Civil War and Reconstruction* (Tampa: University of Tampa Press, 2000), 54–55.

34. Rivers, *Slavery in Florida*, 245–47.

35. *Tallahassee Florida Sentinel*, May 6, 1862; Larry E. Rivers, "Madison County, Florida—1830–1860: A Case Study in Land, Labor, and Prosperity," *Journal of Negro History* 78 (Fall 1993): 241; Rawick, *Florida Slave Narratives*, 247; *The Acts and Resolutions of the General Assembly of Florida at Its Eleventh Session, Begun and Held at the Capitol, in the City of Tallahassee, on Monday, November 18, 1861* (Tallahassee: Dyke and Carlisle, 1862), 38–43; Amon DeLaughter Journal, October 1, 1859, November 5, May 26, September 10, October 6, 1860, transcript in collection of Elizabeth H. Sims, Madison County, Fla., xerographic copy in collection of the author.

36. Rawick, *Florida Slave Narratives*, 80–81, 178, 245, 351.

37. Larry E. Rivers and Canter Brown Jr., *Laborers in the Vineyard of the Lord: The Beginnings of the AME Church in Florida, 1865–1895* (Gainesville: University Press of Florida), 16–19; J. V. Drake, *The Florida Legislature (Twelfth Session): The Official Directory of State Government* (Jacksonville: Times-Union and Job Office, 1883), 37–38; Rawick, *Florida Slave Narratives*, 214, 359; Clifton Paisley, *Red Hills of Florida, 1528–1865* (Tuscaloosa: University of Alabama Press, 1989), 201; John P. Ingle, ed., "Soldiering with the Second Florida Regiment," *Florida Historical Quarterly* 59 (January 1981): 336–37; Charles Joyner, *Down by the Riverside: A South Carolina Slave Community* (Urbana: University of Illinois Press, 1984), 225.

38. *Tallahassee Florida Sentinel*, May 6, 1862; Revels, "Grander in Her Daughters," 261–82; Johns, *Florida during the Civil War*, 307–8; Susan Bradford Eppes, *Through Some Eventful Years* (Macon: J. W. Burke Company, 1926), 163; Susan Bradford Eppes, *The Negro of the Old South: A Bit of Period History* (Chicago: Joseph G. Branch, 1925), 109–11.

39. Peter Kolchin, *American Slavery: 1619–1877* (New York: Hill and Wang, 1993), 203–5; M. N. Fletcher to Dear Son, April 29, 1865, Zabud Fletcher Family Papers, M90-15, Florida State Archives, Tallahassee.

40. Rabun Scarborough to Sissy, ca. November 22–27, 1861, and to My Dearest Sister, November 29, 1861, Rabun Scarborough Letters, Strozier Library, Florida State University, Tallahassee.

41. Catherine Cooper Hopely (pseud. Sarah L. Jones), *Life in the South from the Commencement of the War, by a Blockade English Subject*, 2 vols. (London: Chapman and Hall, 1863), 2:279–85; J. F. Dovell, *Florida Historic, Dramatic, Contemporary*, 4 vols. (New York: Lewis Historical Publishing, 1952), 1:503; Drew Faust, "Slavery in the American Experience," in *Before Freedom Came: African American Life in the Antebellum South*, ed. Edward D. C. Campbell Jr. and Kym S. Price (Charlottesville: University of Virginia Press, 1991), 18–19.

42. Eppes, *Negro of the Old South*, 115–17.

43. Rawick, *Florida Slave Narratives*, 254; M. N. Fletcher to Dear Son, April 29, 1865, Zabud Fletcher Family Papers.

Afterword

1. Wilma King, *Stolen Childhood: Slave Youth in Nineteenth-Century America* (Bloomington: Indiana University Press, 1995), 71, 103; Maria Jenkins Schwartz, *Born in Bondage: Growing Up Enslaved in the Antebellum South* (Cambridge: Harvard University Press, 2000), 207–8; Eugene D. Genovese, *Roll, Jordan, Roll: The World the Slaves Made* (New York: Pantheon Books, 1974), 36–107.

2. Edward W. Baptist, *Creating an Old South: Middle Florida's Plantation Frontier before the Civil War* (Chapel Hill: University of North Carolina Press, 2002), 61–87, 191–218.

3. Jacqueline Jones, *Labor of Love, Labor of Sorrow: Black Women, Work, and the Family from Slavery to the Present* (New York: Basic Books, 1985), 11–43.

4. Douglas R. Egerton, Alison Games, Jane G. Landers, Kris Lane, and Donald R. Wright, *The Atlantic World: A History, 1400–1888* (Wheeling, W.V.: Harlan Davidson, 2007), 1–37.

5. Jane Landers, *Black Society in Spanish Florida* (Urbana: University of Illinois Press, 1999), 4–5.

6. Merton Dillon, *Slavery Attacked: Southern Slaves and Their Allies, 1619–1865* (Baton Rouge: Louisiana State University Press, 1990), 269–70; Donorena Harris, "Abolitionist Sentiment in Florida, 1821–1860" (master's thesis, Florida State University, 1989), 1–15.

7. Canter Brown Jr., "Race Relations in Territorial Florida, 1821–1845," *Florida Historical Quarterly* 73 (January 1995): 304; Kenneth W. Porter, *Negro on the American Frontier* (New York: Arno Press, 1971), 266–75; J. B. Bird, "Part 1: The Largest Slave Rebellion in US History" and "Tally of Plantation Slaves in the Black Seminole Slave Rebellion, with Sources," at www.johnhorse.com.

8. For an excellent study of how people remember or disremember the Civil War, see David W. Blight, *Race and Reunion: The Civil War in American Memory* (Cambridge: Harvard University Press, 2001), 381–97; Thomas Wentworth Higginson, *Army Life in a Black Regiment* (Boston: Fields, Osgood, 1870; Boston: Beacon Books, 1962), 19–20; Daniel L. Schafer, "Freedom Was as Close as the River: African Americans and the Civil War in

Northeast Florida," in *The African American Heritage of Florida*, ed. David R. Colburn and Jane L. Landers (Gainesville: University Press of Florida, 1995), 157–71; Charles Sumner Long, *History of the A.M.E. Church in Florida* (Philadelphia: AME Book Concern, 1939), 75; Canter Brown Jr., *Florida's Black Public Officials, 1867–1924* (Tuscaloosa: University of Alabama Press, 1998), 105–6; Canter Brown Jr., *African Americans on the Tampa Bay Frontier* (Tampa,: Tampa Bay History Center, 1997), 39; David J. Coles, "'They Fought Like Devils': Black Troops in Florida during the Civil War," in *Florida's Heritage of Diversity: Essays in Honor of Samuel Proctor* (Tallahassee: Sentry Press, 1997), 37; and David J. Coles, "'Far from Fields of Glory': Military Operations in Florida during the Civil War, 1864–1865" (Ph.D. diss., Florida State University, 1996), 155–85.

Index

LARRY EUGENE RIVERS is president of Fort Valley State University in central Georgia and the author of *Slavery in Florida: Territorial Days to Emancipation.*

The New Black Studies Series

Beyond Bondage: Free Women of Color in the Americas
Edited by David Barry Gaspar and Darlene Clark Hine

The Early Black History Movement, Carter G. Woodson, and Lorenzo Johnston Greene *Pero Gaglo Dagbovie*

"Baad Bitches" and Sassy Supermamas: Black Power Action Films
Stephane Dunn

Black Maverick: T. R. M. Howard's Fight for Civil Rights and Economic Power *David T. Beito and Linda Royster Beito*

Beyond the Black Lady: Sexuality and the New African American Middle Class *Lisa B. Thompson*

Extending the Diaspora: New Histories of Black People
Dawne Y. Curry, Eric D. Duke, and Marshanda A. Smith

Activist Sentiments: Reading Black Women in the Nineteenth Century
P. Gabrielle Foreman

Black Europe and the African Diaspora *Edited by Darlene Clark Hine, Trica Danielle Keaton, and Stephen Small*

Freeing Charles: The Struggle to Free a Slave on the Eve of the Civil War
Scott Christianson

African American History Reconsidered *Pero Gaglo Dagbovie*

Freud Upside Down: African American Literature and Psychoanalytic Culture
Badia Sahar Ahad

A. Philip Randolph and the Struggle for Civil Rights *Cornelius L. Bynum*

Queer Pollen: White Seduction, Black Male Homosexuality, and the Cinematic
David A. Gerstner

The Rise of Chicago's Black Metropolis, 1920–1929 *Christopher Robert Reed*

Living with Lynching: African American Lynching Plays, Performance, and Citizenship, 1890–1930 *Koritha Mitchell*

Africans to Spanish America: Expanding the Diaspora *Edited by Sherwin K. Bryant, Rachel Sarah O'Toole, & Ben Vinson III*

Rebels and Runaways: Slave Resistance in Nineteenth-Century Florida
Larry Eugene Rivers

The University of Illinois Press
is a founding member of the
Association of American University Presses.

University of Illinois Press
1325 South Oak Street
Champaign, IL 61820-6903
www.press.uillinois.edu